Blake's Prophetic Psychology

Brenda S. Webster

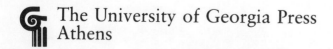
The University of Georgia Press
Athens

Published in 1983 in the USA by
THE UNIVERSITY OF GEORGIA PRESS
Athens, Georgia 30602

ISBN 0–8203–0658–4

Printed in Great Britain

For my mother
Ethel Schwabacher
a visionary artist

Contents

List of Illustrations

Acknowledgements

For permission to reproduce illuminated pages and drawings in their
collections I am indebted to the Auckland Public Library (plates from
America, copy N, and *Europe*, copy I); the Beinecke Rare Book and
Manuscript Library, Yale University (a plate from *America*, copy K);
the Henry W. and Albert A. Berg Collection, New York Public
Library, Astor, Lenox and Tilden Foundations (a plate from *Visions
of the Daughters of Albion*, copy K); the Bodleian Library (a plate
from *Marriage*); the trustees of the British Museum (a plate from
Thel, copy D; plates from *Book of Los*, copy A, and *Milton*, copy A;
a plate from *Tiriel*; drawings from *Vala* and Blake's Notebook);
Cambridge University Library (plates from *Tiriel*); the Fitzwilliam
Museum (plates from *Marriage of Heaven and Hell*, copy I; a plate
from *Tiriel*); the Houghton Library, Harvard University (plates from
Jerusalem, copy D; plates from *Songs of Innocence and of Experience*); the Huntington Library, San Marino, California (a plate
from *America*; plates from *Europe*, *Urizen*, and *Thel*, copy L);
Sir Geoffrey Keynes (plates from *Marriage of Heaven and Hell*,
copy E; plates from *Tiriel*); Paul Mellon (a plate from *Jerusalem*,
copy E); the Paul Mellon Collection, Yale Center for British Art
(plates from *For Children: The Gates of Paradise*, copy E); Oxford
University Press (plates from G. E. Bentley's *Blake's Tiriel*); the
Pierpont Morgan Library (a plate from *Marriage*, copy C; a plate
from *Urizen*, copy B; and a plate from *Europe*, plate iia); the Lessing
J. Rosenwald Collection, Library of Congress (plates from *Visions of
the Daughters of Albion*, copy J; plates from *Urizen*, copy G; a plate
from *America*, plate c, cancelled plate); the Whitworth Art Gallery,
Manchester (*War and the Fear of Invasion*).

I am indebted to several friends, particularly Robert Cole and

Frederick Crews, for help at times amounting to collaboration; to Robert Alter, Carol Cosman, Kurt Eissler, Sandra Gilbert, Bruce Golden, Eric Johannesson, Ira Lapidus, Ellie Ragland-Sullivan and Bernard Wishey for their suggestions and critical reading of various parts of the manuscript; to David Erdman for generously allowing me to use his Blake photographs; to Page Wickland for cutting and editing an early draft; to Grace O'Connol and Florence Myers for superb typing; and to Mrs Danton at Herrick Hospital for her cheerful help in getting books.

List of Abbreviations

Ah	*The Book of Ahania*
A	*America a Prophecy*
E	*The Poetry and Prose of William Blake*, ed. David V. Erdman
E	*Europe a Prophecy*
FZ	*The Four Zoas*
GP	*The Gates of Paradise*
IB	David V. Erdman, *The Illuminated Blake*
IM	*An Island in the Moon*
J	*Jerusalem*
L	*The Book of Los*
M	*Milton*
MHH	*The Marriage of Heaven and Hell*
N	Notebook
SE	*Songs of Experience*
T	*Tiriel*
Th	*The Book of Thel*
U	*The Book of Urizen*
V	*Vala*
VDA	*Visions of the Daughters of Albion*

Unless otherwise indicated, all references given in the text to Blake's works are to David V. Erdman (ed.), *The Poetry and Prose of William Blake* (New York: Anchor Books, 1970). Citations are given by work, plate or page number (for *An Island in the Moon*, chapter number), and line number(s) where appropriate, followed by the page number in Erdman. For example, *VDA* 2:10–15, E 45 means *Visions of the Daughters of Albion*, plate 2, lines 10–15, page 45 of Erdman. For shorter poems identified in the text that are not divided into plates or pages, no title abbreviation is given and only line numbers follow the quotations.

Unless otherwise indicated, all references given in the text to Blake's illustrations are to David V. Erdman, *The Illuminated Blake* (New York: Anchor Books, 1974). Citations are given by poem and plate number, followed by the page number in *The Illuminated Blake* (*IB*). For example, *Th 5, IB* 39 means plate 5 of *Thel*, page 39 of *The Illuminated Blake*.

Introduction

It is no longer possible to refer to Blake, as Southey did, as 'this insane and erratic genius'.[1] Critics have tended progressively over the years to normalise our image of Blake and to deny any irrationality or morbidity. Statements such as Southey's, common among Blake's contemporaries, are now ignored by critics with historical interests, who see him, instead, firmly rooted in his eighteenth-century world of engravers, antiquarians and political radicals. Even his utopian visions are brought into relation with eighteenth-century reality: 'Blake's vision of Paradise is no lost traveller's dream but the sunny side of eighteenth-century London life as experienced by a boy . . . living in an indulgent family in a Broad Street on a square named Golden'[2] – a correspondence his contemporaries never saw. And, unlike the earliest critics, who saw Blake as an otherworldly mystic caring less for art than for enlightenment, recent critics with a formalist or religious perspective have insisted that his symbolic system is artistically valid, rationally understandable, and an effective setting for a redemptive message. His works are related to his philosophy; his purpose is 'to express a vision of a created and fallen world which has been redeemed by a divine sacrifice and is proceeding to regeneration'.[3] Such critics do not concede Blake's emotional involvement with even his near-pornographic material; they see him as portraying degradations of erotic life so that error may be clarified and redemption achieved.[4]

Of course, both historical–biographical and formalist or religious critics have enabled us to get closer to Blake in important ways. It is impossible to study a poet who has nothing to offer but a personal meaning, who is, in Southey's words, 'insane'; such a poet's works would be meaningful only to psychologists. The traditional approaches

1

to Blake give an objective basis for our belief that there are real and shared meanings in his work: Blake followed the great public events taking place around him and reflected them in his political prophecies. Blake consciously worked within a prophetic tradition and considered his message crucial to his readers' salvation. He thought of himself as a poetic innovator, and, by taking his claims seriously and reading him closely, formalist critics have revealed patterns and ambiguities that can serve as material for future interpretations.

Still, critics in their efforts to bridge the distance between Blake and his reader and get as far away as possible from the idea that he was mad may have become almost too Blakean. There is a tendency to accept his prophetic assertions at face value and submit to his obscurities as rightfully imposed tests of one's worthiness as a reader. Even this close identification with Blake's perspective has its advantages, because, although it brings with it a loss of critical distance, it also offers a heightened awareness of what Blake may have intended his readers to experience. And participation in a struggle for salvation need not be the only form for critical interest in reader-response; it might also be extended in another direction, that of reader-response to emotional content.

With few exceptions, there has been a tendency to ignore the intensely personal emotional components of Blake's work, its bitter combat with 'the torments of love and Jealousy'.[5] Psychological approaches, unless they follow Blake's own mystical propensities rather closely, seem curiously but widely ignored.[6] His work is valuable because it enables us 'to appreciate . . . the ultimate truth that we *are* the human form Divine'[7] and to join Blake in a condemnation of our materialist and rationalist society. In this mood, even Blake's own obvious biographical references are ignored when they would conflict with a high view of Blake's character or the sublimity of his purpose. One critic, for example, analysing *Milton*, rejects a biographical interpretation because it would convict Blake of being self-righteous, vindictive, and obscurantist into the bargain — '"mad Blake" indeed'.[8] Since such demeaning accusations are difficult to reconcile with an uplifting view of Blake as a writer of 'sublime Allegory' for times to come, the accusations themselves are ridiculed and denied.

The normalisation of Blake springs not from the emergence of new 'hard facts' but from an unwillingness to look at Blake's private self, the self that is not encompassed by the public facts that he worked steadily, lived simply, and was liked by his neighbours. For example, many agree that there is a shift in his poetry from libidinal revolutionary to radical Christian views. But the attempt to explain this shift as being simply Blake's reaction to an external event, such as the failure of the French Revolution, is insufficient. Those who instead emphasise Christian purpose in the early work may come closer to Blake's private self simply because there is in Christian attitudes, as there is in Blake, an ambivalence toward sexuality.[9] But it is more fruitful to recognise from the beginning what was uniquely Blake's as a person; in this instance, that his work shows oppressive feelings of guilt even when he is defending against them through manic advocacy of sexual liberation. Seeing Blake's ambivalence in the light of personal psychology enriches our understanding both of Blake and of the correspondence between his thinking and Christian ideas. Blake was psychosexually involved in his art to the highest degree, and he suffered, as do his tormented characters, from the self-divisions of 'shame and doubt'.

When Blake's emotional significance is ignored, he can become boring and frustrating to read. Concentrating on his conscious manipulation of the reader, one is forced to conclude that he spent his time creating 'rhetorical barriers' and other traps for the reader. In *Jerusalem*, for example, the narrative itself is 'an obscuring veil . . . that, if investigated by a reasoning reader, becomes a tormenting and eternal labor of frustration'.[10] Other readers find Blake obsessed with mathematical schema:

> *Jerusalem* discloses the following seven structures: a primary structure of four divisions . . . a two-part structure delineating the marked contrast between Ulro and Eden; a three-part structure whose pivots are climactic representations of the fallen state; a threefold and fourfold division within each chapter stressing the dialectical mode of the poem; a sixfold division emphasizing the continuity of the major events; a second three-part structure, derived from the sixfold . . . .[11]

While there are those who believe that Blake's schematisations repay serious study, for most readers Blake's numerological propensities, along with his detailed 'geographies' of Britain and Israel and much of his cataloguing of opposing 'forces', are the least rewarding part of his poetry.

The power in Blake's work comes from his very recognition and description of demonic forces (the eighteenth-century equivalent of unconscious drives) that influence every phase of human relationships, particularly sexuality. Blake's work exhibits the repetitious behaviour-patterns set in motion by these forces in our lives and in history. Blake is consciously concerned to describe a certain type of rational and moralistic 'civilised' man struggling against impulse. In his repeated portrayals of this man, Blake suggests that rationality and morality have a defensive purpose: they develop in reaction to fear, rage and desire and serve to control them.[12] Though Blake's description of rational man is deliberate, defences in his work appear as dramatisations, not descriptions – dramatisations done with varying degrees of consciousness, ranging from the subtlety of a master psychologist in some of the early prophecies to a compulsive re-enacting of infantile experience in the later.

If we accept at least hypothetically the importance of psychosexual conflict in Blake's work, and if we are to go beyond impressionism or commonsense psychology, we need a theory of mental functioning to serve both as a framework for clarifying our responses to Blake and as a technique for exposing the psychic preoccupations behind his defences. Such exposure is not to explain or to explain away his art, but to suggest the power of his images for him and for us. It is also vital if we are to follow the inner logic of his development from advocate of sexual revolution to radical Christian.

Of the available psychologies, Freudian psychoanalysis seems the most productive for studying Blake. The psychoanalytic emphasis on Oedipal conflict and motives of 'love and Jealousy' is in many respects similar to Blake's own. Moreover, particularly in Blake's late work, his manifest emphasis begs to be described as 'Freudian'. His diffuse narratives are given what coherence they have by a linked series of fantasies made familiar by psychoanalysis. In works like *Vala*, Blake literally depicts the staples of the Freudian view of the psyche. For example, he shows children watching adults copulate (the primal scene), he describes acts of incest, he presents a woman with a penis (the phallic woman) and a man without one. These images are not just bizarre accidents and they need to be confronted and dealt with as an important component of his art. The application of psychoanalytic insights to Blake's work, therefore, needs to be systematic and central if we are to do justice to its emotional content. So far, however, when Blake criticism has considered the similarity between Blake and Freud, it has for the most part contented itself with superficial references to Freud that isolate Freudian 'meaning' in a particular figure or work. Orc's hatred for his father (Los), for example, becomes tagged as 'the situation . . . later named by Freud as "the Oedipus Complex"'.[13]

Blake's emotional content, particularly his sexuality, has created a variety of problems for critics. Failure to confront these problems directly leads to serious omissions and bias in attempts to describe his work. For instance, early commentators, such as S. Foster Damon in the 1920s, felt it necessary to separate Blake's ideas from his behaviour. Damon defended Blake's shocking boldness and apparent 'justification of illicit ways'.[14] 'Blake, one of the most pure-souled of men, wrote as he did not because he was over-erotic'; his preoccupation with sex was 'determined not by any aberrations of temperament, but by a search for the highest ideal, which became an essential part of his philosophic system'.[15] In such comments we feel strongly the unsettling effect of Blake's ideas and the critics' need to defend both Blake and his reader against them. Rather than urge the reader to take Blake seriously about sexual matters, Damon assures us that Blake himself did not follow his teachings. As evidence for his case, Damon approvingly describes Blake's marriage: 'He was ideally married. Mrs Blake was a wife of the Pauline and Miltonic type, one entirely submitted to her husband, as he in turn was submitted to his God.'[16] Damon's insistence on a split between Blake's ideas and his behaviour leads this otherwise astute critic to idealise and Christianise Blake's underlying meaning beyond what the text will support.

More recently, there is a tendency to see Blake as anticipating twentieth-century attitudes toward sex in a healthy, 'unrepressed' way. But, here again, the full force of Blake's sexuality creates problems for the critics which they do not adequately handle. Blake calls for a total abolition of repression, including the prohibition against incest. When even this demand is noted, it is in such a way as to deny its emotional implications: 'Blake shared Shelley's belief in [incest's] innocence, and indeed considered it the very root of marriage.'[17] It is important to note here that Blake's earlier critics tended to ignore his radical sexual ideas and fantasies, while his later critics have tended to ignore his guilt over these fantasies. But understanding of his guilt is crucial to an understanding of his poetry. If we are to understand Blake at all, we must recognise and deal with both his fantasies and his defences, his exhortations and his denials. These seemingly contradictory aspects of his character all find expression in his poetry. In the chapters that follow, we shall see that Blake struggles with his desire for incest and his guilt about that desire throughout his poetry and ultimately forges only an uneasy compromise between, on the one hand, his deepest instinctual needs and self-aggrandising desires and, on the other, Christian ideals of self-sacrifice.

Blake's emotional content can distort understanding of Blake for the critic who responds to it sympathetically as well as those who avoid its significance. Perhaps the most fascinating of the sympathetic Blakeans is Norman O. Brown. Brown is instructive as the extraordinary case of a man who reacted to the emotional content of Blake's ideas by creating his own system. Although he is at times taken as exposing Freudian elements in Blake, his writing is really an exposition of his own views, not an analysis of either Freud or Blake. Blake becomes for Brown a saviour who shows the way to undo repression and return to the idealised body of childhood. Brown, like Blake and unlike Freud, is not cowed by the demands of the reality-principle:

> 'Animism, magic and omnipotence of thought' – the child, the savage and the neurotic are right. . . . That 'advance', that 'adaptation to reality', which consists in the child's learning to distinguish between the wish and the deed, between external facts and his feeling about them has to be undone, or overcome. 'Mental Things are alone Real.'[18]

Basing his optimism on this Blakean view of the omnipotent imagination ('Mental Things are alone Real'), Brown thinks it should be possible to create a new ego for man that is not tied to the repressive reality-principle, a new 'Dionysian Ego [which] would be freed from genital organisation'.[19] This is feasible because Brown denies Freud's conclusion that the infant's development through various psycho-sexual stages – oral, anal, phallic – is biologically determined.

Brown is fascinating as a reader of Blake partly because he gives reasons for his adherence to Blakean ideas (like the necessity to transcend genital intercourse) which are illuminating in showing how such ideas function as defences or 'solutions' for our conflict. Brown's quotations from Blake in *Love's Body* suggest the extent of his own preoccupation with oppressive fathers, socially, politically and sexually. What particularly offends him is a feeling that the son, in duplicating the father's intercourse with the mother (the primal scene), has to imitate the father even in the sex act; the son never has priority. Brown rejects genital intercourse quite specifically because it is 'fantasied incest',[20] and for the same reason he shares Blake's identification with Christ because 'Christ is "a son of God who is without a father . . . the Oedipus Complex transcended"'.[21] Frederick Crews ably points out the limitations of Brown's declaration of independence, arguing that what it really shows is an attempt to manoeuvre oneself out of the Oedipal situation.[22] Regardless of the degree to which Brown's views can be seen as defences against guilt and conflict, the effect of a reader's personal involvement with Blake, who did use such ideas defensively, is instructive.

Harold Bloom, whose interests run parallel to my own, has created an imaginative application of a Freudian concept to Blake. Bloom believes Blake is 'the most profound and original theorist of revisionism to appear since the Enlightenment and an inevitable aid to the development of a new theory of Poetic Influence'.[23] The ramifications of Bloom's theory of the poet's radical reaction to his predecessors are complex but its essence is clear: influence is Oedipal struggle on a literary plane, 'Battle between strong equals, father and son as mighty opposites, Laius and Oedipus at the crossroads.'[24] Poets as poets refuse to accept the priority of their poetic fathers and continue to struggle against it by misinterpretation and revisionary creation. Bloom's analysis of Blake's contest with Milton makes us see aspects of Blake's struggle with tradition that Frye and others had smoothed over. Bloom shows us the extent to which Blake and the Romantics were obsessed with priority and origins. Nevertheless, Bloom is interested in different problems from those that will engage us. The terms in which Bloom explains psychic conflict are those of a literary conflict between artists. Blake's revisionary struggles with Milton must also be seen as a part of the younger poet's real obsession with fathers and sons – an obsession generated by personal experience with particular individuals and one that should be treated in its own right as a psychological theme.

Blake's projections of Oedipal conflict in all its variations do foreshadow Freud. And, just as in Freud the question of fathers and sons is not dealt with in isolation, so in Blake it is tied to a great many psychological themes of equal importance. Freudian insights help us to connect these themes dynamically and show how they give structure to Blake's ideas.

The body of Blake's work is an astonishingly translucent description of the unconscious. Not only is he profoundly in touch with the unconscious, but he also reveals it at a level of reality that even the most courageous minds have not been able to reach. Moreover, he reveals it with great depth and clarity, and in such a way as to re-enact, often in a reverse chronological direction, the most basic stages in the development of the human infant. Gradually, through the medium of his work, he forced himself or was drawn into earlier and earlier life-stages in his efforts to resolve his Oedipal dilemma. Father-and-son conflict is the most pervasive of his themes, but equally powerful are his images of developmentally earlier needs and fears. With a thoroughness unparalleled by other artists, Blake evokes important stages of man's early life-cycle, such as the infant's experience at the breast, the child's experience of body functions, and the older child's phallic assertiveness and struggle with the father as replayed in adolescence. Each stage evoked by Blake has its own cluster of body-images that vividly suggest the relations, noted by Freud, between infantile sexuality and certain character-traits and ideas. In addition, Blake re-creates the child's thinking and animistic ways of perception. Being an artist and not a clinician, Blake does not move through these experiences in order. Rather, his forward, backward, and at times obsessive progress suggests attempts to revive and work through early experiences that remained effectively present.

1 *An Island in the Moon*: Images of Dirt and Purity

An Island in the Moon is generally held in low esteem as art, but it is highly relevant for our purposes because it presents major themes and emotional preoccupations of the later prophecies in a relatively stark form. It therefore is of considerable help in understanding problems in the more complex and developed works.

This fragmentary early satire does not fit easily into any formal division of Blake's work, but its conjunction of exquisite lyrics with the scatological imagery abundantly available to eighteenth-century satirists has baffled critics of every perspective. Critics such as S. Foster Damon and Mark Schorer find the nonsense unrelated to the poetry. When Obtuse Angle in *Island* sings the first Song of Innocence, it produces in critics the effect of a pearl found on a dunghill: it is 'one of the great, unexpected moments of literary history'.[1] Damon suggests that the poetry appeared despite Blake's conscious intentions to write satire.[2] David V. Erdman, attempting to connect the two, argues that the Songs continue the satire in a latent form.[3]

It would be more satisfying if an analysis of *Island* could not only reveal Blake's emotions that, repeated as they are, link seemingly random fragments, but also indicate an inner logic behind his juxtaposing pure lyric and gargantuan smut. A tendency carefully to isolate dirty and pure elements from each other caused an early reader to accuse Blake of a 'morbid brain state' when he joined them.[4] But the conjunction, which continues to confuse readers, can be understood as an artistically flawed but still characteristically Blakean effort to resolve recurrent internal conflicts. Moreover, there are precise links between the scatological imagery and the early Songs that involve something quite different from a cleverly disguised continuation of satire.

9

In order to understand the underlying relation between the scatological nonsense and lyric poetry in *Island*, we must first look more closely at the satire as a whole. Since the episodes shift confusedly, a brief summary of the plot might be helpful. The satire has no plot in the usual sense – it consists of a series of social occasions at the islanders' homes – but it seems to fall roughly into two parts and a final fragmentary episode. The first part (chs 1–7) introduces Blake's recurring theme of rivalry, as the three main characters – Quid the Cynic, Suction the Epicurean, and Sipsop the Pythagorean – and a group of islanders are satirised for rivalry and hypocrisy. Their rivalry suggests Blake's larger anxiety about success and failure and, more specifically perhaps, his ambitions as a history-painter. Traditional figures of authority are a main target of hostility. Sipsop, for example, abuses Plutarch and wishes he had been cut up. Sipsop's sadistic idea leads into a song about surgery that traces his hostility back to its source; in the song, it is a mother who, by refusing her son the breast, turns him into a murderous surgeon. The section ends naturally with a renewed 'dissection' of rivals, this time by Quid and Suction.

In the second part (chs 8–11), one Steelyard is the butt of satire. Although he is a contemporary of the hero, Quid, Steelyard's moralism and sense of duty make him seem a conscience, much like that a father or older brother might exert over a family underling. Blake satirises Steelyard, however; he shows that his apparent strength is really weakness. His true master is the woman, imposingly weaponed with a 'sharp tongue'. Woman here is both venomous and, as Quid's misogynic song 'Hail Matrimony' makes clear, intent on entrapping the male for her sexual satisfaction. In this part, then, both Steelyard and the female object of traditional male rivalry are degraded.

The figure who implicitly suffers from male–female hostility is the child (as in the Surgery Song) and his defender, the poet. When Quid is thwarted in his attempt to deal with his frustrated anger through satire of matrimony, he bursts into a childish temper-tantrum. Against this background of uncontrollable anger, the Songs of Innocence that follow show children suffering without cause or resentment. The children's anger is ostensibly suppressed, although, as we shall see, it is expressed in the imagery and syntax. Anger again breaks out openly in the final episode, which ends with his promise to show people the truth by hollowing and stamping, that is, having a temper-tantrum.

David V. Erdman has established that the actual persons satirised in *Island* were friends, not, as had been thought earlier, people Blake angrily regarded as enemies. The most illuminating identifications are of John Flaxman, a fellow artist, as Steelyard, and Blake's brother Robert as Suction. Erdman finds the satire's motive force in Blake's current (1784) anticipation of success in a business-venture which made him sensitive to the opportunism in others.[5] But this explanation does not seem sufficient. Blake's earlier sketches and verses, such as *King Edward the Third*, suggest that he had always been sensitive to the ambitions of others. However, his father's death the year before and his attempt then to make himself independent seem to have focused his characteristic aggressive strivings and corresponding fears of others' hostility.

The perennial problems with *Island* seem best understood by recognising that it deals with Blake's conflicting feelings of rivalry and envy as well as his inability as yet to find adequate art-forms to control them. In 'then She bore Pale desire', an early fragment, Blake himself describes satire not as an artistic device but as a derivative of envy:

Envy hath a Serpents head of fearful bulk . . . her poisnous breath breeds Satire foul Contagion from which none are free. oer whelmd by ever During Thirst She Swalloweth her own Poison. which consumes her nether Parts. from whence a River Springs. Most Black & loathsom through the land it Runs Rolling with furious Noise. . . . tis at this Rivers fount . . . My Cup is fill'd with Envy's Rankest Draught a miracle No less can set me Right. Desire Still pines but for one Cooling Drop and tis Deny'd. while others in Contentments downy Nest do sleep, it is the Cursed thorn wounding my breast that makes me sing. however sweet tis Envy that Inspires my Song. prickt. by the fame of others how I mourn . . . but O could I at Envy Shake my hands. my notes Should Rise to meet the New Born Day.   (30–44, E 437)

The poet must drink the serpent's excrement while longing for the 'Cooling Drop' he imagines is enjoyed by 'others'. That these others are emotionally associated with imagined siblings is suggested by Blake's later association in 'The Ecchoing Green' of nestlings with 'sisters and brothers' round their mothers' laps 'Like birds in their nest' (25–7, E 8). The 'Cooling Drop', following by contented sleep in a nest – which is granted 'others' but denied the frantic poet – suggests specific envy of a rival at the breast – that phenomenon described long before Freud by St Augustine: 'I myself have seen and observed a little baby to be already jealous; and before it could speak, what an angry and bitter look it would cast at another child that sucked away its milk from it.'[6]

Blake's fragment shows, however, that rivalry over the breast has more than negative connotations. Envy can be expressed in sweet song, which indicates that the poet identifies himself with the breast as nourishing and sweet. But being a nourisher is costly: the thorn, envy, that releases the song also releases the poet's lifeblood, a masochistic outpouring that replaces the desired 'Drop' with the poet's spirit and substance. The psychological implication of giving up one's lifeblood to make poetry is that dying is the appropriate punishment for envy and relieves the poet of guilt. If the poet instead of dying turns his anger outward and expresses it directly, envy comes out as his poisoning excrement. In this case, guilt remains with the 'satiric' poet, who then views himself as the locus of filth and spreader of filth. In short, then, the psychological effect of jealous desire for the breast and identification with it is a series of alternating feelings: at some point the feelings of self-loathing generated by a jealous envy are alleviated by the expression of sweetness, which soon gives way again to jealous rage. As we shall see in more detail, this alternating set of guilt-producing and guilt-alleviating feelings in the child and in Blake's recapitulation of early life corresponds with surprising near-precision to the alternation of scatological and lyrical material in *Island*.

Blake thus overtly expresses his envy and rivalry by hurling metaphorical dirt on himself and on others. The language used to describe Quid's brother islanders recalls the abusive anal language of young children. The islanders are described as small, dirty animals, envious of all with higher 'abilities than their nasty, filthy Selves' (*IM* 11, E 456).[7] Patriarchal figures like Voltaire are similarly dirtied or degraded. Scientists are derided as people who engage in dangerous play with 'bog water'. Even Phebus, god of poetry, is besmirched, directly through scatological imagery and indirectly through being portrayed as a merchant concerned with 'filthy lucre'.

The treatment of Phebus functions on two levels. It shifts between serving as a device for satirising the failure of the islanders (and of the eighteenth century in general) to understand the god of poetry and as a device for degrading Quid–Blake's ambitions as poet. Quid's song begins 'In the Moon as Phebus stood over his oriental Gardening' (*IM* 3, E 442). Blake regards Quid's attempts at mythic grandeur with some humour here, but this episode and Quid's later ambitions to outdo Shakespeare and Milton (ch. 7) psychologically prefigure Blake's own ambition in the prophecies. Blake as aspiring painter is linked with Phebus by defining him as 'God of Physic, Painting Perspective Geometry' (*IM* 3, E 442), a list corresponding, as Erdman notes, to the requirements of an eighteenth-century history-painter.[8] The connection is strengthened when Aradobo asks if Phebus understands engraving – Blake's craft.

Thus, it is both as one identified with Phebus and as singer about him that Quid is interrupted by Suction's remark, 'The trumpeter shit in his hat', to which the Pythagorean adds, '& clapt it on his head' (*IM* 3, E 442). These unfraternal remarks disrupt the song and ridicule the singer (much as a raspberry would today). They also work a crude comparison of Quid's song with excrement. One of Blake's late satiric verses, 'When Klopstock England defied', draws its humour from a similar connection between poetry, rivalry and excrement. In that poem, which like Suction's remark also contains the anal image of a trumpet, Blake calls on God while evacuating and binds his rival's soul in his bowels 'Till to the last trumpet it was farted' in trumpetlike response. Implicit is the idea that his rival will be verbally bound as well. Blake ends triumphantly, 'If Blake could do this when he rose up from shite / What might he not do if he sat down to write' (31–2, E 491). The effect of a rival's poetry on Blake is also illustrated by his remark to Crabb Robinson that a passage of Wordsworth's 'caused him a bowel complaint which nearly killed him. . . . Does Mr Wordsworth think his mind can surpass Jehovah?'[9] And, as Abrams acutely remarks, Blake took offence not because of Wordsworth's audacity but because his enterprise paralleled Blake's own. Blake's persistent connection of poetic rivalry with excrement seems to involve two points: One is that his jealous anger had symptomatic expression both in his bodily feelings and in his writing; he expressed anger by writing about excrement, which he almost literally acknowledges in his image of the serpent Envy spreading rivers of filth. In psychodynamics, excrement expresses anger and becomes a metaphor when anger is expressed in words. The second point is that Blake implicitly denigrates satire as excrement and perhaps suggests his guilt at feeling anger or expressing it in satire. In any event, the stage is set for the guilt-relieving alternation with song.

At first, then, Blake associates excrement with Phebus and Quid through Suction's scatological remark. When Quid later resumes his song, he himself degrades Phebus by making him into a swollen-bellied auctioneer. And, just as Blake equates excreting with anger or satire, retention is now equated with hoarding of money: as Phebus says, 'I wont let it go at only so & so' (*IM* 3, E 442). Phebus as the money-god – that is, the god of rententive anality – is then associated with the tyrannically oppressive Jehovah, and both are damned by Sipsop. Although Blake does not develop this image fully in *Island*, the suggestion that retention (and its tyrannical father-figure symbols) is antithetical to creativity – which, by contrast, is again confirmed as letting go – provides the rationale for the presence of this episode here.

Although Blake damns both selfish retentiveness and oppression at the end of the Phebus episode, his own ambition and envy lead him to want to crush his rivals. Intent on success, he identifies in some sense with the aggressors. This ambivalence becomes clear when Quid is contrasted with Chatterton. Chatterton shares Quid–Blake's link with Phebus; he is defined by a list burlesquing Phebus's attributes. As brother poet, he functions as a foil to Quid's extraordinary confidence: Chatterton is the brother who fails and dies. Quid–Blake seems determined not to share Chatterton's fate, even if aggression is the only alternative.

Quid's aggression is plain. When he calls Plutarch a 'nasty ignorant puppy' (*IM* 6, E 444), the apparently mild Sipsop seconds him by wishing that Jack Tearguts (a take-off on John Hunter, a famous surgeon with whom Blake was probably acquainted) could cut Plutarch. 'He understands anatomy better than any of the Ancients hell plunge his knife up to the hilt in a single drive and thrust his fist in . . . he does not mind their crying' (*IM* 6, E 445). Quid takes up Sipsop's aggressive thought in a song tracing the desire to slice up rivals (or patients) to infantile anger against a depriving mother, expressed in the form of a parable of the infant's rejection and his subsequent rage, all in delightfully incongruous meter:

> For flesh & he could neer agree
> She would not let him suck
> . . . .

And this he always kept in mind
And formd a crooked knife
And ran about with bloody hands
To seek his mothers life.

(*IM* 6, E 445)

Surgery's anger, deflected from his mother by a love-affair with 'a dead woman', falls on his sons, 'Scurvy & spotted fever'. He decides to experiment on them and, tying Scurvy down, 'stopt up all its vents', thus discovering dropsy; he discovers guts by cutting out Fever's spots.

Blake thus illustrates the formation of a vicious psychological cycle. The mother's unjust refusal to let the infant suck – presumably caused by his biting – is followed by even greater aggression and creates a sadistic cycle continuing through the generations. Each member is victim and aggressor in turn, and the mode of aggression of each recapitulates the other's as the surgeon's cutting is the adult enactment of the infant's biting. In fact, the cycle is even more detailed, for *Island* also suggests the origins of the mother's rejection of the infant in a comic primal scene where father, 'old corruption', defiles mother flesh.

Adornd in yellow vest
He committed on flesh a whoredom
O what a wicked beast

(*IM* 6, E 445)[10]

Although Blake is at this point more interested in the development of the sadist than in this violent beginning, it seems that the mother's rejection of her male infant is, in part at least, retaliation for the rape. That, in turn, aggravates the cycle of retaliation, for it justifies the son's seeing his father as his rival, the source of his deprivation.

In *Island*, the surgery myth provides a paradigm of the paradoxical relationships of fathers and sons (as well as suggesting the serious roots of *Island*'s comic misogyny). Through Sipsop, Blake portrays the problem of identification with and ambivalence toward an oppressive father. After Quid's Surgery Song, Sipsop affirms his identification with his surgeon father: 'I do it [surgery] because I like it. My father does what he likes & so do I' (*IM* 6, E 446). But Sipsop has evident difficulty mastering his feelings of sympathetic identification with the victim: 'I think some how Ill leave it off there was a woman having her cancer cut & she shriekd so, that I was quite sick' (*IM* 6, E 446). Sipsop's concern about his calling's obvious sadism helps us see Quid's as similarly sadistic. That there is this inner connection between Sipsop and Quid is suggested in Sipsop's remark to Quid: 'you think we are rascals & we think you [painters, poets] are' (*IM* 6, E 446). Each perceives the mixed motives of the other to be similar to his own.

The hostile component in Quid's practice of his art becomes clearer in the next episode (ch. 7). Here, his verbal scalpel is turned against his literary forebears, Homer, Shakespeare and Milton. Each has faults. Milton, who could most nearly be considered as Blake's poetic father, is dismissed as having no feelings – a trait shared by Jack Tearguts. In conclusion, Quid boasts that all three great poets 'might be easily outdone' (*IM* 7, E 446). Suction joins Quid in his rivalry, and another enemy of Blake's, Sir Joshua Reynolds, is added to the list of men to be outdone.

> If I dont knock them all up next year in the Exhibition Ill be hangd said Suction. hang Philosophy . . . do all by your feelings. . . . Im hangd if I dont get up to morrow morning by four o clock & work Sir Joshua – Before ten years are at an end said Quid how I will work these poor milk sop devils.   (*IM* 7, E 446)

Suction functions in part as a mirror of Quid–Blake – even their words run together making it difficult to tell them apart – but several things clearly differentiate him as a younger brother. His name suggests his volatile oral character, and his impulsiveness contrasts with Milton's lack of feeling. If Milton's feelings are overcontrolled, Suction's lack control: 'do all by your feelings and never think at all about it' (*IM* 7, E 446). The differentiation between the brothers makes it possible to move from the theme of rivalry with the father to that of sibling-rivalry. But sibling-rivalry is not an independent concept – the brother, like the father, is a rival for the mother's favour.

Blake's choice of the name 'Suction' for his brother and his presentation of Suction's freedom in expressing feelings suggest an older child's jealous view of a younger one's privileges. And, although Blake undoubtedly loved his younger brother, there must have been times in his childhood when he was intensely jealous.[11]

His work suggests that he felt particularly angry at seeing the newcomer sucking from his mother's breast. By nurturing his brother in his adult life as he did, Blake might have dealt with his early rivalry and derived some satisfaction of his own need for nurture. But some ambivalence naturally persisted. There are hints of fraternal rivalry, for example, in the drawing on the last page of *Island* and in the theme of the pictures Blake sent to the Academy in 1785. The *Island* drawing suggests a playful contest on a serious subject: which brother is the English genius. Robert's laurel-crowned profile is threatened by a goat. Blake's profile is crossed out; the brothers' names are reciprocally smudged.[12] In *Island*, therefore, when Suction hopes his paintings for the Exhibition will 'knock them all up' (*IM* 7, E 446), one wonders whether Blake was representing what he felt, consciously or unconsciously, to be Robert's competition with him. Although they are close in *Island* (as in life), Suction does interrupt Quid's song with his remark about the faecal trumpeter, a type of mildly aggressive, anal humour resembling the name and face smudging of the *Island* drawing. In reality, it was Blake who sent the paintings, not Suction–Robert.

The pictures Blake sent are of the Joseph story, and they may represent aspects of his feelings toward both Robert and James, his oldest brother who had recently inherited his father's business. The question of inheritance, important in the Joseph story, was relevant to Blake's life. His father had died in 1783, and Erdman suggests that there was probably some unpleasantness with James over dividing the inheritance.[13] Blake's only surviving letter to James shows Blake defensively explaining his plans for making profits. To some extent, James has assumed the paternal role and is thus caught in Blake's rivalry with his father. Blake's paintings *Joseph's Brethren Bowing before Him* and *Joseph Ordering Simeon to Be Bound*, suggest fantasies of triumph and revenge as well as the self-justification Erdman sees in them.[14]

Blake's relation to Robert, on the other hand, was that of a teacher or parent. Robert, Blake's junior, lived in his household, shared William's sketchbook and had similar ambitions. The Joseph story contains a division like that in the Blake family between hostile older brothers (in Blake's case, James was perhaps only disapproving) and the true brother of Joseph's soul, Benjamin. But the Joseph story also suggests Joseph's ambivalence toward Benjamin: Joseph sentences the boy to death for stealing his silver cup. The cup hints both at the primitive source of ambivalence in the competition for nurture, and at the ceremonial quality of winning parental favour. Joseph's action serves as a warning to Benjamin not to usurp his power, even as he (Joseph) had done with his elder brothers. For his third painting, Blake chooses the moment when forgiveness has won over other feelings, *The Bard, Joseph Making Himself Known to His Brethren*. This emphasis on forgiveness adumbrates the solution of the mature Blake to the problem of rivalry.

Island's male characters are on a spectrum from the untrammelled Suction to the repressed figure of Steelyard. The satire's first part ends with Quid and Suction's shared rivalry toward paternal figures. The second part introduces Steelyard – a type of father or elder brother. As we shall see, the shift of subject from Quid and his ambitions to Steelyard's moralism foreshadows later allegoric shifts in Blake's work between the poet Los and the moralistic Urizen.

The character of Steelyard reveals Blake's feelings toward the artist John Flaxman, who played an important role in Blake's life at the time. Flaxman, although only two years Blake's senior, seems from the beginning to have helped and promoted him.[15] He introduced Blake to his own patroness, Mrs Matthew, and helped to publish Blake's *Poetical Sketches* in 1783. Flaxman obtained a commission for Blake from Mr Hawkins. In April 1784 he wrote to his new friend, Hayley, praising Blake and adding that Mr Hawkins was raising a subscription to send Blake to Rome to study. Although in fact it was Flaxman who went abroad, he was obviously a real friend, going beyond words of friendship to energetic support of Blake. Blake's portrayal of Flaxman is fuller than most of the others and is particularly interesting because it shows Blake's mixed feelings toward someone taking the role of elder brother or father.

Blake not only accepted Flaxman's patronage but was emotionally dependent on him. He later said that he survived the terrors of revolution only because of his 'conjunction with Flaxman, who knows how to forgive Nervous Fear'.[16] However, he clearly felt ambivalent about his dependence. The name 'Steelyard the Lawgiver' suggests not only strength but also harshness and inflexibility. Moreover, through the character of Steelyard Blake implies that Flaxman has both serious weaknesses and a tendency toward oppression. Though Steelyard passively submits to ideas of religious duty, his name indicates that the other side of this passivity is tyranny. And, here, Blake suggests the way certain traits, like masochism and sadism, exist together in individuals, with one or the other being dominant for a time or indefinitely.

Steelyard has an unflattering image of himself derived from Christian themes of self-abasement. He sees men as St Jerome did, 'poor crawling reptiles' (IM 8, E 447), with no claim to happiness. His god is the sadistic Jehovah of Hervey's Judgement Day sermons. Ideas of duty and religion restrain Steelyard's impulses. Because of his domestic responsibilities, he feels unable to 'knock up his rivals'. His hostility is transformed into an apocalyptic longing for total destruction – 'the wreck of matter & the crush of worlds' (IM 8, E 447) – a solution that would destroy him along with his rivals.

Steelyard not only abases himself before a harsh God but also allows himself to be tongue-lashed by a woman (Miss Gittipin), and Blake connects the two phenomena, both standing for the parents. The satire of Steelyard is interwoven with a satire of women, and Blake demonstrates how Steelyard's excessive self-control reinforces what he later called the 'female will'. His saintly tolerance only indicates his willingness to be walked on: 'They call women the weakest vessel but I think they are the strongest. A girl has always more tongue than a boy' (IM 8, E 447).

Blake's own attitude toward woman was that she ought to be sheep to man's lion or, as he put it in his annotations to Lavater, 'the female life lives from the light of the male' (E 585). Blake also seems to have acted on such views. According to Gilchrist, when Blake's wife offended his brother Robert, Blake made her kneel and beg forgiveness. In Island Blake not only explores Steelyard's weakness in the face of women but also suggests that the tradition of courtly love and its religious counterpart, Mariolatry, conspire to give women generally a false strength. To illustrate the unmanning effects of the female will, Blake follows Miss Gittipin's provocative speech with a parodic pastoral version of a courtly love-song:

> Phebe drest like beauties Queen
> Jellicoe in faint peagreen.
> (IM 8, E 448)

As the 'jelly' in Jellicoe's name and the pun on 'faint' imply, the hero is turned to jelly by the heroine. Jellicoe's relation to Phebe cum Venus is a comic preview of the Fall of Man when, in Vala, Man melts weakly on Vala's breast.

After this song comes an interlude of scatological imagery and aggression – a duet between Quid and Suction that indicates their rejection of what came before. The duet is about men in competition and has homosexual overtones.

> QUID: O ho Said Doctor Johnson
> To Scipio Africanus
> If you dont own me a Philosopher
> Ill kick your Roman Anus
>
> SUCTION: A ha To Doctor Johnson
> Said Scipio Africanus
> Lift up my Roman Petticoatt
> And kiss my Roman Anus.
> (*IM* 9, E 448–9)

With this incursion of rather forced humour, Blake returns to the problem of male rivalry. Argument between the rationalist Johnson and the visionary Scipio is seen in terms of kicking or kissing posteriors.

The duet is followed by a street-song and great confusion. To restore order, Suction calls on Steelyard, who sings a romantic ballad, an idealisation befitting his inhibited character:

> O there did I spy a young maiden sweet
> Among the Violets that smell so sweet
> (*IM* 9, E 449)

Just as the philosophers' duet presented a contrasting attitude to the courtly love-song, an explicit parody of the pretensions of romantic love follows Steelyard's ballad. The lover is now reduced to a fool 'blinded by love' and the woman to molasses from which it is difficult to disentangle oneself.

Joe Bradley saw for he had but one eye saw a treacle Jar   So he goes of his blind side & dips his hand up to the shoulder in treacle. here lick lick lick said he.   (*IM* 9, E 449)

The humorous substitution of sticky treacle for womanly sweetness suggests Blake's more serious views of the dangerous devouring or excremental aspects of love. As Blake wrote in *Jerusalem*, 'I will make their places of joy & love, excrementitious' (*J* 88:39).

The sequence from the duet to the treacle-pot is connected by metaphors suggesting incorrect use of the senses. The rational Dr Johnson is compared to a bat 'Winking & blinking' – an image that Blake eventually develops into the spiritually blind Spectre. The theme of seeing or not seeing continues with Steelyard's spying of the maiden (her setting among violets is an alliterative suggestion of his desire to violate her)[17] and culminates in one-eyed Joe going 'of his blind side' to consummate his love with the treacle-pot. Images of smell and taste also occur throughout the sequence. The sweet, entrapping treacle reveals the dangerous possibilities of the alluring and seemingly innocent sweet violets and maiden. Scopprell's refrain, 'I ask the Gods no more', sung after the story of Joe, ironically comments on the desires of fallen man.

At this low point of the chapter, Quid interrupts with a song on matrimony, bringing the theme of woman's degradation (and man's danger) to a climax. Quid's 'fingerfooted' women 'Formed to suckle all Mankind' are clearly, albeit humorously, beasts. Starved for sex, they require Matrimony's 'universal Poultice' to make them resemble cheerful birds. Matrimony in Quid's view is not 'made of Love' but made of unsatisfied sexual desires, both of the woman and of the lover who 'panteth for a Bride'. So strong are these desires that he overlooks the bride's deformities.

> For if a Damsel's blind or lame
> Or Nature's hand has crooked her frame
> Or if she's deaf or is wall eyed
> Yet if her heart is well inclined
> Some tender lover she shall find.
> (*IM* 9, E 450–1)

Blake's early song 'How sweet I roam'd' (E 404) suggests that the caged male is unhappy after his initial satisfaction. His Notebook poems suggest that he felt trapped in monogamy. Perhaps this is why, when Scopprell questions Quid's right to make fun of matrimony, Quid erupts with fury. Blake's deletion of the exchange with Scopprell and Miss Gittipin's remark that Quid 'always spoils good company in this manner' (*IM* 9, E 451) indicate, as Erdman notes, that here the mirror came too close for comfort.[18]

But what exactly is being mirrored? There is more to Blake's strain of misogyny than a reflection of his marriage difficulties. His imagery in *Island* suggests that he is preoccupied with homosexual ideas and fantasies and that degrading women is only part of a larger problem. In the first section, homosexual ideas (along with sadistic hetero-sexual ones) are present in Sipsop's description of his father plunging his knife and fist into his patient's body. Quid's complementary song about a surgeon also includes both homosexual and sadistic hetero-sexual ideas: the surgeon cuts up his sons, symbolically impregnating one by inducing a swelling dropsy, and the surgeon tries to cut his mother 'flesh' with his knife, imitating his father Corruption's original rape of her. Sipsop's dilemma is to decide whether to be like the father and cut/penetrate another person or be like the mother, as his effeminate 'sissy' name implies he is, and have it done to him. The issue takes this particular form because Blake is depicting the problems of male identity and male–female relations partly from the viewpoint of a child at a pregenital stage of development, when sex is often misapprehended as an act of sadistic violence. The alternative sexual directions Blake presents seem equally depressing: primal rage at the mother for withholding the breast (and later for denying sexual favour) works toward a passive and eventually homosexual choice, while terror at being emasculated (cut) works against it.

In the second section of *Island*, Blake continues to depict rela-tionships from perspectives of early childhood. He creates the ingredients of an Oedipal triangle comprising Steelyard, the law-giving father, the seductive mother and the aggressive poet–son, but, instead of having the male characters struggle over a woman (or women) as he does later with, say, Bromion and Theotormon, Blake shows an emasculated father who relates to women like a meek and frightened 'well-trained' child still subject to maternal tongue-lash-ings, rather than an adult man. Quid–Blake's role as son is not spelled out in *Island*; instead it is Blake as author of the satire who combats the father by depicting him as feminised and weak.

Though Blake clearly disapproves of Steelyard's being childish or womanish, he is ambivalent about the possibility of egalitarian male homosexuality which will dispense with women altogether. In the section dealing with male–female relations, Blake creates a locker-room atmosphere in which men deal with their fears of women through aggressive joking. The joking where the homosexual over-tones are most clearly physical – in the duet about Dr Johnson – comes after a song about a man being turned to jelly by a woman.

Quid's outburst against Miss Gittipin breaks off all talk of women. Returning to the relations between men – this time in society – Blake seems to be attempting to alleviate anxiety by replacing anger and envy with sympathy and love. Obtuse Angle's song about a charity hospital is ambiguous. On the one hand, it suggests a movement away from individual rivalry and hatred: Obtuse asks the company to consider instead the model of charity presented by Sutton's construction of a home 'for aged men & youth' (*IM* 9, E 451). On the other hand, as Erdman notes, Obtuse concentrates more on the sanitary facilities than on genuine sympathy.[19] Blake's ambiguous presentation may stem from his feelings about Sutton as a paternal figure caring for dependent wards. These 'helpless sick' are the first people in *Island* whom Blake treats without satire. What satire there is in Obtuse's song is directed against the paternal figure's lack of love. But, owing to Blake's ambivalence, the satire is not clearly communicated, and critics such as Martha W. England, for example, are able to read the poem as 'a tribute to Thomas Sutton, who by building a hospital did more for humanity than Locke'.[20]

Steelyard likes Obtuse's song very much and begs to have it repeated. If there is irony in Steelyard's request and in his being chosen as the next singer, it strongly suggests Blake's ambivalence toward Flaxman, for here there is also a reflection of Flaxman's piety and actual generosity toward Blake. The underlying link between Sutton and Flaxman–Steelyard seems to be that, although they did good, they were deficient in love. Steelyard's song 'This city & this country' (*IM* 9, E 452) continues the strain of irony that shows ambivalence, and, again, Blake's satiric intention is obscure. This song, in which the wealthy mayors invite the hungry poor for a feast, is read by some critics as simple praise of English hospitality. Yet there is certainly an ironic contrast between the well-fed fathers of society and the hungry children. As Beer sensitively remarks, the song contains mixed feelings: 'irony . . . but . . . also nostalgia, for the lawgiver is . . . yearning for the generosity of true justice'.[21]

After Steelyard's song, Inflammable Gass, the scientist, has a fit of rage paralleling Quid's earlier one; the songs of charity are thus explicitly bracketed by fits of rage before and after their appearance. Quid's rage had led to two songs that present sympathy and charity as alternatives to envy and rage, but rage persisted in the suggestion that there is not enough real sympathy and love. Inflammable's outburst is more cataclysmic than Quid's, but it too leads to a counter-image. His angry breaking of the bottle of wind represents in one apocalyptic image the satire's persistent themes of dirt and aggression and contrasts with the defensive cleanliness of the charity hospital, where gutters and sinks safeguard against pestilence. And Blake suggests again, as he did with the serpent of Envy, that outer disease is a manifestation of inner anger, by making Inflammable's rage result directly in pestilence.

Inflammable, as furious scientist, complements Quid as furious poet. Earlier, Blake described the surgeon's sadism; here, his imagery suggests that scientific curiosity derives from an earlier concern with faeces: Inflammable and scientists in general are shown to be preoccupied with nastiness and dirt ('heres the bottle of wind that I took up in the bog house'). Inflammable refers to his experiments as his 'puppets', which hints at a more-or-less separate connotation connecting science with autoerotic activity. The idea that scientists play with dirt may help to explain Blake's hostility to science. In any event, it seems fairly clear that the pestilence not only is the concrete expression of Inflammable's anger but also symbolises a punishment for anger and perhaps for play with forbidden matter.[22]

The explosion of plague-air depresses the islanders; at their next meeting the dirty air seems to be still in their thoughts as they try 'every method to get good humour' (*IM* 11, E 453). In this context, the lyric 'Upon a holy thursday' serves to banish bad thoughts of forbidden activity and punishment and temporarily to provide 'good humour' by evoking the innocence of childhood. The poem's metaphors reverse the previous 'dirty' imagery. The children's clean faces and pure song contrast with Inflammable's bog-wind and with the scatological songs and satire. Blake's pastoral imagery builds up the contrast and adds to the relief felt at finally being free of filth.

Blake's clean, peaceful images gain power from their connection with their unconscious opposites – the dirt and rage they deny. Critical insistence (with the notable exception of Erdman) on the gulf between *Island*'s scatology and the innocent Songs and failure to relate these to their contexts omits what critically links them; that is, that Blake was insisting on the children's purity and goodness as a defence against the filth he had just spread. Open expression of rage by the children would have defeated Blake's psychological need to bring 'good cheer' and, more generally, to induce feelings of goodness. This arrangement, however, has masochistic undertones: the children respond to their fate, as deprived orphans, only by singing pious hymns. But anger is nevertheless implied by Blake's use of syntax and images which evoke ideas of rage elsewhere in his work.

Thousands of little girls & Boys raising their innocent hands

Then like a mighty wind they raise to heavn the voice of song.
(*IM* 11, E 453)

For example, the line 'The hum of multitudes were there [i.e., in the church] but multitudes of lambs' (*IM* 11, E 453) suggests that elsewhere multitudes are not singing meekly. In Blake's poem about the French Revolution, they were revolutionary crowds, and later, in *Vala*, in an apocalyptic moment, a group of deprived children express their rage fully. The multitude of lambs is transformed into the angry multitude hinted at by the earlier syntax:

a mighty multitude rage furious
. . . .
Rend limb from limb the Warrior & the tyrant . . .
The furious wind still rends.[23]

The 'mighty wind' of the children's voices has become the 'furious wind' rending oppressors. Blake's capacity and predilection later to transform the early images is adumbrated by the initial ambiguous comparison of the children's peaceful song to a strong wind and mighty thunder. Moreover, these images not only suggest the power of rage under the cloak of innocence but also recall Blake's earlier aggressive excretory images, most particularly Gass's bog-wind.

The nature of this transformation becomes clearer when the images are contrasted with those in Blake's sketch of Envy. The watery flow of clean-faced children is in direct contrast to the 'Black & loathsom' river issuing from Envy's 'nether Parts'. Moreover, the children move in orderly fashion behind their guardians, and the Thames is contained by its banks; in contrast, the river of Envy rolls wildly over the land. Its 'furious Noise' contrasts with the 'harmonious thunderings' of the children's song, resounding among 'the seats of heavn'. The essence of the transformation is thus a displacement from below upwards: the filthy nether-parts become clean faces and mouths and the river of excrement becomes a stream of sweet song. One result of the transformation is that Blake's anger against the parental guardians becomes repressed and deflected into more acceptable moral forms.

The idealised image of a good and pure child in 'Upon a holy thursday' can be seen to cover an image of a dirty and hostile child that emerges in the following songs. In Mrs Nannicantipot's song, hostility is projected outward as the dangers of night that the mother–nurse feels threaten the child. Quid's song 'O Father' (*IM* 11, E 454) is more complex; here, Blake represents a child's feelings of being dirty and unworthy of love. Blake evokes with nightmarish intensity the child's complete dependence on an unpredictable adult and his terror of being abandoned. The reason for the father's quick step and implied anger is not clear. It is not even clear whether the father is real or only a dream-image, but the child's anxiety is evident and he wakes in wet and mire to find his fears confirmed, his father gone. The situation suggests early memories of incontinence and parental anger, but the wet and mire has more general relevance as an objectification of feelings of dirtiness or unworthiness.

Overall, the evidence is clear that rage, expressed in excremental imagery, is the chief impulse in *Island*. Blake also begins to explore ways of coping with envy, rivalry and other dangerous impulses. This entailed considerable conflict. Blake himself probably felt dirty when he envied or was angry, and it is this conflict that appears beneath the surface of 'Upon a holy thursday' and 'O Father'. Thus, perhaps the self-critical adult Blake harbours within an earlier Blake, suggested particularly in 'O Father', who is afraid of loss of love and external punishment. Such an interpretation is strengthened by the next song, 'O I say you Joe', which indicates the reasons a boy might fear abandonment. Here dirty actions are coupled with aggression, and the poem's child narrator assumes the place of the abandoning father. He will leave, not be left.

> Ive a good mind to go
> And leave you all
> I never saw saw such a bowler
> To bowl the ball in a turd [*first version*]
> And to clean it with my handkercher.
>   (*IM* 11, E 454)

The narrator's other friend is also a 'bad' child. He has given the narrator (who sounds somewhat like a childhood version of the pious Steelyard) a black eye, 'knockd down the wicket / And broke the stumps' (*IM* 11, E 454). The narrating child is assuming the father's attitudes – perhaps as Blake's reasonable elder brother James did in their childhood.

Such realism in depicting children in their essential ambivalence is rare in Blake. The lack of such realism may be explained in part by the strength of Blake's forces of denial. The *Songs of Innocence*, which grow from the songs in *Island*, show idealised children who are notably free of envy or anger against their often cruel fate. Blake becomes the champion of these 'good' children in *Songs of Experience*, reworking his own rage and envy in the larger context of legitimate protest against the exploitation of children which was all too frequent in eighteenth-century England. Within *Island*, however, the denial of anger present in the innocent songs, while foreshadowing Blake's later ideas of forgiveness, does not maintain its hold beyond the songs themselves. *Island*'s concluding dialogue, the most violent in the satire, shows Blake both experiencing and projecting his anger. Whoever will not have his *Songs of Innocence* 'will be ignorant fools and will not deserve to live'.

> . . . their nasty hearts poor devils are eat up with envy – they envy me my abilities & all the Women envy your abilities my dear they hate people who are of higher abilities than their nasty filthy Selves.   (*IM* 11, E 456)

In these spiteful outbursts (by Quid and his conversational partner) we see clearly the streak of paranoia that opposed Blake's attempts to resolve conflict. This adumbration of paranoia in *Island* is not surprising considering the extreme ambivalence and archaic attitudes toward objects that are exhibited there and which form the basis for ideas of persecution that plagued Blake until the end of his life.

Island contains in rudimentary form almost all the psychological themes of Blake's later work. There are both his pervasive theme of inevitable rivalry between brothers, fathers and sons and his equally strong theme of fear and dislike of the sought-after female. In *Island*, Blake seems to be working his way back to childhood memories, recapitulating relations to parents and siblings and stages of development. The excremental nature of much of the material suggests the process of regression, perhaps triggered by his father's death the year before. Blake depicts relationships of rivalry with father and brothers in the language of anality and in terms of the sado-masochistic impulses appropriate to that stage. Anger is expressed metaphorically as spreading filth or disease. Similarly, guilt over sadistic impulses is expressed by images of dirt and unworthiness. Blake does not concentrate on only one stage of development, however, but moves between them describing similar tendencies in the language of earlier or later stages of development: the sadism expressed in images of surgical cutting is related to the earlier anger of the biting infant as well as to later homosexual desires to penetrate another man.

Early in *Island*, Blake's depiction of peer-rivalry leads him to recall or evoke deprivation at the breast as a source of anger and envy. The act of writing in this context appears as a belated attempt to do in one's rivals: satire is the literary surrogate for attacking with dirt or faeces. In this first part, Blake actively deals with rivalry by identifying with the aggressor and sadistically cutting up others as he fears being cut. But this extreme aggressiveness arouses guilt and fears of retaliation.

In the second part, Blake sets up Flaxman as a father with whom it is dangerous to identify for the converse reason, because he is self-castrating and subservient to the female. Blake sketches out her seductive and threatening nature in his misogynistic song and then shows his male characters retreating from dangerous heterosexuality into homosexual jesting. The comic images of kissing or kicking posteriors continue in sexual terms the earlier vacillation between cutting and being cut. However, as a solution, submitting to one's rival sexually is unsatisfactory because it means being feminised like Steelyard, and vulnerable to female abuse.

In Blake's concluding section, he depicts a possible way out of rivalry through a sublimation of homosexual feelings. He shows men engaged in charitable and nurturing activities that prefigure his later poet Los's creation and care of infants. The alternation of mood here, between anger and innocent love or goodness, expressed in alternating imagery of dirt and purity, exemplifies an important structural pattern in Blake's work — expression of impulse followed by either defensive denial or symbolic punishment, or a combination of both. Impulse in the form of Quid's childish temper-tantrum begins the concluding section. The following defensive song about the charity hospital suggests, in its emphasis on sanitising the youth and the sick, the adult's wish to clean essentially corrupt children. Blake's sympathy with this urge to help others is qualified by his identification with the recipients of the charity, and the persistence of some anger, in this case against the adult figures who self-righteously presume to clean up the victims. This anger breaks out in the text in a second tantrum by Inflammable Gass in which he literally releases pestilential filth. Both tantrums suggest a child's rage at being thought bad or corrupt, and in a deleted passage Quid is actually rebuked like a child by Miss Gittipin for characteristically spoiling 'good company' with his outbursts. Gass's tantrum leads directly to Blake's defensive insistence that children are naturally innocent, clean, and implicitly victimised by unfeeling parental guardians. Feelings of dirtiness and of being unworthy of parental love denied by Blake's insistence on innocence then re-emerge in songs about dirty, bad and forsaken children, after which the manuscript breaks off with Quid's preparing to have another tantrum.

If *Island* is an identification with the child, if it is written with the feelings of a certain time of childhood, and if fears of loss of love because of one's anger and badness are the underlying problems which it attempts to resolve, then both its dirt and its innocence are relevant modes of expression. Furthermore, their strange alternation is itself relevant because it expresses the alternation of bad feelings and wishes with good feelings and defensive attempts to see oneself as good and clean. At the same time, it is significant that the 'clean' children are shown at the mercy of guardians and their fate a fate which, though seemingly undeserved, functions as a punishment for, as well as a denial of, ugly and angry feelings.

Seeing *Island* as an evocation of early problems and stages of development rationalises its organisation. But it does not make *Island* art, and this may be what underlies the critics' general unwillingness to find any rationale for the work. Perhaps they wanted an explanation which would also show the work is good. Certainly, one might ask why *Island* is not a work of art if it reflects the deep experience of early childhood, since the ability to evoke such experience often gives power to art. The answer would seem to be not that Blake's themes or concerns are insubstantial, but rather that, except for the Songs of Innocence, there is a lack of aesthetic distance and control. Blake represents experience in modes too close to the child's – a stream of good and bad feelings punctuated by tantrums and lacking the organising insights of later life. Moreover, the satiric mudslinging and anal humour not only lack artistic elaboration but operate at cross-purposes to the desperate quality of Blake's concern with questions of envy and sexual identity. Later, Blake combines *Island*'s anal imagery with the characteristics of Steelyard to create the obsessed 'anal' personality of Urizen, this time with psychological and artistic effectiveness. Urizen's repressive writings (which Blake depicted as black blobs) are created from the same source as Quid's satire. But, in Urizen's case, Blake projects the impulses he disapproved of into a clearly delineated character instead of spilling them throughout a chaotic text, and he is able both to analyse and to repudiate them rather than simplistically to enact them.

2 *Tiriel* and *Thel*: Forms of Devouring and Self-sacrifice

The Book of Thel, one of Blake's loveliest lyrical narratives, was written at about the same time (1789) as *Tiriel*,[1] a portrait of an envious tyrant. On the surface, *Thel* and *Tiriel* present contrasting modes of being, but they have an internal connection that illuminates both. The core of both poems is the same psychological issue: the relations beteen parents and children. Blake's imagery sketches out alternate views of love, as devouring greed or as self-sacrifice, and suggests ways in which the infant's experiences form the basis for adult behaviour.

In Blake's *Thel*, a youthful protagonist, worried about death and her function in life, is introduced to a world without conflict where nurturing figures, an imaginatively humanised Lilly, Cloud and Clod, voluntarily sacrifice themselves to the world's infants (flowers, lamb and worm). In *Tiriel* the central conflict between father and children is evident from even the briefest summary. King Tiriel, blind and banished by his sons, returns to curse them. Thereafter, Tiriel visits his childhood home, and we learn of a similar conflict with his own father. Finally, after again cursing his sons, Tiriel leaves them dead, curses his own repressive father, and dies.

In *Tiriel*, the father–son conflict is expressed through a rich variety of oral imagery, particularly that of devouring or being devoured. This imagery, although explicit, has not been given critical attention. It runs from the opening scene, where Tiriel curses his sons for draining their mother and wishing to devour his flesh, to the end, where he remembers his own deprived and hungry infancy. This cannibalistic imagery, so obvious in *Tiriel*, also occurs in *Thel*. In *Thel*, however, the connotations of the imagery are reversed: ideal-ised mother–infant relations become the model for Christian self-

31

sacrifice. Thus, in *Thel*, the mother selflessly allows her children to devour her. But, although one set of images is negative and the other positive, the same fantasies lie behind both. Since it is easier to recognise these fantasies in *Tiriel*, let us begin by analysing the negative vision.

Because *Tiriel* portrays a cruel tyrant who abuses his sons, it encourages interpretations solely in terms of the implications of the father's role. It can be seen as an allegory of the failure of reason or moral virtue,[2] or as a portrayal of the state of experience, as distinct from innocence. But *Tiriel* makes more sense as an attempt to deal with a unified psychological reality in which both parents are critical because each creates conflict in the other's relationship to the child. The psychological connections need not be expressed in plot alone; in *Tiriel*, the father dominates the plot, while ideas about the mother dominate the imagery. Plot and imagery are generated by fantasies that, although often not well integrated or consistent, embody dynamic relationships between mother, father and sons. Similarly, the roughly contemporaneous *Songs of Innocence*, which seem to be about one parent only, take their character from the effect of the other parent's situation: for Blake, *Songs* can present a happy mother–child relationship precisely and solely because the father does not appear; hence, no conflict occurs between him and the child or between him and the mother.

The conflict in *Tiriel*, then, like the lack of it in *Songs*, implicitly involves both parents as actors in the family drama. Their conduct is naturally susceptible to moral evaluation, but it does not follow that Blake can be read in *Tiriel* simply as condemning the father's conduct. Blake treats conflict as occurring within the mind of each individual as well as between individuals; he therefore cannot isolate an offending part of the mind and condemn it, a point he stresses in his later theory of contraries. The figure of Tiriel represents the judgemental or censorious part of the mind in conflict with its other parts. In *Tiriel* Blake explores the way this part of the mind is formed and passed on from father to son.

In the poem's initial scene, Tiriel, exhibiting the dying Myratana to his sons, tries to make them accept the guilt for their mother's death. His accusations are couched in terms of nurture and oral greed: 'Nourishd with milk ye serpents, nourishd with mothers tears & cares' (27); 'The serpents sprung from her own bowels have draind her dry as this' (32).[3] Blake presents the mother, rather as in a morality play, as an emblem of guilt the sons must absorb through their senses. Where they originally felt pleasure, these senses are made to feel trauma. Tiriel first orders his sons to 'look on her that bore you . . . see the death of Myratana' (8–10), then to 'Listen & hear your mothers groans' (24), and finally to touch her body. The sense of smell is invoked in Tiriel's wish that his sons 'may lie as now your mother lies like dogs cast out / The stink of your dead carcases annoying man & beast' (45–6). Of all the senses, 'devouring' taste is imagined as the most guilty, not only of draining the mother dry but also of wishing to devour the father's flesh. In his curse, Tiriel symbolically punishes this wish to devour: instead of the once-desired milk, he asks that 'the heavens rain wrath / As thick as northern fogs around your gates to choke you up' (43–4).

These fantasies of devouring the mother occur within a larger structure determined by fantasies of Oedipal conflict: Tiriel's sons have rebelled against their father and cast him out. Blake's illustration of the sons being cursed (Illus. 1 – G. E. Bentley's plate 1) merges symbols of orality with ideas of Oedipal crime. The plate shows a struggle with feelings of guilt denied by the text. The stiff figures of the sons seem passive, as Bentley notes, rather than boldly rebellious,

Illus. 1   *Tiriel: Tiriel Supporting Myratana*

and their frozen positions further suggest the immobilising presence of opposing impulses of attack and restraint. Heuxos, the eldest son, shows this tension in both his hands and his feet. One hand is slightly raised towards his father; the other, palm down, seems to cancel the gesture of threat or entreaty. The same indecision is shown by the feet – one rooted to the spot, the other suggesting possible forward motion.

The sons' attributes indicate different types of relation with their father and mother. Heuxos's crown marks him as the usurper of his father's kingship. Tiriel's contrasting bald skull is an image of his son's guilty desire: the wish to dispossess the father. If King Heuxos is the son who, identifying with the father, succeeds him, the second son, with his sensitive face and laurel wreath, suggests the poet. Although no poet is alluded to in the text, this almost feminine figure is an older version of the vulnerable child–poet in Tiriel's final speech, the victim of his violent father, who 'scourges off all youthful fancies from the newborn man' (381). This illustration of the laurel-wreathed poet son, shrinking from the paternal curse, prefigures, as we shall see later, the thorn-crowned crucified Christ of *Vala*. Bacchic vineleaves in the third son's hair, although unexplained by the text, link him with Tiriel's images of devouring and drinking dry and suggest that he represents the infantile oral character. Together, the three sons suggest comparison with the similar trinity in *Island* of lawgiver (Flaxman or James), poet (Blake), and the impulsive oral personality Suction (Robert).

The opening text and illustration having sketched a pattern of father–son conflict, the second section of *Tiriel* (lines 53–152) explores the origin of conflict in childhood. The oral imagery that Blake used to describe Oedipal conflict is psychologically more relevant to this earlier stage of childhood. Evidently, Blake felt an overlapping connection between these two stages; perhaps Oedipal conflict simply reminded him of other feelings of conflict; or perhaps he saw repression by the father in the later Oedipal situation as justified by the son's earlier oral greed. In any event, Tiriel moves back from being the father to his own past in the vale of his father Har. Though Blake gives no reason for Tiriel's seeking out his father after cursing his sons, the two actions are dynamically connected: Tiriel's cursing both arouses a need for forgiveness and reminds him of his father's reaction to his own rebellion. Blake's perspective shifts between seeing Tiriel as a harsh agent of justice and as a self-doubting seeker for a sense of justification. The ingenious effect of Har's childlike senility is to suggest a son's feeling toward his father; expected roles are reversed, with the senile father feeling the child's fearfulness. At other times, Har is again Tiriel's old father. With Har's ambiguous, shifting age, Blake expresses in a double image the child's fear of his father and the aged patriarch's fear of his sexually mature son.

At the outset, Blake describes Har and his wife Heva as 'like two children' (57), deleting a later explicit reference to 'aged father and mother' that interfered with this view of them. The aged couple play like young children, and are 'delighted with infant dreams' (61). Blake stresses their helpless dependence on their mother–nurse Mnetha. At the first sight of Tiriel they run 'weeping like frighted infants for refuge in Mnethas arms' (64).

Tiriel enacts the role of a threatening paternal figure approaching the child's (Har's) beloved mother (Mnetha). Here Blake projects a fantasy of triumph over the father: Har fears Tiriel's aggression against Har's mother as the child Tiriel once presumably feared Har's against Tiriel's mother. Although no sexual act is explicit, Har's fear of aggression against the mother corresponds to a common childhood misperception of such acts as aggressive, striking or wounding.[4] Har specifically fears Tiriel's aggression and magical powers of penetration despite his eyeless state.

> He wanders without eyes & passes thro thick walls & doors
> Thou shalt not smite my mother Mnetha O thou eyeless man.
>
> (77–8)

Tiriel responds to Har's fears by indicating his own impotence: he throws away his staff and kneels. Har's blessing, a response to Tiriel's helplessness, centres, as Nancy Bogen notes, on Tiriel's defects.[5] The blessing implies that Har can accept Tiriel only when he is helpless and impotent:

> God bless thy shriveld beard . . .
> Thou has no teeth old man & thus I kiss thy sleek bald head.
>
> (88–9)

Har's fear of energy and vigour is manifested also in his invitation to Tiriel to join him in a great bird-cage, an image that recalls the restraining cages of matrimony in *Island*. In Blake's text, then, Har is both the aged father, fearful of his son's potency, and a fearful child who evokes aspects of the child Tiriel. Along with Blake's evocation of a child's fear is an evocation of the child's sense that parental sexuality inexplicably gives pleasure to his mother, which the child would like to share. Two of the illustrations (Bentley's plates II and VIII) project fantasies of the parents' pleasure and the child's participation. In these, Har, a robust godlike figure, appears with his mother Mnetha and wife Heva, who are both portrayed as beautiful young women. To Bentley, the discrepancy between these illustrations and the text and other illustrations showing Har and Heva in advanced age indicates that Blake found life in the vale of Har 'more important and attractive . . . than he could easily show in the poem alone'.[6] These illustrations suggest the eruption of material that, although dynamically connected to the other fantasies that Blake presents, is not well integrated into his fable. This material involves issues concerning females that appear in various sections of *Tiriel*; an analysis of these issues requires us to depart temporarily from Tiriel's narrative.

What emerges from an analysis of the illustrations in relation to the text seems to be an erotic dream of union with a sister–wife, who is a double of the mother, while mother watches. In Bentley's plate II (Illus. 2), Har and Heva sit naked in a shallow stream, gazing hypnotically into each other's eyes and partially embracing. Mnetha lies behind them on a bank, dressed in a Grecian gown with one breast bare. Her body, with its elongated legs, stretches across the page, conveying the impression that she protects or encloses the couple.

In Bentley's plate VIII (Illus. 3) this young and beautiful Mnetha watches over Har and Heva sleeping embraced. The striking similarity of Mnetha and Heva suggests that mother and daughter–consort are interchangeable. Moreover, Heva's youthfulness in relation to Har foreshadows Blake's presentation of Tiriel's relationship to his daughter Hela, with its incestuous connotations. Mnetha's benevolent expression suggests she would sanction their lovemaking, as does the winged cupid in the background. The underlying fantasy appears more clearly in Blake's use of a similar triangle, in *Vala*, of Vala and her two adult children, Enion and Tharmas. There, when Vala as mother puts her children to bed, the scene involves an open permission to incestuous sexuality. Thus Blake's fantasy here appears

Illus. 2 *Tiriel: Har and Heva Bathing*

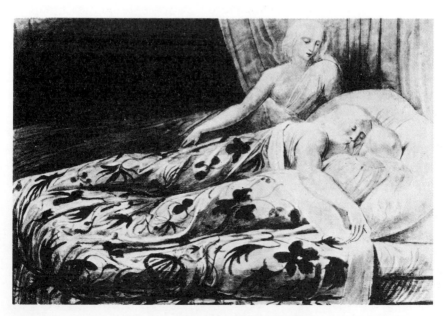

Illus. 3 *Tiriel: Har and Heva Asleep*

to centre on incest that is both permitted and enjoyed by the mother. The structure of this fantasy can be seen in several situations of untabooed love in Blake's other early works. In *Visions of the Daughters of Albion*, for example, it is masked under the guise of a mistress Oothoon, who would bring girls to her lover and enjoy the sight of his 'lovely copulation'. Ahania is similarly glad when her husband Urizen enjoys his daughters while she enjoys her sons. What made Blake devote a disproportionate number of his *Tiriel* illustrations to Lower Paradise seems to have been just this image of guiltless incest. It is a fantasy that persists throughout Blake's work.[7]

Tiriel, as we have seen, contains two main fantasy characterisations of the mother. Mnetha, watching over Har and Heva, is essentially protective and benign. Later in the text, when Mnetha confronts Tiriel with drawn bow and arrows, she assumes the threatening aspect that her bare-breasted Amazon dress suggests. This beautiful but armed and feared mother is the negative side of the sexually permissive mother and her image is presumably inspired by guilt over the earlier vision. In *Vala*, Blake divides the images of nurturing and of threatening mother by time-sequence: before her redemption, Vala is a warrior goddess; afterwards, she is a benevolent mother. In *Tiriel*, the images are superimposed (as in Har's shifts in age) without any real synthesis. In part, this lack of synthesis explains the poem's aesthetic failure. Readers tend to concentrate on one image and block out the rest – Nancy Bogen sees Mnetha as a sex-goddess while Mary Hall, with equal justice, notes her similarity to an Amazon queen of the Gorgons[8] – or, like Bentley, to observe discrepancies without being able to resolve them within Blake's framework of the child's dynamically reciprocating perceptions of and desires for his mother.

Hela, Tiriel's youngest daughter, also has a characteristically Blakean double aspect; she is both nurturing and threatening. Thus, later in the narrative, when Tiriel has cursed his sons a second time, he chooses Hela to lead him back to the vale of Har. Tiriel asks for Hela's obedience and receives curses and abuse instead. To punish her, Tiriel causes snakes to spring from her head. In these sequences, Hela represents both the loving care Tiriel desires and rejection. Tiriel's disappointment – the difference between desire and fact – is what turns Hela into a Medusa. In Blake's later reworking of the theme in *Vala*, Urizen curses his three daughters with snakes when they refuse to let him drink from their stream. Blake's choice of snakes as a way of making women monsters would seem to call for some further explanation. Freud argues that Medusa's snake-covered head serves to deny woman's frightening lack of a penis.[9] That Blake tried to deny this lack is suggested by his presenting Mnetha as an Amazon with a spear and in his later work by his drawings of women with snakes between their legs or, more explicitly, with an actual penis. It is characteristic of Blake's defensive handling of disturbing material that he presents the horrifying sight not as passively experienced but as actively produced by Tiriel's (or Urizen's) curse. The man seems in control and justified in perceiving (or making) women to be monsters.

Tiriel's frustrated relations with Hela mirror his earlier frustrations as an infant. But, whereas the infant lacks power to compel attention to his needs, Tiriel as king can abduct his daughter. Her physical similarity to his wife suggests that Tiriel sees her as a replacement, and her function as a mothering figure is equally important. By killing off all possible rivals and isolating himself with her, Tiriel enacts an infantile wish for total possession of the mother; now that the curse has devoured his 'guilty sons', he can live in peace with Hela. Some critics, like David Erdman,[10] see Tiriel as exclusively obsessed with sex, but, although sexual and specifically incestuous desire is obviously present, more is involved. Tiriel not only wants to possess Hela; he wants her to be a cherished part of him – his eyes – and thus to give him renewed sight as though, through her, he could erase earlier neglect. In later work, Blake stresses seeing and being seen as sources and forms of guilty feelings. Seen in that light, his desire for the woman-figure to see for him is a means by which Tiriel would be freed of guilt. When she rejects him, he reacts with rage and curses.

Hela not only rejects Tiriel but also wants him to feel the special pain of his own father's curse. She leads Tiriel to Har in the hope that Har will curse him, fearing at the same time that Tiriel will again escape punishment:

> O they [Har and Heva] are holy & forgiving filld with
>   loving mercy
> Forgetting the offences of their most rebellious children
> Or else thou wouldest not have livd to curse thy helpless
>   children.

(303–5)

The reason for Har's earlier forbearance is important in interpreting his relationship to Tiriel. Bentley suggests that Har represents 'passive benevolence based on an innocent world of loving'.[11] But this interpretation seems mistaken. The distant Har may seem kind in contrast to Tiriel, but Hela is too angry at her father to be a reliable commentator on Har's qualities. Moreover, Har's gruesome blessing of Tiriel earlier revealed the destructive impotence of his 'benevolence'. He resembles not the innocent inhabitants of *Songs*, but the priests and hypocrite parents who speak softly of Heaven and keep their charges in Hell.

So far, in tracing Tiriel's story, we have seen Blake treating two general subjects. The first was the problematic relationship of Tiriel with his sons, which is characterised by his efforts to make them feel guilty both for their greedy attitude toward their mother and for their filial rebelliousness. The second main subject, in which ideas about the mother play a more central role, has been the relationship between Har and Heva, imagined by Blake from the viewpoint of their son. The son perceives his mother – and Blake portrays her this way in his illustrations – as infinitely desirable but necessarily fears that she will punish him for his incestuous wishes. Blake's treatment of both these subjects suggests the double quality of a child's attitude toward the parents, one in which he feels loved and cared for and one in which he feels threatened. This duality is implemented by a technique in which individual characters are seen in double aspects and also by pervasive references to the contrast between youth and age.

We may now return to the narrative of *Tiriel*. After he has received Har's ambiguous blessing, Tiriel next encounters his savage brother Ijim. Blake has just suggested the mixed fear and affection between father and son. Now, with Ijim, he presents another paradigm of ambivalence. Ijim violently insists that Tiriel is a 'foul fiend' hypocritically claiming to be his brother. Outraged, Ijim carries Tiriel to his palace hoping to confront the hypocrite with the beloved 'real' brother. Ijim's hatred of the fiend expresses his unconscious hostility toward his brother, while his love is expressed in open admiration for Tiriel as brother king. Since Ijim cannot find his loved brother, however, hostility seems to win. Ijim's dual attitude also expresses Blake's ambivalence toward Tiriel as father: Tiriel as tyrant or fiend is an object of hatred, but there is also Tiriel as a model and object of love and Tiriel as childlike victim with whom Blake identifies. The

Ijim episode expresses the Blakean theme that hostility invariably produces evil; in this case Ijim's hostility produces a 'fiend', a distortion of reality. Finally, this episode and the preceding scene with Har and Heva express ambivalence in terms of personal identity. In the Ijim scene, Tiriel wants to be loved for himself but goes unrecognised. In the preceding scene, Tiriel is offered love but refuses to accept it by denying his identity.

After Ijim withdraws, Tiriel curses his sons a second time. The illustration (Bentley's plate VI) echoes that of the original curse (Bentley's plate I), but several significant alterations have been made (see Illus. 4*a*). For example, one son now closely resembles Ijim. This suggests that a part of Ijim unconsciously joins the sons in their rebellion, while another part of him, reflecting his ambivalence, is horrified at what they have done. It is this horror, as well as the sight of their blind and exiled father, that makes the sons finally accept their guilt. As Blake saw, a curse depends on guilt for its efficacy. Guilt evokes punishment; the sons prepare to die. Bentley's plate I showed Heuxos with his two brothers; here, Blake provides Tiriel with another son and five daughters. Next to Heuxos is the dark-bearded figure resembling Ijim who seems to replace the Bacchic son of plate I. The third, a smooth-haired figure, resembles the poet of plate I, as does a classic profile faintly drawn behind Heuxos's left shoulder. Heuxos looks older than in plate I and has a slightly more distorted expression. The most significant change is in the smooth-haired figure. He is drawn with hand hidden as before, but unerased sketchlines show another gesture: his hand clutches his head as if fearing decapitation.

Blake later reworked this illustration several times, reversing its meaning so that the sons become tyrants and Tiriel becomes a helpless victim of war. The illustration's still later development into an engraving about the Last Judgement is important because it not only clarifies aspects of the Oedipal fantasy (through reversal and projection) that were only implicit in the early versions, but also shows the continuity of Blake's struggle with guilt and the characteristic defences employed in his work. Three versions of this illustration are reproduced in Illus. 4*a*, *b* and *c*. Blake's pencil drawing (Illus. 4*b*), dated 1790, still has the configuration of *Tiriel* plate VI (Illus. 4*a*) – an old man gestures toward three younger male figures, but some negative symbolic details have been added. The sword in the first son's hand contrasts ironically with his impotent fleshiness; the

Illus. 4(*a*)   *Tiriel: Tiriel Denouncing his Four Sons and Five Daughters*

Illus. 4(*b*)   *War and the Fear of Invasion*

Illus. 4(c)   *The Marriage of Heaven and Hell*, plate i

second figure clutches his crowned head, while a snake circles his
waist; and the third is clad in mail. Their horrified expressions
border on caricature. Although they still suggest sons being cursed or
repelled by an angry father, Blake was in the process of metamor-
phosing them, through the negative detail, into oppressors.[12] In a
1793 engraving (Illus. 4c), the three male figures have clearly become
tyrants. Blake's change of the configuration of sons accused of
murdering a parent into grotesque patriarchal tyrants awaiting their
doom indicates a method, common throughout his work, of denying
filial guilt by accusing the father.

The shift from guilty child to guilty parent also serves to deny
fear.[13] The doomed tyrants assume the distress of Tiriel's sons, who
wait 'Desolate, Loathed, Dumb Astonishd' (277) for death. A final
version of the plate, probably engraved after the sedition trial which
encouraged Blake's paranoid ideas, mythicises the three figures as a
satanic trinity of accuser, judge and executioner. The stress is on
accusation, and the message is that fathers who accuse their sons of
parricidal crimes are themselves guilty and will be punished.[14]
Within *Tiriel* itself there are hints of similar reversals. The figure of
Earthquake, for example, whom Tiriel invokes to rise against his
sons with 'dark & burning visage', foreshadows the revolutionary
Orc in *America*, who bursts out to topple kings. Not every element in
Tiriel's curse ends up neatly reversed in later works. Some associations in the curse are consistent throughout his writings. Thus,
pestilence here prefigures Blake's murderous maternal figures – his
pestilential queens. Tiriel invokes pestilence as the appropriately
tailored punishment for the cannibalistic crimes of which he accuses
his sons. Using pestilence to avenge the mother here is especially apt,
for the vaporous poisons dropping from Pestilence's garments are a
version of the fogs that Tiriel invoked earlier to choke the sons who
drained their mother dry. Pestilence, who sits and smiles into the
sons' faces as they inhale her poison, becomes thus a demonic parody
of the nursing mother.[15] Illustrating again Blake's consistent ambivalence, however, he also has a positive counterimage for pestilence, as
we shall see in *Thel*, where the Lilly gives off perfume from her 'milky
garments' and, accepting the infantile greed even if it means her
destruction, smiles in the face of the infant lamb while he crops her
blossoms.

Leaving his sons with Pestilence, Tiriel is again compelled to seek
out Har, thus continuing the poem's pattern of alternating states of

anger and self-pity, states expressed dramatically in back-and-forth shifts of location. Tiriel's expression of anger is specifically associated with retribution here, for it takes the form of a punitive curse. His self-pity, both in the Har and Heva episode and in the later one with Hela, is associated through Blake's illustrations and details like Hela's snakes with a child's disappointed wishes and sexual fears. The suggested presence of these wishes, particularly the wish for incest, is followed in Blake's plot by Tiriel's otherwise inexplicably renewed guilt and anger, because justice requires punishment for countenancing incest. There is seemingly no way out. After receiving his parent's blessing, Tiriel angrily returns to curse his sons, and, after failing to get Hela's care, he goes back to curse Har and die.

The final speech (358–93) not only draws together *Tiriel*'s themes and images but gives retrospective meaning and provides a framework for earlier motifs. The speech is addressed to his father. It starts out with Tiriel's identification with his father and then, gradually, as in the work itself, moves backward into the past and relations with his mother. Tiriel's opening words suggest his negative identification with his father. 'Thy laws O Har & Tiriels wisdom end together in a curse' (358). Har is now seen as the original restrictive force, and his laws are connected with another restrictive force, the church.

Both law and church work by instilling a sense of weakness and guilt. In *Island*, Blake casts doubts on this view of man as a 'crawling reptile' by associating it with the weak and sanctimonious Steelyard. When Tiriel asks in his closing speech why men are bound in reptile form, he is ruminating not only on imprisonment in the body but also on why he has to *see* the body as sinful. Answering himself, he describes the serpentine elements in man's nature, chief among them envious rage. Tiriel's description recalls the serpent Envy in 'then She bore Pale desire', whose poison, as we noted earlier, Blake himself had deeply imbibed. The speech thus moves from complaints against being constrained by law and the body to Blake's conclusion that envy causes man to accuse himself and others of sin.

Tiriel divides men into two types, the openly angry man and the more threatening hypocrite, who masks his anger 'in silent deceit' (365). The hypocrites (serpent men) inhale poisons 'from the morning' and rise 'with daggers hid beneath their lips & poison in their tongue' (365–6). The inhaled poison emanates from the demonic maternal figure of Pestilence. The lines suggest that when someone incorporates something bad (poison) instead of benignly offered milk, he either dies, as the sons do, or becomes, like Tiriel himself, a dagger-wielding murderer. The subsequent images of the mouth as a grave and the teeth as 'gates of eternal death' make clear that the dagger (like Surgery's knife) is an adult replacement for the infant's organ of aggression, his teeth. The lines may also contain a limiting suggestion that only the envious find poison in the morning, whereas others find life-giving sustenance. In either case, there is a tension between the need to blame someone outside and the realisation that poison, including, for example, poisonous writing, is the product of an inner state.

The closing speech suddenly shifts from the poisonous adult to the infant, which makes psychological sense, since the shift comes after these oral images: the infant's life centres in his mouth. In the first scene of *Tiriel*, when the tyrant blames his sons for their mother's death, Blake presents the fantasy of a bad infant who damages the mother by aggressive sucking or biting – which makes the infant's aggression responsible for his being deprived. An earlier version of this fantasy appears in *Island*, where the aggressive babe Surgery is refused suck by his mother; the greedy 'Catterpillar on the Leaf' in *The Gates of Paradise*, who symbolically devours the maternal substance, is a later version. In this final speech to his father, Tiriel is exonerating himself, and so he sees himself as a child who is the victim rather than an aggressor against the mother. Both perspectives are Blake's, but he has split them up, and denies the presumably guilt-producing idea of the child hurting the mother by putting Tiriel in his role of accuser and structuring the opening scene in such a way that we join with the sons in denying it too; Tiriel is too tyrannical to be persuasive. Now, in the closing scene, the badness is all in the adult, and Blake stresses the infant's vulnerability and dependence on maternal care.

Tiriel begins his defence of himself with a powerful description of what happens to the dependent child to turn him into a poisonous adult:

The child springs from the womb. The father ready stands
    to form
The infant head while the mother idle plays with her dog
    on her couch

> The young bosom is cold for lack of mothers nourishment
>   & milk
> Is cut off from the weeping mouth with difficulty & pain.
> (375–8)

If, as Erdman suggests,[16] this passage is influenced by Rousseau's description of midwives moulding the child's head, Blake changes it significantly to the repressive father who wants to control the child entirely – from the physical shape of his head to the mental contents. In a similar way, Blake presents the mother who neglects to nurse her baby not, as Rousseau does, as absent in town, but as playing with a small dog. In effect, seeing the little dog as competitor, he presents an archetypal situation of envy, echoing his earlier image ('then She bore Pale desire') of the poet longing for 'one Cooling Drop' while 'others' are fed and content. Moreover, in his unique image, Blake fuses two experiences – that of earliest neglect, which leaves the infant 'cold', and that of weaning, when milk is 'cut off' with pain. Maternal deprivation is coupled with paternal repression.

Ordinarily, we think of the child gradually developing a perception of external reality. Blake ties this perception to the father's repressive function and sees it as forced on the child in place of the forms of his budding imagination.

> The little lids are lifted & the little nostrils opend
> The father forms a whip to rouze the sluggish senses to act
> And scourges off all youthful fancies from the newborn man.
> (379–81)

Blake may well have perceived in a similar light the childhood beating his father gave him for 'seeing' angels in a tree. In Tiriel's case, such punishment turns him into a pious hypocrite. Forbidden his fantasies, Tiriel was 'compelled to pray repugnant & to handle the immortal spirit' (387) until he became a serpent.

Tiriel's final speech offers a summary of his development: he evolves from the infant whose desire for love and nurture turns to envious rage through maternal neglect, to the child whose fantasies are repressed by the father, to the rebellious son, and finally to the cursing father-figure, who will cause the pattern to be repeated in the next generation. Within *Tiriel* as a whole, motifs from early and later stages of development are interwoven, as we have seen, in Tiriel's relations with his children, brother and parents.

The final image of Tiriel as devouring serpent provides a compelling example of the way Blake infused traditional imagery with his own meaning. Blake's Devil–serpent image, used in the context of a developmental analysis, has a different impact from that of similar images in the Bible or Milton. For example, Milton describes Satan and the devils after the Fall as transformed into serpents, compelled by 'scalding thirst' to eat apples that turn to ashes in their mouths.[17] Blake's concluding description of Tiriel,

> I am subtil as a serpent in a paradise
> Consuming all both flowers & fruits insects & warbling birds
> And now my paradise is falln & a drear sandy plain
> Returns my thirsty hissings in a curse on thee O Har
>
> (388–91)

recalls Milton's Satan, but Blake takes the momentary sympathy we feel for Satan (which is submerged by Milton) and expands it. Such sympathy comes from perceiving similar impulses in ourselves. Blake removes envy from the celestial plane and shows its human source in the infant's feelings of deprivation, neglect, and rivalry with competitors for the mother's care.

The issue of devouring with which *Tiriel* ends is central to *Thel*. Critics have interpreted the poem in many ways, and there is a wide divergence of opinion about how to view the character of Thel: vain, spoiled, and fearful of sex; as a lovely girl; or even as a future leader of social protest.[18] The importance of a psychological interpretation is that it sheds light on the nature of the sacrifice being asked of Thel, her reactions to it, and Blake's manipulation of our perception of her character and choice.

As we indicated earlier, *Thel* shows an innocent girl instructed by three nurturing figures who urge her to follow their model of self-sacrifice. In Blake's portrait of the first nurturing figure, the Lilly, whose body feeds the lamb, a rarefied and difficult ideal of Christian self-sacrifice is fused with latent cannibalistic ideas. The reader's distance from these ideas is maintained and they are made pleasing through the use of the pastoral setting, the fairy-tale creatures who inhabit it, and the beauty of Blake's language. Although the lamb devours and kills the Lilly, the lamb is innocent. No overt hostility can be detected. On the contrary, the whole (story and creatures) is bathed in an atmosphere of love and care. Yet when Thel hesitates to accept identification with the Lilly and voices her fear of death, we can understand this not just as vanity but as her unconscious response to the latent meaning.

The psychological centrality of being devoured in the Lilly's way of being becomes clearer if we compare her with Blake's contrasting image of the murderous mother in the figure of Pestilence in *Tiriel*. Blake reverses Pestilence's attributes in the portrait of the Lilly, point by point, as he turns the bad mother into the good one:

Pestilence

Where art thou Pestilence that bathest in fogs & standing lakes
Rise up thy sluggish limbs, & let the loathsomest of poisons
Drop from thy garments as thou walkest wrapt in yellow clouds
Here take thy seat in this wide court. Let it be strown with dead
And sit & smile upon these cursed sons of Tiriel.

(T 250–4)

Lilly

Thy breath doth nourish the innocent lamb, he smells thy
   milky garments,
He crops thy flowers. while thou sittest smiling in his face,
Wiping his mild and meekin mouth from all contagious taints.

(Th 2:4–7, E 4)

In each line the Lilly replaces Pestilence's noxious qualities with beneficent ones. Both figures have the watery substance Blake often associates with female nature, but the Lilly's water is free-flowing, while Pestilence bathes in disease-bearing 'fogs & standing lakes' and her opaque cloud covering contrasts with the Lilly's garment of light. Pestilence's spiritual pride – she will sit 'enthroned' – is opposed to the Lilly's modesty, her love of 'lowly vales'. Even the Lilly's beauty, whiteness and perfume are prized not for themselves but for the pleasure they give the infant lamb who smells her 'milky garments' before he crops her blossoms. Most important is the Lilly's relation to the lamb as contrasted with Pestilence's to the sons. The Lilly welcomes the lamb's greedy feeding with a loving smile even though it means her death. In what constitutes a final contrast between the two figures, the cropped Lilly wipes the lamb's mouth of all contagious taints.

The contrasting images of Pestilence and Lilly are perhaps Blake's earliest portrayal of the two types of feminine nature that became so important in his myth. His effort to create an ideally satisfying figure to counter inner fantasies of a murderous mother had to be continually renewed. As we shall see, the paradoxically smiling Pestilence develops in later poems into a series of wicked females whose smiles promise love but proffer death.

As *Thel* progresses, various aspects of nurturing love and sexuality come into focus along with accompanying fantasies suggesting the two types of feminine nature. The virginal Lilly contrasts meaningfully with Pestilence, who is invoked by, and thus under the aegis of, the tyrannical father.[19] Thel's second teacher, the Cloud, is also portrayed primarily as an asexual innocent. The Cloud's union with the dew suggests a pregenital merger rather than adult sexuality. Their fusion does not produce children but results in their bodily dissolution into nurturing showers for the flower–infants. Finally, and unlike Lilly and Cloud, the Clod symbolises the genital mother with her dark pit. The characterisation of the Clod is ambiguous; she is both nurturing and threatening. Sexuality, in her, is not clearly opposed to nurture of children. But the imagery suggests ways in which it will be in the future.

The Cloud provides food with his body, and thus suggests Christ in the traditional symbolism of the Eucharist and in such iconographic examples as, for instance, those portraying him as a pelican feeding its young with its blood. But for Blake, identification with Christlike sacrifice seems to mean identification with the feminine – that is, becoming like an ideal mother and allowing oneself to be devoured.[20] Blake, in fact, made the Cloud's gender ambiguous. Although ostensibly male, he closely resembles Thel in the illustration (*Th* 4, *IB* 38 – Illus. 5). Blake's image of the Cloud is positive in tone, but the idea of nurture as involving dissolution is a fearful one and is associated in Blake's mind with equally negative ideas of being unmanned and forcefully made womanlike. In later works, the female 'melts' the male into womanish helplessness through intercourse. The inner connection between nourishing a hungry infant and losing one's vital fluid to a 'hungry' womb lies behind Blake's later use of the Cloud to image the male sperm in *Europe*. Similarly, in later prophecies Blake associates the ideas of crucifixion and castration.

III.

Then Thel astonish'd view'd the Worm upon its dewy bed.

Art thou a Worm? image of weakness. art thou but a Worm?
I see thee like an infant wrapped in the Lillys leaf:
Ah weep not little voice. thou canst not speak. but thou canst weep;
Is this a Worm? I see thee lay helpless & naked: weeping,
And none to answer. none to cherish thee with mothers smiles.

The Clod of Clay heard the Worms voice, & raisd her pitying head:
She bowd over the weeping infant. and her life exhald
In milky fondness. then on Thel she fixd her humble eyes.

O beauty of the vales of Har. we live not for ourselves.
Thou seest me the meanest thing, and so I am indeed;
My bosom of itself is cold. and of itself is dark,

Illus. 5   *The Book of Thel*, plate 4

Thel responds primarily to the Cloud's self-sacrificing provision of food.

> I fear that I am not like thee;
> For I walk through the vales of Har. and smell the sweetest
>   flowers;
> But I feed not the little flowers: I hear the warbling birds,
> But I feed not the warbling birds. they fly and seek their food.
>   (*Th* 3:17–20, E 5)

For the first time she thinks of feeding in connection with herself and spontaneously envisions the worms who will eat her body.

> And all shall say, without a use this shining woman liv'd,
> Or did she only live. to be at death the food of worms.
>   (*Th* 3:22–3, E 5)

The Cloud has no trouble with this question: It is good to be used by worms. The worm, on the most obvious level, is a grave-worm, but it is also a symbol of the phallus and an image of the devouring infant. On the surface, the lines accurately depict what happens to the body after death – their brutality is muted by lyrical beauty and by the biblical resonance of Blake's statement. The worm's sexual connotations have long been noted by critics who see it as symbolic of the sexuality Thel fears. The reaction of most of these readers to Thel's reluctance is to preach at her – as the Cloud does – and insist that she ought to give herself freely.[21] These readers do not seem to appreciate that the prospect of being eaten by worms – death as a devouring – might be terrifying to anyone; nor do they perceive behind Blake's moral tone ('if thou art the food of worms. O Virgin of the skies, / How great thy use. how great thy blessing' – *Th* 3:25–6, E 5) the implicit degradation and forced submission of the woman. These evils, implicitly seen as virtues by Blake, are represented as horrible and demeaning (even if inevitable) in Andrew Marvell's address to his Coy Mistress. If she refuses him, he argues, and preserves her body intact until death, she must eventually submit to violation: 'then Worms shall try / That long preserv'd Virginity'.[22] In the speeches of both Thel and the Cloud, the theme of degradation is condensed in the opposition of high and low, shining virgin and earthworm. Yeats, Blake's great disciple, used a similar opposition in his play *A Full Moon in March*, where a frigid Queen accepts desecration and the lover's night. There, the sado-masochistic intent is explicit; in *Thel*, the fantasy of degradation is concealed by the ideals of Christian self-abasement.

The worm's sexual connotations are inseparable from its relation to the ideas of devouring at the poem's core. When Thel imagines her body being devoured by worms, she is not only describing her fears of death and sexuality (seen as death) but she is also bringing the idea of the cannibalistic infant to the surface. It is the idea of cannibalism that fuels her revulsion at the self-sacrificing ideals of the Lilly and Clod. But the worm who materialises as if answering her thought is portrayed as a helpless infant. His materialisation in this form effectively changes Thel's attitude toward her own destruction or, more subtly, makes her unaware of it by awakening her love for the infant worm. When she sees the worm, she is struck with amazement at the helpless human appearance of what she so greatly feared. 'Art thou a Worm? . . . art thou but a Worm? / I see thee like an infant wrapped in the Lillys leaf' (*Th* 4:2–3, E 5). Her thought shifts from her earlier fear and disgust to concern with the neglected infant's needs, 'helpless & naked: weeping, / And none to answer, none to cherish thee with mothers smiles' (*Th* 4:5–6, E 5). A similar reversal of perspective occurs in *Tiriel*: when Tiriel is angry at his sons, he sees them as devouring serpents; when he remembers his own infancy, he identifies with the child's helplessness and deprivation. Thel's double view of the worm indicates the way conflicting emotions can alter perception – a topic central to Blake. What seems a threat when someone is afraid or angry is seen as need when he is secure and loving.

The Clod, arising to succour the infant worm, exemplifies this ideally secure love. Like the Lilly, the Clod accepts her nurturing task even though this means her death: 'She bow'd over the weeping infant, and her life exhal'd / In milky fondness' (*Th* 4:8–9, E 5). But unlike the Lilly, the Clod, appearing after the Cloud's discourse on generation, presents a sexual being – mother earth – and sexuality is presented as dangerous. The Clod's darkness suggests a connection between sexuality and death. The Clod's interior is an enveloping grave ('thy cold bed') foreshadowing Urizen's ambivalent presentation of his consort Ahania as 'a cavern . . . dark cool and deadly' (*FZ* 43:14, E 322). But possibly frightening aspects of the Clod's sexuality are checked by her absolute self-abnegation and grateful dependence on Christ's love. The Clod's darkness — including her sexuality — is an obedient darkness lightened by unquestioned faith and love. That the woman's self-abnegation should control a prospect of fear in the poem suggests that Blake sees the dark pit from a particularly male point of view in which intercourse is death, that is, castration — unless he who enters is entirely in charge and the woman is utterly passive. It is no accident that the woman's love of Christ, whom Blake later pictured as feminised, should function as an assurance that the Clod will not castrate others. Christ neutralises woman's threat because he has already undergone the feared punishment. The Clod's 'ideal' marriage to Christ sharply contrasts with the voice Thel hears within the Clod's depths. There, the virgin finds no self-abnegation but a Hell and hears a sorrowful voice from her own grave-plot.

Earlier in the poem, Blake had shown two examples of selfless nurturing which left Thel unconvinced because the nurturing role means her death. In the third example of nurture, Thel and the poem change: The creature to be nourished becomes a clear sexual symbol and the act of nurture becomes also the act of sex. When Thel enters the pit in the concluding plate, her action suggests intercourse, which would change her role from female to male.[23] The voice she hears in the pit has the point of view of a male. Simultaneously, the imagery becomes less idyllic and more frightening. Thel's ambivalence toward nurture ends up as ambivalence toward sex. Blake's own ambivalence toward sex becomes more evident here as the tone of the work takes on an explicitly male quality.

The psychological structure of Thel's narrative suggests a libidinal odyssey. In the poem's opening sequence, Blake's voracious drive to satisfy his needs is expressed in terms of an infantile need for nurture. He insists to the woman that in satisfying his need she will also fulfil herself and hence not truly die at all. The resulting picture of happy child, happy mother is unstable for Blake, both because it conflicted with his sense of unworthiness, and because implicit in his fantasy of satisfaction was the idea that he was killing his mother. Furthermore, his mother's nurturing seems inevitably associated with equally guilt-producing ideas of her satisfying his sexual need as well. Blake seems to express guilt by projecting it onto punishing female figures. Thus Blake, in the final plate, assumes the identity of innocent, ambivalent Thel, who enters the Clod. The voice's description of the sexual action he is implicitly doing there frightens him away, an appropriate sanction for the greedy fantasies he has just enjoyed.

On another level, Blake's fantasy of a totally acquiescent nurturer counteracts a perception of the relationship between mother and son, woman and man as fiercely competitive, a combat in which the giver loses all. Blake's view of sexual intercourse, when not fantasised into a cost-free idyll, is haunted by fears of castration, or alternately seen as rape. The point seems to be to avoid being a giver, because if one gives the other takes. Moreover, the fantasy requires women to be the givers. But unfortunately, to be a taker is not a reliable way out because it arouses guilt.

In this scheme of things, Christ presents a very special issue for Blake. Christ was a giver and he was male, and his being both is unarguably not only good but divine. He therefore is of compelling fascination for Blake as the one who might redeem him from the hopeless trap of competition. Yet, in *Thel*, Blake does not explore Christ's role in depth. Instead, Christ is either implicitly unmasculine (is not a taker), or he functions simply as a prop who makes Blake's argument come true by rewarding nurturing females after death, or he functions as a scapegoat, distracting females from castrating more mortal men. (In *Jerusalem* such females are shown literally dancing with severed organs.)

Plate 6 of *Thel* elaborates these themes, apart from the question of Christ's role, more fully. The plate, organised as a series of questions about the murderous conflict between the sexes, seems to be a late addition, and in it Blake returns to the mood and themes of *Tiriel*. He freely transforms Tiriel's questions about men's murderous duplicity into the parallel questions about sexuality asked by the voice from the pit. The plate throws into relief the message of the earlier parts of the poem: For human harmony to exist, one has continually to be sacrificed to another; ideally, the woman should be sacrificed. The good Lilly, Cloud and Clod all joyfully accept this sacrificial devouring, and the imagery works to make Thel accept it too. In the final plate we see what happens when the woman will not accept destruction and both sexes try to destroy each other.

Plate 6 is not well integrated with the rest of the poem. The horrifying view of sex, particularly its hostility, disturbs our previous perceptions of Thel's non-hostile, pastoral world and arouses doubts about its absence of conflict. It has been argued that Blake's artistic lapse here is a result of the pressure of new ideas about social involvement,[24] but the inner reasons for the juxtaposition of sexual hatreds with maternal sacrifice seem more cogent. *Thel* attempts to

present a world of mutual sacrifice without hostility, but what is
sublimated beneath this ideal is the infantile one-sided, uncompromising wish for a mother's unlimited giving to her infant even if it
means her death. In *Tiriel*, the tyrant relates his adult need to devour
to being deprived as an infant of his mother's milk and love; the
implication was that if he had been satisfied he would have been
different. In a sense, *Thel* is a compensatory fantasy: it suggests the
ideal mother Tiriel needed to keep him from becoming a serpent
man. But the excessive wish for the mother has the further consequence of generating guilt and justifying retaliation. Thus, woman's
dangerous sexuality in plate 6 was to be expected. It is the punishment for the greedy wish for her perfect acquiescence.

   The final plate of *Thel* suggests that sexual need, like the need for
nurture in the preceding sections, must be satisfied without restraint
if the serpent is to be kept tame. But here the fantasy of perfect
satisfaction is overborne by a sequence of fearful images. The female
has become recalcitrant and dangerous. The courtly metaphors used
by the voice from the pit evoke a sexual battleground of seduction
and denial. *Tiriel*'s dark images of guilt and fear return in sexual
rather than cannibalistic form. The sexual and oral images are linked
by the common concept of fearful harm from bodily incorporation of
that which ought to nourish or please. The poisonous female
suggested by the courtly language resembles Pestilence, whose poison
one ingests. The voice's questions about man's vulnerability specifically recall Pestilence's smile as she choked Tiriel's sons. 'Why cannot
the Ear be closed to its own destruction? / Or the glistning Eye to the
poison of a smile!' (*Th* 6:11–12, E 6). Because of the intensity of
desire in Blake's imagination, there can be no middle ground between
the Clod's complete submission and the castrating intent of what he
later called the 'Female Will'. Plate 6 develops the image of a
seductress with honeyed tongue and an eye that lures the unwary into
ambush. A further image of the ear as a whirlpool that fiercely
'draws creation in' is linked to the Clod's womb–grave and foreshadows Blake's view of the ravenous earth–mother Enion, who tries to
draw all existence into her void. The image is especially dangerous to
poets, of course, whose songs this ear destroys. The woman has
fearful restrictive tools as well as these terrible engulfing ones. The
Female Will's restraining aspects are alluded to in the famous lines
about the restrictive maidenhead and its 'tender curb' on the burning
boy. These lines contrast with an earlier situation in which the Lilly

tames the fire-breathing steed with her freely given perfume, and perhaps anticipate the concluding illustration of the phallic serpent being happily ridden by children. Giving oneself in loving self-sacrifice seems to be the only way to control the beast.

Although the final plate, with its emphasis on a dangerous sexuality, was added later, sexual imagery occurs throughout *Thel*, particularly in the illustrations. Thel's initial pallor and isolation suggest that her descent itself is motivated by sexual frustration and curiosity that urge her to seek the 'secret air'. The sexuality she observes emphasises the female's submission to the male's exuberant force and seems to be associated with ideas of rape. Presumably the first thing Thel sees (title-page, *IB* 34 – Illus. 6) is a naked youth leaping from a voluptuous blossom to embrace a maiden, gowned like Thel, whose arms are thrown up in an ambiguous gesture that suggests horror as much as it does pleasure. Erasmus Darwin's 'Loves of the Plants', a poetically written guide to the sexual life of flowers, was one of Blake's pictorial and metaphorical sources for *Thel*. As Erdman notes, 'Darwin's emphasis on sexual encounter and aggressive masculinity seems particularly relevant' (*IB* 33). When the Cloud courts the dew, for example, he exhibits vigorous activity, while the dew kneels weeping. Sexuality here, as in the illustrations of suggestively positioned flowers that hover over Thel on plate 5 (*IB* 39), involves male aggression and female willingness to undergo incorporation or penetration.

Much later, in his concept of Beulah, Blake systematised his views of ideal female receptivity to male force. Beulah exists to provide sex and comfort to the energetic male creator of Eden. Har's vales have often been compared to Beulah and there are important similarities. Not least of these is the similarity of Christ's relation to Lilly and Clod with that of the female in Beulah to the Male Genius. In *Thel* the Lilly and Clod give their lives for their infant charges and are rewarded by Christ's love and care. Christ functions here as a superior mother. Rewarding the Lilly, he clothes her in light and feeds her with morning manna. For Clod, Christ is a caring bridegroom; the Clod is bound in nuptial bands, crowned, and cherished with oil. The sacrifices of *Thel* are primarily maternal, but Blake describes the sexual self-abnegation of Beulah's females in imagery suggesting the close connection between maternal and sexual sacrifice: 'every Female delights to give her maiden to her husband / The Female searches sea & land for gratifications to the

Illus. 6   *The Book of Thel*, plate ii, title-page

Male Genius' (*J* 69:15–17, E 221). In return for this self-denial and concern with the male's boundless appetite, he, like Christ, 'clothes her in gems & gold / And feeds her with the food of Eden. hence all her beauty beams' (*J* 69:17–18, E 221). Blake himself was obviously the prototype for the fiery 'Male Genius' and his wife for aspects of the beaming females of Beulah. He describes Catherine as 'like a flame of many colors of precious jewels'; but her flame is clearly dependent on his: 'my fingers Emit sparks of fire with Expectation of my future labors'.[25] As he explained elsewhere, 'the female life lives from the light of the male' (Blake's marginalia, E 585). Of herself, then, Catherine would be dull and dark like the Clod.

When Thel shrieks and returns to the Beulah-like vale of Har in the poem's problematic ending, Blake seems, in his complex attitude toward her, no longer to identify her with him but rather to see her again as entirely female; he seems, by making her flee the manifestations of the Female Will revealed in the pit, to be forcing her to accept the role of sacrificial nurturer. Her natural tendency might have been to put her own needs first, for her tendency to think first of some self-preserving use for herself is suggested throughout the poem and in fact gives her a certain resemblance both to Blake's self-portrait in *Island* and to Tiriel. Because of this self-interest, Gleckner calls her a prototypical Tiriel.[26] It would be fairer to see her as only ordinarily selfish, but Blake makes it difficult to see her in perspective. His insistence on characterising woman as all-nurturing or all-castrating forces Thel out of a possibly balanced choice and into the either/or world of alternating fantasies. Blake rationalises our earlier censure of Thel by reference to Christian ideals, but motivates us to censure her by involving us emotionally in a fantasy of our complete gratification by Thel. Our intended outrage at her 'selfishness' is fuelled by the threat she poses to a lingering infantile wish.

Although *Tiriel* and *Thel* both contain fantasies of devouring, these fantasies bear very different relations to their respective texts and have different effects on us as readers. In *Tiriel* the wish to devour appears directly: You sons killed your mother. However, the wish, although presented directly, is denied at the same time by making it an accusation by a character we are supposed to dislike and disbelieve. We take the part of the sons. In the same way, the image of the devouring mother occurs in Tiriel's curse, seemingly evoked by his malice – but the imagery makes clear that it is in retaliation for infantile hostility. Blake's mode of dealing with oral

sadistic wishes here, then, is to present them only to deny and escape
blame for them. And in his presentation he suggests, as Freud did, the
relation of these wishes to the frustration of early infantile needs.

Thel shows a more complex and confusing use of the fantasy, the
understanding of which is enlarged by its direct expression in *Tiriel*.
In *Thel*, no hostile wishes are expressed or denied by the characters;
rather, we are presented with a world of harmony where one gives
unstintingly to another. When we look more closely at this world,
however, we see that the wish to devour is, as it were, built into it. In
Thel, an infant can blissfully incorporate his mother without guilt.
Blake stresses the infant's innocence and helplessness. The question
of guilt or blame is directed away from the infant and finds an altered
expression in the sacrificial atonement of the maternal figures. Thus,
Blake offers us at the same time pictures of the highest form of
human altruism and the boundless egoism of the infant. Moreover,
he does this in such a way that, when Thel wants to escape
self-sacrifice and voices her fear of being eaten, we are supposed to
deny the validity of her fear and blame her, not the devouring worm,
for her selfishness.

3 The Case for Impulse

The works we have discussed so far are clearly minor. *Tiriel* and *Island* are unfinished as well, and their psychological themes are relatively accessible. With *The Marriage of Heaven and Hell*, however, we are dealing with a work of acknowledged importance that appears consistent thematically as well as in religious, historical, or philosophic terms.[1] The question now is whether Blake in his successful work continues to express the strong psychological preoccupations we found earlier and whether the emotional content continues to structure the work. One may also ask if aspects of this content have been ignored by critics using a more traditional approach. One is struck primarily by the extent to which most interpretations deny hostile intent on Blake's part and discuss the work under quite different categories. Blake's attacks on figures of authority are seen as necessary to his moral purpose. Northrop Frye, for example, brilliantly rationalises Blake's expressions of hostility as self-defence: a fearful society indeed seeks to destroy the poet. David Erdman similarly justifies Blake on the grounds of his social conscience. Others simply ignore hostility while concentrating on sexual aspects of the poem. Robert Gleckner is an exception. He senses Blake's irrational hostility, particularly toward Swedenborg, and concludes that 'with passion as its basis, the artistic subtlety characteristic of Blake's other works is understandably lacking'.[2]

Marriage insists that received moral categories of good and evil need to be revised. To understand Blake's attacks on morality, it may not be adequate simply to analyse them under moral or religious categories. We must first examine the content of these attacks; they may be best understood not as moral arguments at all so much as choices of external targets for hostility of internal origin. Even those positions that can be appropriately discussed in moral or social terms are better understood when their hostile motivations are first made clear.

In *Marriage*, Blake's continued struggle with impulses of rage and desire is focused by his strengthened sense of vocation in opposition to Swedenborg. *Marriage* shares *Island*'s central theme of rivalry and its concern with the management of impulses and their relation to art. There are also striking structural and verbal parallels between the works. In *Island*, for example, conflict with rivals and the moralistic Flaxman concludes in a promise to give the reader *Songs* as fruit of Blake's impulsive genius; in *Marriage*, after similarly demolishing the moral authority of Milton (and Swedenborg), Blake promises the reader another book, the Bible of Hell.

Although *Marriage*, unlike *Island*, can at least be given coherence by reference to moral and social concepts, its underlying order is still psychological. The opening lyric 'Argument' and concluding 'Song of Liberty' serve as a frame for *Marriage*'s diverse prose-sections. Both lyric 'Argument' and 'Song' offer, as we shall see, dramatically biased paradigms of father–son conflict. Within this frame, Blake presents his central project of return to Paradise, which contains at its heart the desire for a sexually unrepressed, 'renewed' body and entails a struggle with civilised morality. Blake's quarrel is primarily with his predecessors Milton and Swedenborg, whom he attacks as defenders of repression. Blake's attitude toward each of these figures, particularly toward Milton, re-enacts the classical Oedipal attitude toward the father: loving admiration on the one hand, hostility on the other. Much of Blake's brilliant outpouring of ideas, his construction of a world diametrically opposed to that of the authorities, serves a wish to triumph over these paternal figures. His most famous idea, the theory of contraries, justifies Blake's own ambivalence by establishing it as a principle: hatred is as necessary as love.[3]

Throughout *Marriage*, rivalry and envy seem to fight with love. In reinterpreting Milton (plate 5), Blake denies influence and dependency. Love seems admissible only from a position of dominance; otherwise, his imagery suggests, he would feel crucified. After Milton has been put down, Blake can admit their kinship as co-members of the Devil's party because it is on his terms. By didacticism, by actively reinterpreting and teaching, Blake defends himself against passivity and submission.[4]

Blake's concluding attack on Swedenborg suggests that in defending himself against his predecessor's influence Blake defends against fantasies of homosexual submission. Blake is particularly ruthless here, using every means to degrade Swedenborg and shake off his influence. The reverse side of Blake's bravado and criticism of Swedenborg appears in the episode's final illustration, which shows the Blakean Devil's vanquished angelic opponent being shot in the breast by an archer. Forcibly 'influencing' another man is equated with penetrating him. Being influenced would correspondingly make Blake the womanlike object of penetration, an idea he resisted with all the force of his masculine rhetoric.

The battle of ideas in *Marriage*'s opening and concluding prose-sections (plates 1–5 and 21–8), then, explores love–hate relations between competing men. The central section (plates 6–21) offers a vision of creativity. Blake leads the reader into a hell that temporarily substitutes for the lost Paradise. Here, driven by sexual desire, the poet imagines or recreates the return. The omnipotence of the poet's desiring imagination is crucial: nature must subordinate itself to thought. Blake's model of omnipotent imagination linked to extraordinarily expanded senses is not created, as it were, *ex nihilo*, but evokes, with the resources of mature art, childhood experiences in which fantasy infuses reality and governs perception of it.

Blake's exploration of omnipotent imagination is followed by his central allegory of the creative process. Blake's sacred place, around which the whole work revolves, is the printing-press of Hell. Blake's metaphors for the creative process, however, apply equally well to sexual experience and the body. The maternal earth-cave of the Clod in *Thel* becomes a series of caves that represent the maternal body. In an astonishing sequence, Blake shows the mother's body penetrated and re-created *from within* by the poet–son. In a sense, his creative activities substitute for lost or insufficient experiences of pleasure and closeness. Thus the word-making in Blake's printing-press is also lovemaking. He describes the poet's work with the Prima Materia and, at the same time, likens the caves and the creative processes within them to bodily functions that play an important part in our early life. Both sexual and the bodily analogies emphasise restoration, whereas constriction characterises the following vision of actual moral history. Between his presentation of the two visions, which show alternative modes – creative and moralistic – of relating to the world, Blake attempts to deal with his fears of being devoured. The devourer becomes a harmless and necessary counterpart to 'the prolific'.

Marriage ends as Blake assumes a paternal role – the world will have his works 'whether they will or no' (*MHH* 24, E 43) – and warns of the consequences if the world, particularly its father, does not listen. In the initial 'Argument', the prophet–son raged in the wilds; the final plate (*MHH* 24, *IB* 121) shows his enemy, the fallen King Nebuchadnezzar, on all fours, naked and terror-stricken. One cycle has ended.

Because both the shifts in feeling and the cumulative effect of imagery are essential to understanding this complicated work, we shall deal with the individual sections in the order in which Blake presents them. In the opening 'Argument', Blake presents an archetypal event, expulsion from Paradise, in such a way that we see the expelled man as good and the one who expelled him as a usurping hypocrite. In striking contrast to the biblical and Miltonic accounts of 'loss of Eden', which emphasise man's sin, Blake stresses the expelled man's innocence:[5]

> Once meek, and in a perilous path,
> The just man kept his course along
> The vale of death.
> (*MHH* 2:3–5, E 33)

The just man is also a Blakean artist. He transforms a hostile nature, and the magically blooming landscape suggests the magical strength of his creativity. In addition, he re-creates man through the 'living fluids' of his imagination – Isaiah's springs and streams. Blake's description of the artist as the 'just man' parries an inner accusation of sin associated with his creative activity. Blake uses Isaiah's imagery to support his defence by stressing the artist's godlike creative power and goodness. This idea reverses Isaiah's emphasis on man's sin and God's punishment. Blake's artist, in effect, takes God's place as creator–redeemer, and the artist's sinfulness as a man is actively denied. Blake's insistence on the just man's meekness parallels his earlier insistence in *Island* on the children's meekness and cleanness. Similarly, it denies aggression, which, as we shall see, is a major feature of *Marriage*. Blake's denial of creativity's aggressive components, and his association of justice and meekness with the artist, stem from his own uncomfortable feeling that, for him, creativity and aggression were connected. This can occasionally be confirmed outside his work. For example, in a letter to Thomas

Butts, Blake shows how his personality swings between elated assertiveness and 'meek' depression in which he repudiated his art.[6]

The first step in Blake's argument is thus that the artist's creative activity does not justify his expulsion from Paradise. The next step seems to be to establish the 'villain's' envious motives for expelling him. The paradigmatic source of envy is suggested more clearly elsewhere: in the drafts of 'Infant Sorrow', which offer an illuminating analogy to the conflict of the artist and the villain, a desired woman is the source of conflict between father and son. The father–priest steals his son's beloved (the myrtle-tree) and, in rage, the youth murders him. As in the 'Argument', Blake seemingly defends against impulses of rage and rivalry by projecting the crime's initiation onto someone else, so that his own violence is justified. In addition, his enemy's violence is implicitly greater than his own. The action of the 'Argument' is ominously bracketed by Rintrah, a counter-revolutionary figure of paternal authority, roaring and shaking his fist.[7] The motive force for the 'Argument', then, would seem to be Blake's feelings of rage. If he can show that the rage is a response to unjust treatment, he can then show that the existence of these feelings does not prove his lack of worth or that he could have been considered a threat to his father.

Blake begins *Marriage* proper by simultaneously attacking Swedenborg and dramatising his own innocence. By alluding to Swedenborg's prophecy of a New Jerusalem to begin in 1757, the year of Blake's birth, Blake becomes a saviour who will not only escape crucifixion but will be the agent of Christ's resurrection. Swedenborg's writings become Christ's grave-clothes – now superfluous and restrictive of the free energy and new pleasure-giving body that Blake is imaginatively creating for him. The identification of Blake with a reborn Christ recalls the pairing of Blake and Chatterton in *Island*, where Chatterton was the failed and crucified brother poet. There, Blake's aggressive satire covered fears of being similarly 'crucified'. An important part of Blake's self-appointed task in *Marriage* is to 'undo' Christ's crucifixion and transform his threatening passivity into Blakean activity. At the poem's end, Blake resurrects Christ as an impulsive diabolist, and passive suffering is transferred to the father as fallen King Nebuchadnezzar.

In the doctrine of contraries which follows the attack on Swedenborg, Blake seems to establish the pre-eminence of activity over passivity: by describing man as a being in conflict and by giving value to emotions usually perceived negatively ('Repulsion . . . Energy . . . and Hate are necessary to Human existence' – *MHH* 3, E 34). In his depiction of energy's struggle with restraining reason, Blake's partiality towards energy clearly includes its negative components.[8] His formulation both describes ambivalence (two contrary emotions toward the same object) and exalts it. Blake elsewhere insists, as Freud did, that the infant is born with conflicting emotions of love and hate ('Desire, Love, Rage, Envy' – E 591). Blake's sketch of infant-development also anticipates Freud's concept of a thinking ego evolved through frustrations ('Thought is not natural to Man it is acquired by means of Suffering' – E 591). The Blakean infant is forced to reason, rather than simply feel or wish, by a harsh, intrusive reality, whereas imagination or vision naturally expresses his inner world of emotion. In ordinary development, Freud argues, the primary process, visual or pre-verbal thinking, is followed as the child matures by the secondary process, logical thought. Blake, although acknowledging a similar type of progress, repudiates it. Logical thought, learned through suffering, is used to promulgate religious teachings that are alienated equally from the body and from imaginative vision. Through these repressive teachings man becomes passive and suffering instead of active and joyful. 'Good is the passive that obeys Reason. Evil is the active springing from Energy. Good is Heaven. Evil is Hell' (*MHH* 3, E 34). Such is the received wisdom.

Blake extends his theory of psychic contraries in 'The voice of the Devil' (plate 4) to include religious contraries. Thus, the traditional religious concepts – that body and soul are divided, that the body's energy is evil (and punishable) and the soul's reason is good – are held to be false and are opposed by their 'true' contraries – that the body and soul cannot be divided, that life is energy which reason merely limits and that energy itself is 'Eternal Delight'. Blake suggests here a spatial metaphor similar to Freud's early model of the rational ego as a thin layer on top of the id, where sexual energy is bounded by reason. Blake differs radically from Freud in the valuation he places on the unequally proportioned contraries ('Energy is Eternal Delight'), thus laying the groundwork for such modern Blakeans as Norman O. Brown and Herbert Marcuse, who confidently exalt early stages of development into ideals, undeterred by the intense anxieties to which the infant's mode of perception and weak ego leave him vulnerable.

The exaltation of early childhood modes of perception along with the epistemological apparatus of *Marriage* are crucial to Blake's depiction of the poet–son's Oedipal struggle. *Marriage* does not – and in the nature of Blake's larger enterprise could not – offer a 'neutral' philosophy of mind (and it is thus not surprising that he should appeal to radical critics of the idea of neutrality). Soon we shall see Blake, through Isaiah and Ezekiel, confirming the imagination as the first principle of human perception. We shall also find him attacking something seemingly so basic as the ordinary person's use of the senses, especially the eyes. Blake regards reason, ordinary visual perception (conceived as rational perception), logical and verbal thinking, and abstraction all as repressive, both in experience and in their origin. Man is born innocent of reason and in creative 'pre-logical' communication with reality. Reason is imposed on him by the regime of justice and morality, as the instrument by which the regime maintains its power. Blake makes it entirely clear that reason is the father's weapon. Imagination, in contrast, is the weapon of the poet–son. The father has used reason to work on his son an injustice of monumental proportions: he has deprived the son of access to reality. A striking example of Blake's theories concerns eyesight as it is practised by the ordinary person, as contrasted with the imaginative genius. Throughout his work Blake refers to the evils of being seen and seeing. To be seen (by the parent) is to be judged; to see (the primal scene, perhaps) is to be guilty. The ordinary person's seeing is not a spontaneous perception of reality but an intellectualised part of a structured regime of control. For Blake the man, these theories must have been a lifeline: they justified his self-concept as an artist using vision and a poet using language and dissociated him emphatically from those artists and writers whose use of perception and imagination seemed part of the traditional paternalistic regime.

In the next section, Blake prepares to reinterpret Milton. Concentrating on the libido aspect of energy – desire – Blake associates self-control with weakness and passivity (as he did in *Island* with Flaxman).

> Those who restrain desire, do so because theirs is weak enough to be restrained; and the restrainer or reason usurps its place & governs the unwilling.
> And being restraind it by degrees becomes passive. . . .
>
> (*MHH* 5, E 34)

Blake's rhetoric evokes fears of passivity in his readers, which works to increase their generally sympathetic response to his condemnation of restraint. But it is important to see that Blake's view of reason is distorted first by his identification of it with conscience or superego and second by the threatening, primitive way in which conscience is perceived. The implacable nature of Blake's 'restrainer' resembles the child's experience of a rigid, overwhelming conscience (superego) before he is able rationally to examine and modify its prohibitions or to experience its benign, comforting aspects. The superego's extreme punitive tendencies are now recognised to be just as irrational as the drives they oppose; moreover, the superego can be modified by reason, which Blake instead identified with it.

Blake's analysis of *Paradise Lost* carries on the initial thrust of his 'Argument', where a priestly villain usurps the just man's primary place. Here reason (the Messiah) casts out desire (Milton's Devil). In Blake's reinterpretation of the Fall, desire – or the traditional Devil – is as innocent as the just man. The Devil's brother, the Messiah, is really the fallen one: 'The Messiah fell. & formed a heaven of what he stole from the Abyss' (*MHH* 5–6, E 34). Against the background we have so far developed and taken with the more direct Oedipal material of 'Infant Sorrow', Blake's insistence on the Devil's priority and innocence suggests the extent of his defensive need to project guilt onto a repressive, thieving father or brother. Blake's attempts in *Marriage* to free himself of the influence of Swedenborg and Milton – to deny what he had taken from them – apparently strengthened his need to be judged innocent and is consistent with Harold Bloom's theory of literary Oedipal conflict.[9] Blake augments his own power by correcting Milton's intellectual position, and at the same time he shows affectionate feeling for his predecessor by analysing his unconscious motives in such a way as to identify Milton with Blake. 'The reason Milton wrote in fetters when he wrote of Angels & God, and at liberty when of Devils & Hell, is because he was a true Poet and of the Devils party without knowing it' (*MHH* 6, E 35).

'A Memorable Fancy' plunges Blake directly into the hellfires of sexual energy which he associates with creativity. In Hell, the Devil, duplicating Blake's own engraving process, is engraving on a rock; Blake, like a modern folklorist, collects proverbs. The Devil's engraved sentence, 'How do you know but ev'ry Bird that cuts the airy way, / Is an immense world of delight, clos'd by your senses five?' (*MHH* 7, E 35), alludes to Chatterton's 'How dydd I know that ev'ry darte / That cutte the airie waie, / Myghte nott fynde passage toe my harte, / And close myne eyes for aie.'[10] Significantly, since Chatterton was for Blake a threatening example of failure, Blake reworks this image of sexually tinged vulnerability as a positive statement. He replaces Chatterton's masochistic passivity – waiting for the 'darte' – with a triumphant identification with the active bird. The latent connection between being cut by a dart and homosexual penetration is transformed by Blake into a connection between aggression or rage, phallic sexuality and creativity: sex as cutting is aggression, and the bird that cuts the air is both the phallus and the engraving tool, which opens a 'world of delight'.

The Devil's verse-sentence appropriately introduces the 'Proverbs of Hell', which express feelings of rage, sexual desire, and the creative artist's omnipotence. The emotionally immediate connection between rage and sexuality makes sense in terms of the Oedipal situation, as we have seen. The Proverbs dramatise the proposition that what has traditionally been thought evil is not only good but also God. The paternalistic injustice of previous thinking about morality enrages Blake and leads him under the theory of contraries to exalt rage as necessary. However, rage in real life is antisocial. This exaltation of rage thus leads Blake into difficulty when faced by rage's actual destructive force ('The roaring of lions, . . . the raging of the stormy sea, and the destructive sword' – *MHH* 8:27–8, E 36). He avoids the dilemma by asserting that these manifestations of rage – in form attributed to nature but actually also his own – are beyond his understanding ('[these] are portions of eternity too great for the eye of man' – *MHH* 8:27, E 36). Blake's rage against parental figures and his counterbalancing creativity become the model for an eternity in which raging hunger is met and nourished. Here, as in Blake's defence of 'hate', he justifies hostile emotions that are usually suppressed or denied.

Blake's needs and his rage when thwarted seem stronger than those of ordinary people. He sees himself as a fierce predator, lion or eagle, while others are seen as scavenging foxes or crows. As he did in *Island*, Blake here resents those who are less driven by desire, but the Devil in *Marriage*, unlike Quid–Blake, maintains his control and suggests that criticism can be used to strengthen one's self-esteem: 'Listen to the fools reproach! it is a kingly title' (*MHH* 9:47, E 36). Blake's anger against the world is just as great as it was in *Island*, but his artistic distance is greater.

Nevertheless, Blake's resistance to being influenced by others becomes a principle in a group of proverbs that deal with individuality. 'The eagle never lost so much time. as when he submitted to learn of the crow' (*MHH* 8:39, E 36). Just as the influence of the weak should be shunned by the strong and gifted, traditional Christian virtues of meekness and humility should be replaced by pride and exhibitionism as positive virtues. 'The pride of the peacock is the glory of God' (*MHH* 8:22, E 36). Blake anticipates Freud's view of shame as a defensive reaction against an original impulse of pride: 'Shame is Prides cloke' (*MHH* 7:20, E 36). He wants to undo such hypocritical and, to him, unnecessary defences and return to the impulses. And, since pride was originally of one's body and genitals, Blake returns it there: 'The head Sublime, the heart Pathos, the genitals Beauty, the hands & feet Proportion' (*MHH* 10:61, E 37). The aesthetic quality, the beauty, of the genitals is determined by the investment of desire in them. Similarly, Freud in *Three Contributions to the Theory of Sex* suggests that sense of beauty was originally a reflection of sexual excitation.[11] These proverbs seem to be part of Blake's own struggle against sensations of shame, described poignantly in *Jerusalem*:

> We reared mighty Stones: we danced naked around them:
> Thinking to bring Love into light of day . . .
> Displaying our Giant limbs to all the winds of heaven! Sudden
> Shame seizd us, we could not look on one-another for
>   abhorrence . . .[12]
>
> (*J* 24:4–7, E 167)

The largest group of proverbs, which provides the tone for the whole section, insists that sexual desire should be obeyed without restraint. These statements are made particularly striking by Blake's control of the aphoristic form so often used for moral teaching. As Nurmi notes, Blake's proverbs are the infernal counterpart of the biblical Book of Proverbs.[13] Blake's exaltation of desire reverses the reasoned control recommended by Lavater, whose aphorisms Blake had carefully annotated. In viewing sex as both good and healthy, Blake anticipates the modern view that neurosis is caused by repressed desire: 'He who desires but acts not, breeds pestilence' (*MHH* 7:5, E 35). Pestilence was connected with syphilis as an obvious (and at that time deadly) punishment of sexuality. In *Tiriel*,

Pestilence punishes Tiriel's sons' forbidden desires. Now, defending against guilt and fear of punishment through reversal, Blake makes pestilence arise from restraint, which also weakens a man and subjects him to the castrating or devouring female. Blake uses every rhetorical resource to stress the evils of restraint: 'Sooner murder an infant in its cradle than nurse unacted desires' (*MHH* 10:67, E 37). Blake's choice of infanticide here is not fortuitous in a poem structured by rivalry over paradisal 'inheritance'. Just as restraining desire makes one ill, following desire not only becomes a virtue but 'leads to the palace of wisdom' (*MHH* 7:3, E 35). Moderation is correspondingly seen as impotence: 'Prudence is a rich ugly old maid courted by Incapacity' (*MHH* 7:4, E 35).

Implicit in the exaltation of desire is a release of aggression against parental figures who oppose gratification. At the same time, Blake analyses the motives of these figures. We are to feel, for instance, that the pleasure-forbidding priests restrain desire because of a wish to enjoy it themselves: 'As the catterpiller chooses the fairest leaves to lay her eggs on, so the priest lays his curse on the fairest joys' (*MHH* 9:55, E 37). Blake's implicit comparison of infant caterpillars devouring the nurturing leaf with curses that similarly destroy their object not only suggests that the forbidden joys are *of* the maternal body but also concisely illustrates a dynamic progression we observed in Tiriel's growth from deprived infant to serpent man.[14] To put it another way, the comparison between blind instinct and abstract curses is remarkable in suggesting a repressed component of the priest's behaviour.

His perceptive analysis of other people's aggressive motives did not effect Blake's sense of justified anger against authority which builds prisons 'with stones of Law, Brothels with bricks of Religion' (*MHH* 8:21, E 36). Blake reverses the usual order of crime and punishment. It is law and religion that by their prohibitions cause crime and perverse sexuality; if desire were not restrained, it would flow in untroublesome channels. This idea finds a modern spokesman in Marcuse, who pictures desire channelling itself productively once 'surplus-repression' is removed.[15]

Blake's anger against personal and poetic fathers appears less directly in the highly condensed proverb 'Drive your cart and your plow over the bones of the dead' (*MHH* 7:2, E 35). Bloom suggests that this is an image of the sexual act; we may also note that, by symbolising the destruction of Blake's predecessor's (or father's) remains, the plough is aggressive as well as sexual.[16] Blake reassures himself against fears of retaliation with proverbs like 'A dead body. revenges not injuries' (*MHH* 7:16, E 35) and 'The cut worm forgives the plow' (*MHH* 7:6, E 35), which, as Bloom again notes, has a sexual connotation.[17] Although the idea of aggression against the father seems almost required by the unleashing of desire, Blake consciously denies that such aggression is necessary. He rejects acts that 'hinder' another, such as murder or theft; in fact, he would like to think that only fathers commit such acts. But aggression denied appears constantly – in Blake's attacks on Swedenborg and others, in his metaphors, illustrations, and use of satire.

Freedom from sexual restraint is a cognate of Blake's belief in the omnipotence of the imagination, which enabled him to assert the possibility of forbidden or impossible acts ('Every thing possible to be believ'd is an image of truth' – *MHH* 8:38, E 36). Aside from the general relation of this belief to childhood perception, Blake's specific experience of confrontation with the reality-principle in the person of his father, who punished him for imagining angels in a tree, is evoked by an interlinear illustration of a small boy regarding a tree. Blake's faith in imagination gave him the necessary courage to create a life-enhancing, if perhaps illusory, image of a future based on the living body rather than, say, the machine. But Blake's world of imagination has nothing in common with political democracy. It is strictly hierarchic. What the genius Blake perceives is intrinsically more valuable than the ordinary man's perceptions. 'A fool sees not the same tree that a wise man sees' (*MHH* 7:8, E 35).

One last group of proverbs concerns the sense of time and creative work. Submission to time is seen as a weakness equal to the acceptance of sexual restraint. Attitudes toward time, money and success are, as Freud points out, unconsciously linked to original attitudes toward body-products. The so-called anal personality (orderly, retentive, punctual) develops in reaction to strong pleasure in untrammelled anal functioning. Blake later portrays Urizen–Satan as an overcontrolled, anal character like his earlier prototype, Flaxman. Just as Blake's demands for sexual freedom in *Marriage* are the moral premises for realising incestuous fantasies of overcoming the father, his demands for freedom from the dominance of time and rule suggest conflict over the necessity of controlling body-functions and abandoning related pleasurable or sadistic fantasies. Earlier-established controls for regularity are repudiated: only docile fools allow their production to be measured 'by the clock', for the hours 'of wisdom: no clock can measure' (*MHH* 7:12, E 35). Personifying eternity as an exalted parent whose appreciation of Blake's works raises his self-esteem, he says that 'Eternity is in love with the productions of time' (*MHH* 7:10, E 35). This proverb has the same effect as Blake's remark in his letters that angels spend their leisure studying his books. Blake's insistence on a spontaneous, totally subjective view of time and his own inner freedom may serve, like his remark about angels, to defend against a painful tendency to obsessive brooding and self-doubt. In his letters Blake speaks of filling up time to counter depressing thoughts, and the final proverb in this group (which has the tone of a nursery maxim) suggests a defensive rather than a free relation to time: 'The busy bee has no time for sorrow' (*MHH* 7:11, E 35). Defensiveness is similarly implicit in the aggressive self-justification one senses in the proverbs about individuality, in which the creatively energetic person is superior to ordinary, obedient people. The creative person's insecurity is latent, too, in his asserted superiority to the rules the timid obey and, finally, in his suggested sexual superiority to the source of rules, the father.

The 'Proverbs of Hell' illustrate the varieties of impulse that constitute the energetic 'fire' genius inhabits. Blake's method there is to project impulse or emotion onto clearly defined objects or creatures, which are thereby humanised. As in fables, projection facilitates the expression of dangerous or experimental ideas. The formality of proverbial diction also lends distance to such expression. In the plate (plate 11) following the Proverbs, Blake describes how this method of projecting parts of the self outward was used to create a religion and the idea of God.

The ancient Poets animated all sensible objects with Gods or Geniuses. . . . Till a system was formed . . . [which abstracted] the mental deities from their objects. . . . And at length they pronounced that the Gods had orderd such things. Thus men forgot that All deities reside in the human breast. (*MHH* 11, E 37)

This description of the development of religious myth parallels Piaget's description of the child's psychological development[18] and Freud's description of the development of primitive religion.[19]

Blake's illustration (*MHH* 11, *IB* 108 – Illus. 7) shows the connection between animating imagination and unconscious fantasy. Nature appears as a family: a mother and child observed by an old man (father) in a stump. The mother's ambiguous 'portrait' as a mermaid evokes childhood speculation about the maternal body. The lower leg (in some versions a leg, in others a tail or tail-like appendage) suggests connections with the phallic serpent women who are important in Blake's later work. Similarly, the changing perception of the father in different versions – phallic waterspout or splintered tree-trunk – reflects Blake's portrayal of the father as alternately

Illus. 7   *The Marriage of Heaven and Hell*, plate 11

threatening and weak or old. In all versions, the emphasis on mother
and child and the isolation of the trapped old man suggest Blake's
view of a happy solution to Oedipal rivalry. Blake is consciously
illustrating the pagan process of projection while projecting his
unconscious fantasies. At the bottom of the page, Blake presents the
contrary religious view, in which the old man (as God creating
Adam) is central and the mother and child are unimportant.

In the next section, the second 'Memorable Fancy' (plates 12 and
13), Blake dines with the prophets Isaiah and Ezekiel. The central
theme continues to be the omnipotence of creative thought. Blake
asks, 'Does a firm perswasion that a thing is so, make it so?', and
Isaiah replies, 'All poets believe that it does.' The prophets, as Blake
sees them, are poets. According to Blake's Ezekiel, 'The Poetic
Genius . . . was the first principle [of human perception] . . . and all
the others merely derivative' (*MHH* 12, E 38). God here becomes the
equivalent of the poetic genius or imagination – a revelation that was
prepared for in the preceding section by 'All deities reside in the
human breast.' The fusing of prophet and poet aids Blake in his
moralisation of the poet's task into a duty to enlarge perception (by
fusing it with fantasy): 'Is he honest who resists his genius or
conscience, only for the sake of present ease or gratification?'
(*MHH* 13, E 38). Blake also moralises and justifies his own angry
denunciations through identification with Isaiah's belief that 'the
voice of honest indignation is the voice of God' (*MHH* 12, E 38).
Blake both denies and expresses his own aggression by perceiving it
as godlike indignation, not personal aggression. A similar dignifica-
tion of motive is accorded Ezekiel's eating dung in order to raise man
'into a perception of the infinite' (*MHH* 13, E 38). Earlier, in 'then
She bore Pale desire', Blake had described his struggle with envious
rage in terms of drinking filth from the serpent Envy – evidently
before he could rationalise the act as morally worthy instead of
shameful.

Having shown God reabsorbed into the self as the poetic genius,
Blake prepares for a return to Paradise (plate 14). If God is
recognised as a mental entity whose 'creation' is linked with human
desires and fears, a major barrier to return disappears. 'The cherub
with his flaming sword is hereby commanded to leave his guard at
the tree of life, and when he does, the whole creation will be
consumed, and appear infinite. and holy' (*MHH* 14, E 38). In
connecting free access to the tree of life with a destroying fire, Blake's

apocalyptic imagery fuses desire and rage. Together they burn away the disappointing aspects of the world, which will reappear as an image of the poetic imagination.

The 'Printing house in Hell' section (plate 15) is of central importance in *Marriage* and a fitting climax to the denial of God's external and punitive existence. Blake's vision here must be read against his polemical vision of religious history, in which creation and sexuality are opposed to a morality divorced from the body. Blake, fighting to expunge 'the notion that man has a body distinct from his soul' (*MHH* 14, E 38) illustrates here the incestuous wishes intimately connected with art. His purpose is to describe the creative process as an alternative world view to the received moral view of experience.

Blake clearly describes art, in terms of sexuality, beginning with the first stanza, where a dragon man clears away 'the rubbish from a caves mouth' while others hollow it out. These dragon men have long been recognised as phallic figures; Erdman notes that they are pictured in the illustration (*MHH* 15, *IB* 112) as engraving-tools, thus equating tool and phallus. Less obvious is a fantasy that appears in the next stanza, of restoring or renewing the body-contents after penetration. Blake shows a viper adorning the cave with gold, silver, and precious stones. Blake's choice of the viper suggests hostility to the maternal body such as is explicit in the legend of the viper who kills its mother by eating its way out.[20] The act of adornment, however, suggests an effort to overcome hostility and Blake illustrates it in a positive way: graceful human figures stand or recline with books and a viper-shaped scroll. Here, as in Beulah, where the male genius adorns the females with gold and jewels (*J* 69:17, E 221), adornment suggests restitutional giving rather than hoarding of one's precious substance.

The winged eagle men in the third chamber suggest the creative inspiration whose prototype is the winged phallus.[21] They defy gravity and are not bound by the constraining female space that they extend infinitely. They are also not bound to adorn it, however, beautifully; instead, they create their own substitute spaces – their palaces or works of art. The illustrations show that the cliff-face in which palaces are constructed is the copper-plate, and the eagle's activity parallels the phallic–aggressive activity of the Devil and bird at Hell's entrance.[22]

In the fourth chamber, we return to anal–urethral components of creation. The viper's precious metals are transformed into their unconscious equivalent, 'living fluids' of the body, by raging lions – a constructive use of aggressive energy. Ultimately these fluids are cast out into the expanse and gathered in books. Given the sexual locale, the process suggests a reworking of fantasies of anal birth, with the book seen as the infant. Blake, like many artists, thought of his books as children and referred to them as his sons. These final stages of creation are characterised by confidence and vigour, which oppose the constipated vision of traditional religious history and shows that what is given generously is not lost but only transformed into something equally precious.

The large illustration (plate 15) shows an eagle holding a snake, rising from the cave. The snake penetrates the rock with his tongue and, like the similarly phallic dragon men, seems to want to enter and remain in the maternal cave–body. In this sense the energy he represents is restricted by matter (and the maternal womb), which can be adorned but not changed. The eagle's flight, on the other hand, suggests an inspiration, which, although fuelled by sexuality, rises above matter, foreshadowing Blake's view of a male creativity that transcends sexual organisation.

In plate 16 Blake, having described the creative process with its anal and phallic components, reworks his ideas about reason's dynamic opposition to energy in terms of the obsessive oral fantasies of *Tiriel* and *Thel*. Here Blake removes devouring from the original context of infant and parents and conceptualises an abstract strife between 'two classes of men' who stand in the relation of fathers and sons: all creation is divided into devourers and prolifics. The prolific sons are first seen as the originators of the world ('the causes of its life') and the Tiriel-like devourers as those who enchain them, maintaining an illusion of priority. But Blake moves away from the rhetoric of accusation to suggest that both are necessary and can be satisfied without harming each other: 'The Prolific would cease to be Prolific unless the Devourer as a sea received the excess of his delights' (*MHH* 16, E 39). When the two are in correct relationship, the prolific son is freed from chains to produce. His production does not threaten the father, and the father does not threaten him. The father devours only the son's excess, leaving his body intact, uneaten. This idea brings the son relief from fear of castration. It also relieves guilt over infantile greed, because the father is cast as the devourer while the poet identifies with the good nurturing mother; he is no

longer a devourer but a supreme giver. A negative alternative to this
equilibrium promptly appears in the illustration of an imprisoned old
man with his sons (*MHH* 16, *IB* 113 – Illus. 8). Enchained, the sons
have no energic excess to give the father, who will devour them. In
version G, Blake actually shows this horror; there is a bloody lump
beneath the old man's outstretched arm, the flesh he has been eating.

Blake's concept of prolific and the necessary devourer, like his
theory of interdependent contraries, suggests the possibility of solutions to two problems that obsessed him: first, whether men can live
in mutual harmony rather than competition, and, second, whether a
man can be a 'giver' and still retain his male identity. Earlier, in
Island, *Tiriel* and *Thel*, Blake portrayed the male as a 'taker', in

Illus. 8　*The Marriage of Heaven and Hell*, plate 16

heterosexual relations. Here, he puts himself as poet in a female role; creation is seen as nurturing; the poet becomes a 'giver' to the devouring father. Blake's concept of the poet as 'giver' follows naturally from the final image of the 'birth' of books in the printing-press sequence. Perhaps the problem of competition could be solved only when Blake could view himself in the mother's role. This in turn suggests homosexuality as a latent condition of harmony. In later works such as *Vala* it becomes clear that harmony can exist only when women are segregated or absent. However at this point, when Blake was still extolling liberated sexuality, he vacillated between viewing men as interdependent and viewing them as rivals. Thus his concept of harmony is not sustained here, where it is disrupted by the cannabilistic illustration of plate 16; nor is it sustained in *Marriage* as a whole, which ends with a classic picture of rivalry between father and son.

After Blake's exposition of creation as giving, he introduces a contrasting moral vision. In the fourth 'Memorable Fancy', Blake harshly resumes his criticism of Swedenborg, attempting to demolish conclusively the barriers of religious morality, paternal authority and poetic precedence obstructing a return to Paradise. The 'Fancy' takes off from the discourse of an Angel in Swedenborg's *Scortatory Love*, who tries to reform a lustful young man. Blake's parody combats the concept of the sinful nature of sexual desire and attendant fears of punishment. Fear is turned to laughter in his exaggerated burlesque of the Angel's admonitions. 'An Angel came to me and said O pitiable foolish young man! O horrible! O dreadful state! consider the hot burning dungeon thou art preparing for thyself to all eternity' (*MHH* 17, E 40). The Angel's exhortation, although modelled on Swedenborg, suggests the tone of any father or priest to a young rebel. Blake now turns enforced passivity into active mastery. If the Angel shows him his 'eternal lot' he will retaliate and show the Angel his own 'eternal lot' from a Blakean perspective. In talking to the Angel, Blake's narrator assumes the reasonable tone of an educator: 'We will contemplate together upon it and see' (*MHH* 17, E 40). We may speculate that Blake in this section relives a childhood scene of admonition, but this time with a power he did not previously possess. When Blake's father had threatened to beat him for saying he saw angels in a tree, Blake had been compelled to listen. Now Blake forcefully insists on the rightness of his vision.[23]

The two versions of man's eternal lot (the Angel's and Blake's) reach beyond the satire of Swedenborg to Blake's essential concerns. The Angel goes first. His imagination produces a history of religion paralleling the previous allegory of creation; this historical vision reverses the restorative, expansive process of creation into one of progressive rigidity, abstractness, and alienation from the body. As in the creative vision, in the historical vision a process in time, from Christ's birth to the present, is represented spatially. Blake's movement with the Angel is downward through buildings and structures signifying crucial events. They descend from the stable of Christ's birth with its earthy associations, through a church to a vault (the oppressive institution built over Christ's body), through a mill (sensually impoverished rational thought), to a cave of error, and finally arrive at the Newtonian void, where they hang headfirst over the abyss.[24] Now Blake asks if they should let go, committing themselves to providence. This query concludes Blake's opposition of the creative and rational–moral modes: whereas the creative expands and gives out, the moral restricts and holds on. And, whereas the creative vision begins with penetration and ends with birth, Christ's stable provides the only life in the religious vision. After Christ's birth, the body and its wishes are progressively repressed and denied until, as Blake sees it, only the sterile reasoning mind and an inert bodily shell are left.

Repression, whether by parent or priest, rests on the fear of punishment for bodily impulses. The Angel, therefore, shows the Blakean persona the punishment awaiting him: beneath a hellish black sun, he will be trapped between two groups of famished spiders. This fear of being devoured is clearly Blake's own, but he distances it by placing it in the Angel's vision, enabling him to repudiate it and the related Swedenborgian view that impulses – the spider lusts – are dangerous. The habit of certain female spiders of devouring their mates makes the spider also an apt symbol of the devouring mother: a female parallel to the cannibalistic father (plate 16). Both images suggest that men weakened by repression cannot resist being devoured or castrated – an idea also present in Flaxman's portrait in *Island* and in the portrait of Swedenborg as 'Samson shorn by the Churches' (*Milton* 22:50, E 117).

While observing the spiders, who in the composite image represent both lust and its punishment, the Angel and Blake suddenly witness the eruption of threatened energies as the Leviathan of revolution – a birth that is the aggressive complement of the previous non-destructive birth of books. This vision of revolution supersedes the moral–legal order and thus cancels the Angel's punitive power. Leviathan, as his enormous fanged mouth suggests, will become the punishing devourer. He expresses revolutionary rage and the aggressive components of creation in general. However, Blake is not able or willing to take responsibility for this hostile element in creativity. He blames the serpent's appearance not on his own rage but on the Angel's distorted vision. When the Angel flees, Blake finds himself on a bank listening to a harper singing, 'The man who never alters his opinion is like standing water, & breeds reptiles of the mind' (*MHH* 19, E 41). Besides effectively putting down both Swedenborg and the Angel, this sequence, like the spider-sequence, allows Blake to express rage and revenge and, at the same time, to deny these feelings as products of the Angel's mind. Blake here conclusively asserts his poet's innocence. Not only is he a 'just man' or son provoked to rebellion, but rebellion itself is not really what it seems: aggression becomes transformed through the harper's words into a guilt-free endorsement of growth and change. Blake's narrator blames him for the horror of the vision: 'All that we saw was owing to your metaphysics' (*MHH* 19, E 41). He then proposes to show the Angel *his* eternal lot. When the Angel hesitates, the narrator forces him into the void with an expansive motion opposed to the Angel's frightened clinging. Now the punitive vision will be applied to the one – representative of paternal authority – who first invoked it. What is important here is not so much the possible allegories – whether of rival churches or doctrines or Hobbesian nature – as the overwhelming presence of the theme of devouring in the visions of both the Angel and Blake.

> I took him [the Angel] to the altar . . . and lo! it was a deep pit, into which I descended driving the Angel before me, soon we saw . . . a number of monkeys . . . the weak were caught by the strong and with a grinning aspect, first coupled with & then devourd, by plucking off first one limb and then another till the body was left a helpless trunk. this after grinning & kissing it with seeming fondness they devour too; and here & there I saw one savourily picking the flesh off his own tail . . . (*MHH* 19–20, E 41)

Blake here returns the Angel's punitive vision to him tenfold.[25] The angel saw Blake devoured by spiders; Blake in turn sees the angel devoured, even self-devouring. But Blake's responsibility for this fantasy's anger and fiercely negative sexual images is denied – again the vision is blamed on the angel's metaphysics. Similarly, in *Tiriel* Blake denied fantasies of infantile greed by projecting them onto the negative character of Tiriel. The links observable in *Tiriel* and *Thel* between infantile greed and fear of retaliation are explicit here: coupling is followed by devouring of the body. A gruesome detail links the monkeys more specifically to the smiling but murderous mother in *Tiriel*: the monkeys devour the limbless trunk only after kissing it with seeming fondness.

Whereas in the fourth 'Memorable Fancy' (plates 17–20) Blake struggles with fantasies of being devoured or castrated, combating them in the Swedenborgian Angel, in the next section (plates 21 and 22) he struggles against his envy of and rivalry with his poetic fathers. Having just defended creativity against punishment and his narrative persona against threats of being devoured or castrated, Blake must now repel other attacks on himself for being who he is. Again he projects his feelings outward, his desire for originality appearing as a prominent – though vain – characteristic of Swedenborg. 'Thus Swedenborg boasts that what he writes is new; tho' it is only the Contents or Index of already publish'd books' (*MHH* 21, E 41). Blake attributes Swedenborg's mistaken belief in his originality to two entirely different reasons: a 'confident insolence sprouting from systematic reasoning' and the false pride of a man who 'carried a monkey about for a shew, & because he was a little wiser than the monkey, grew vain, and conceiv'd himself as much wiser than seven men' (*MHH* 21, E 41–2). Swedenborg is placed in the context of the devouring monkeys who degrade sex here and recall the loathsome ape-like mate in *Island*; the image also evokes echoes of Quid–Blake's boasting in *Island*. There it was joined with derogatory comparisons of his fellows to fleas and nasty puppies. The disdain and competitive pride Blake attributes to Swedenborg, as well as the degrading view of sex, were, perhaps, things he felt in himself.

Swedenborg, Blake continues, is vain, unoriginal and wrong. 'Now hear a plain fact: Swedenborg has not written one new truth: . . . he has written all the old falsehoods' (*MHH* 22, E 42). In a reversal of Swedenborg's precedence, Blake becomes the teacher and Swedenborg the pupil whose 'conceited notions' prevent him from accepting Blake's doctrine of sexual energy. This role-reversal fits the general pattern of *Marriage*, in which a previously subdued son triumphs over the father. In his attack, Blake not only denies Swedenborg's real influence and genius but probably also revises early experiences of attempted moral influence by his parents. His temperament was such that he felt any correction as a mortal insult: his parents actually kept him home from school because they felt he would not submit to being thrashed. In *Tiriel*, Blake showed the reasoning, repressive father thrashing fantasy from the growing boy. The conflict carries over strangely into *Marriage* when Blake derides the visionary Swedenborg for Urizenic, 'mechanical talents' and exalts the free poetic imagination over the moral vision. 'Any man of mechanical talents may from the writings of Paracelsus or Jacob Behmen, produce ten thousand volumes of equal value with Swedenborg's . . .' (*MHH* 22, E 42).

The illustrations on plate 21 make a visual connection between the themes of poetic and paternal conflict. Blake's inter-linear portrayal of child-development, noted by Erdman, revises the father-dominated education we observed in *Tiriel*. There the infant was rudely weaned and forced to perceive reality; here, an infant receives spiritual food from a winged female. Paternal brutality is replaced by the image of a child studying with his nurse or mother, and Tiriel's compulsive thinking is countered here by the image of a boy freely employing his mind, absorbed in reading.

The process of growth and education leads, as Erdman notes, to the naked humanity of plate 21 (*IB* 118 – Illus. 9). The naked youth sits on the bank where Blake found himself after Leviathan's disappearance. The figure unites Blake and the harper; Blake seems to be assuring us that he is innocent. But, as Erdman notes, the speaking or singing poet-figure is linked visually with the raging Leviathan by his open mouth and upward-tilting head. Moreover, the youth is sitting not just on a bank but on a grave-mound. His knee is on a protruding skull and his hand holds down a paper, the analytic writings of Swedenborg (or, perhaps, Aristotle). On one level, this image indicates the birth of liberated imagination from the bones of abstract thought; on a more literal level, however, the bones are those of dead fathers, prophetic or real. A later version of the illustration empha-sises the literal meaning: an old man enters death's gates while the same naked youth wakes on top of the mound. The illustration suggests that the son can be free only when the father is dead. The youth's whole posture indicates that he is free from paternal threats. Not only is he naked, showing pleasure in his body, but he sits so as to expose his genitals. The incestuous desire at the centre of father–son conflict is also suggested symbolically in the illustration: the youth's left foot, drawn up in line with his penis, seems about to penetrate a cleft in the maternal earth. This expression of incestuous desire and rivalry grows out of Blake's attacks on Swedenborg. Both those attacks and the illustration defend against the self-accusation that Blake's creativity expresses the desire for incest. The illustration defends against this inner accusation in a typically Blakean manner by making the youth both victorious and innocent. The attacks on Swedenborg defend by translating the son's victory into literary

Illus. 9   *The Marriage of Heaven and Hell*, plate 21

terms. The accusation of lack of originality is relevant because incest, in a naïve but accurate way, is unoriginal: the father has been there first. To defend against that charge of unoriginality, Blake projects it onto a literary father.

Throughout this section dealing with rivalry, Blake symbolically demolishes paternal restrictions while maintaining a childlike innocence. But he also appropriates the paternal language of morality to undo his rivals. Blake's parable of the man and the monkey parodies Swedenborg with one of Swedenborg's favourite teaching-devices. Blake also uses pseudo-rational argument to turn the tables on paternal authority and put the father in the position of being scolded, reasoned at, and forced to submit. This device is particularly evident in Blake's concluding attack on Swedenborg, with its sequences of phrases suggesting rational argument. A general rule is followed by a specific and outrageous example. The scholarly opening, 'I have always found that', leads to the conclusion, 'Thus Swedenborg boasts.' And a sequence of seemingly objective phrases – 'Now hear a plain fact . . . and now hear the reason . . . Have now another plain fact' – contains Blake's most effective exaggerations.

The mixed feelings of love and hate attending this enterprise of debunking are depicted in tiny interlinear illustrations (*MHH* 22, *IB* 119) of a naked archer shooting his arrow at the breast of a figure opening his arms to receive it. The arrow with its sexual and aggressive connotations is yet another version of the bird cutting the airy way. Attacking an older rival is unconsciously experienced as both murdering him and sexually penetrating him. Accepting another's opinion is correspondingly felt as submitting passively to sexual or retaliatory attack. After violently attacking Swedenborg, Blake seems intent on repelling similar attacks against himself: his Devil warns that, since God exists only in man, especially geniuses, envy of great men is hatred of God. We saw in *Island* how Blake's own envy made him quick to feel envied. There, when Blake–Quid felt persecuted by envy he threatened a tantrum. In *Marriage* Blake has greater control – it is the Angel, not the Blakean Devil, who is enraged by Blake's identification of God and the genius. In this rage, the Angel echoes the Christian rhetoric of his angelic predecessor in *Island*, Flaxman. The Angel's assertion that, Jesus aside, men are 'fools, sinners, & nothings' (*MHH* 23, E 42) parallels Flaxman's opinion that 'We are all poor crawling reptiles.' And, just as Blake–Quid had mocked morality as feminine weakness, here Blake makes the radical claim that Jesus mocked the commandments and 'acted from impulse'. Jesus becomes a rebel involved, like Tiriel's sons, in Oedipal conflict. In *Tiriel* and in Blake's illustrations of the accusers, the rebel sons are accused of murder, theft and adultery. Jesus, Blake now tells us, murdered, stole, coveted, and freed the adulteress. Blake's outrageous argument is forced on him by the need to identify Jesus completely with the rebel son.

At this point the Angel is converted, changing from a type of moralising elder brother (a James Blake or Flaxman) to a devoted comrade (such as Robert–Suction). The transformed Angel and Blake now read the Bible together in its 'diabolical sense', just as Quid–Blake and Suction–Robert discussed art and agreed to act impulsively. Moreover, just as the brothers' collaboration in *Island* issued in Blake's announcement of the forthcoming *Songs*, Blake now announces the parallel Bible of Hell. In the earlier work, however, Blake portrayed himself as a child who, though enraged by misunderstanding, could show the 'truth' only through temper-tantrums. Now Blake assumes paternal authority and treats the world as naughty children who will receive his biblical interpretations only 'if they behave well', but who will be forced to take his Bible of Hell 'whether they will or no'. Blake's increasing artistic control is exemplified by his conversion of his angelic opponent through the power of his imagination rather than through a temper-tantrum, but his wish to force his vision on others remains constant. In this, as elsewhere in *Marriage*, he identifies with the aggressor. Moral instruction, once suffered passively, is now actively inflicted on the world, particularly the father.

The theme of instruction pervades *Marriage*, from its initial questioning of the instruction given by Swedenborg to Blake's instructive reinterpretation of Milton, to the use of devices of printing-presses, proverbs and prophets, to specific instances of instruction, of which the Angel's re-education is the most important. Blake seems to have regarded instruction as a fundamental aspect of his male identity and as crucial in his relationship to his father and to men generally. His job as a man was to be a poet who would instruct other men. *Marriage* is a defence of Blake's kind of poetic instruction, including its asserted philosophical foundations in imagination's relationship to reality. He viewed his kind of instruction as peculiarly creative and at the same time as peculiarly moral instruction; doing his kind of poetry led to salvation. Since we have already seen in earlier works a self-concept that wavered between unworthy and supremely good, we should not be surprised that his treatment of instruction here shows deeply ambivalent attitudes. Ambivalence is expressed both in ambiguity about the primacy of father or son and in alternating moods of benevolence and hostility.

The ambivalence in which the son, reversing roles, instructs or chastises and then lovingly embraces the father is subtly highlighted throughout *Marriage* by illustrations suggestive of love and hostility as well as of instruction. The Proverbs' concluding illustration, for example (*MHH* 10, *IB* 107 – Illus. 10) shows a naked, kneeling devil instructing two figures, one of whom resembles Blake and is

Illus. 10   *The Marriage of Heaven and Hell*, plate 10

apparently the impulsive devil's alter ego. The other learner is visually linked, as Erdman notes, to the poem's devouring fathers. The scene of instruction raises (and answers) the question of priority. Both figures seem to have received the message together, but rivalry is suggested by the Blake figure's attempt to observe what is being transcribed by the other learner. A related question of who will submit to whose instruction and what this means emotionally is dealt with in the image of the arrow and related images of the submissive Angel headless or limbless.[26]

Aggression is paramount in *Marriage*'s final illustration, of the fallen Nebuchadnezzar (*MHH* 24, *IB* 121), an attitude that sharply alternates with the immediately preceding benevolence toward the Angel. The father is an accuser or moral teacher no longer. Instead, in an image that condenses all the degraded animal images of *Island* and turns them against the father, he is a terrified beast, himself accused. Blake hereby warns the world, particularly its fathers, what it can expect if it fails to mend its ways.

'A Song of Liberty' is printed as *Marriage*'s coda. In *Marriage* Blake emphasises the legitimacy of creation, which for him subsumes both desire and rage. In this final song, Blake expresses rage imaginatively not through literary creation but through political action, embodied in a conflict between a potentially rebellious 'new born wonder' and a 'jealous king'. The action and the characters sketched here form the base of Blake's myth, tentatively elaborated in *America* – a myth that develops out of *Marriage*'s conflict between Blake as a rebel son and the angelic fathers.

Nurmi wonders why Blake joined this 'political prophecy to his metaphysical credo'.[27] In a general sense, it is because the emotional basis of both the metaphysics and the politics is the same. Blake drastically simplifies revolution, viewing it in terms of his own conflict or central myth, as a struggle between fiery sons and repressive fathers. More particularly, as critics have noted, 'Song' refers directly back to the illustrated story of *Marriage*'s opening plates: a boy's birth, his peril, and a fiery fall. Essick argues that these plates illustrate the themes of 'Song', not of *Marriage*,[28] but they clearly refer to *Marriage*'s latent themes as well. On plate 3 of *Marriage*, Blake's birth signals the beginning of a new Heaven, and the illustration (*MHH* 3, *IB* 100 – Illus. 11) shows a baby boy literally emerging from between his mother's legs. The following illustration (*MHH* 4, *IB* 101 – Illus. 12) introduces the threatening paternal figure: a blind male pursues a naked woman and infant. The figure in flames resembles the jealous king in 'Song', as Essick notes, but this does not mean, as he concludes,[29] that it represents this king in particular: the theme of father–son rivalry, although more obvious in 'Song', is shared by *Marriage*. Plate 5 of *Marriage* (*IB* 102) depicts the climax of Oedipal struggle in an ambiguously illustrated fall, which can be read as either the fall of the father (reason) or of the son (desire). The accompanying text of *Marriage* at this point deals with the precedence of desire over reason and the problem of who (son or father) stole what from whom. 'Song' presents the alternatives in dramatic sequence. The jealous king throws down the infant only to fall himself.

In 'Song', the conflict between males, at the core of *Marriage*, emerges clearly as a fight to the death between father (jealous starry king) and son (infant terror). *Marriage*'s project of return to Paradise

Illus. 11   *The Marriage of Heaven and Hell*, plate 3

Illus. 12   *The Marriage of Heaven and Hell*, plate 4

depends here on the overthrow of paternal power: the bursting of barriers and the taking of keys. In 'Song', the symbolic equation of war with birth is followed by the actual birth of the 'terror' and his confrontation with the king – a confrontation prepared for by the son's hostility implicit in *Marriage*. In choosing a setting for the confrontation – the infinite mountains 'now barr'd out by the atlantic sea' – Blake again recalls the lost Paradise and the barriers to return. Both fall, but the fiery son triumphs. He stamps the Ten Commandments to dust, just as the impulsive Jesus did in *Marriage*. The poem's final chorus commends joyous impulsiveness free from the curse of priests, 'For every thing that lives is Holy.'

4 Fathers and Sons: Impotence or Rebellion

VISIONS OF THE DAUGHTERS OF ALBION

In *Visions of the Daughters of Albion*, roughly contemporaneous with *The Marriage of Heaven and Hell* (1793), Blake depicts the fantasies of impotence underlying *Marriage*'s rebellious attacks against Milton and Swedenborg. In *Marriage*, impotence was denied by establishing desire as a first principle and active hatred as love's necessary contrary. *Visions* presents an archetypal situation of hatred and frustrated desire: a youth, Theotormon, loves a virgin, Oothoon; she decides to give herself to him but is raped instead by the tyrant Bromion, whereupon her lover falls into impotent despair.

The poem has been discussed primarily in relation to its ideas — as a defence of free love or as an attack on slavery — and its plot has been dismissed as derivative, a peg on which to hang the heroine's Blakean rhetoric.[1] My concern here is not primarily the manifest meaning of the text but rather the latent meaning of the characters and the situation. I would thus argue that the poem must be understood in terms of its emotional dynamics, which take the form of a psychic story of thwarted love and traumatic witnessing. Blake later illustrated the story's prototypical situation in *Vala*, where a boy observes his parents' intercourse. Here, in *Visions*, although Theotormon is not Oothoon's son, Blake draws on the imagined feelings and body imagery of a helpless child in order to represent him. In its broad outlines, *Visions* suggest failure in the Oedipal struggle; Oothoon is an incarnation in the hero's adult experience of a virginal mother raped by a sadistic father, Bromion, and Theotormon suggests the impotent son forced to witness their union. Theotormon's reaction, his anger against Oothoon and his self-beat-

ing, suggests rivalry with the mother for the father's sexual atten-
tions. Theotormon's masochistic wishes foredoom any efforts to
'arise' and rebel. Blake expands this inner meaning into an artistically
successful defence of analogous unfortunates: black slaves, children
sold by their parents, and women enslaved by marriage.

That Blake's psychic story works emotionally is partly owing to
the ambiguity of Oothoon's marital status. Blake nowhere explains
whether she is married to Bromion or to Theotormon, or why, if
married, she is a virgin at the time of the rape. This ambiguity
permits Blake to suggest, while perhaps not yet as conscious of it as
he was in later works, the fantasy of possessing the mother before the
father did. The rape evokes the shock of the discovery of parental
intercourse, breaking the dream of priority. The rape's violent sadism
suggests, moreover, a child's perception of intercourse as a hostile
act. Oothoon's apparent arousal and lack of regret represent the
reality denied by the child, because it implies the mother's unfaithfulness to him. This idea of unfaithfulness makes emotional sense of
Theotormon's angry wish to punish Oothoon and for the extreme
jealousy that Oothoon sees as Theotormon's besetting fault. Re-
proaching him, she asserts that, although he is unwilling to share her
with another, she, like a mother choosing her son's wife, would
gladly provide other women for his pleasure.

Turning to the poem's 'Argument', we see that Oothoon unites
traits of earlier maternal figures; her conflict between sexual fear –
her initial hiding in Leutha's vale – and generous desire correspond
to the contrast between frustrating and nurturing mother-figures in
Tiriel and *Thel*. Later, in *Europe*, Blake suggests that murderous
anger as well as fear underlies withholding: Leutha develops into a
'Sweet smiling pestilence' who seduces, then infects (just as in *Tiriel*
Pestilence's smile promised nurture and meant murder). The choice
and development of Blake's illustration for the 'Argument' (*VDA* iii,
IB 128 – Illus. 13) also reflects negative and positive views of a
maternal figure. The mother as whore appears in Vien's engraving,
Blake's visual source.[2] There the well-endowed woman, kneeling and
holding a small cupid by the wings, is a procuress selling loves. Blake
adapts the figures but gives them an opposite meaning. His naked
woman, holding full breasts and kissing a small figure leaping from a
flower, suggests both the incestuous nature and the special
non-possessive quality of Oothoon's love, which combines generosity and lack of restraint.[3]

The Argument

I loved Theotarmon
And I was not ashamed
I trembled in my virgin fears
And I hid in Leutha's vale;

I plucked Leutha's flower,
And I rose up from the vale;
But the terrible thunders tore
My virgin mantle in twain.

Illus. 13   *Visions of the Daughters of Albion*, plate iii

The illustrations at the top of the first plate of the text (*VDA* 1, *IB* 129 – Illus. 14) replace the idealised view of mother and child with sexual fantasies, followed at the bottom of the page by a view of Bromion and Oothoon after the rape. The sexual details are explicit but sufficiently disguised to have remained unnoticed until Erdman's edition of the illuminated works. In the C version, the mother–son

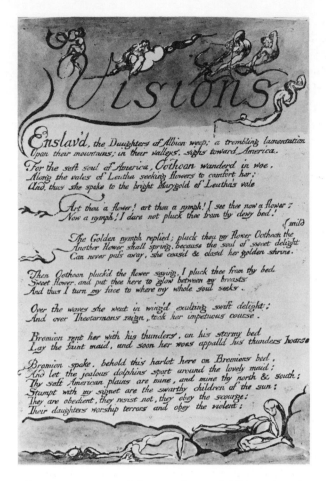

Illus. 14   *Visions of the Daughters of Albion*, plate 1

theme continues in the image of a small naked male angel standing in the lap of a woman riding a cloud horse. The angel's eagle-wings suggest both inspiration and the cruelty of Theotormon's eagles, who tear Oothoon's breast after the rape. The sexual nature of the embrace between woman and small angel is clearly shown by the penis and testicles Blake has drawn emerging between the woman's legs, where we should expect the neck and head of her cloud mount. In some versions Blake adds a beak or bill to the penis, which seems equivalent to biting teeth in its potential to injure the maternal body. The idea of phallus as weapon also appears in the figures of two archers who shoot their arrows down at the figure of Oothoon (at the bottom of the page), who lies in a pose suggesting both torture and sexual gratification.

Sexuality in the top illustration seems exciting, even inspiring, but possibly damaging to the female. The bottom illustration suggests it can also damage the male: Bromion sprawls exhausted, his impotence suggested by the deflated cloud–penis–horse crumpled beside Oothoon's arm. Dangers to both male and female are denied by the text. Oothoon is assured that the plucked flower of her virginity will be replaced, and although Blake refers to the spirit ('the soul of sweet delight / Can never pass away' – *VDA* 1:9–10, E 45), the implication seems to be that the body will suffer no harm or loss. Bromion, after the rape, is described in the text as being full of power and sadistic arrogance.

Blake's concentration on Bromion's proud sadism introduces a rhetoric of blame (not the son but the father has these impulses). Blake's condemnation of Bromion as a slaver is given force by the underlying fantasy of bestial father and virgin mother. The impotent black slaves, 'swarthy children of the sun' (*VDA* 1:21, E 45), are the collective alternative of the son. The implicit connection between Theotormon and Bromion's slaves is strengthened by the juxtaposition of Theotormon's lament with the illustration (*VDA* 2, *IB* 130) of an exhausted black with his tool laid aside. Theotormon is tormented by the voices of slaves and of abandoned children, whose predicament echoes his own. Sitting at the cave's mouth, he pictures them locked deep in 'religious caves', while the fires of Bromion's lust, seen in digestive terms, 'belch incessant from the summits of the earth' (*VDA* 2:11, E 45).

In presenting Theotormon's reaction to the rape itself, Blake uses imagery of excretion to express impotent rage. Theotormon's first act is to surround Bromion and Oothoon with 'black jealous waters' (*VDA* 2:4, E 45). These waters go back to Blake's early image of the serpent Envy discharging a river of filth. Using faeces as weapons is characteristic of very young children; Melanie Klein, for example, cites cases of children who reacted to observation of parental intercourse with angry soiling.[4] From Blake's imagery, one might infer his own repressed memory of such a reaction, but, whatever the source of his insight, as artist Blake was able to conect Theotormon's childishly ineffectual rage with the body imagery that best expressed it.

In Blake's frontispiece illustration (*VDA* i, *IB* 125 – Illus. 15),
Theotormon appears allegorically as black water surrounding 'the
adulterate pair' and humanly as an angry tearful youth covering his
eyes so as to avoid the painful sight of Bromion and Oothoon.
Chained back to back, their union is both denied and expressed
sadistically. Similarly, their posture in this illustration expresses ideas
of punishment and of accusation. Although the text describes the
pair as bestial rapist and victim, the illustration shows Bromion
quailing in open-mouthed horror at something offstage. His expression links him with Blake's painting of the last Judgement, *The
Accusers*. Here, as there, accusation originally directed by the father
against the son is redirected against the paternal figure – a pattern

Illus. 15   *Visions of the Daughters of Albion*, plate i

that explains why Theotormon calls the pair 'adulterate' even though there is no evidence that he and Oothoon are married. Theotormon's effort, plainly similar to Blake's in *Marriage*, to appease his conscience (or deny his aggression) by blaming someone else is unsuccessful. His anger turns inward; instead of attacking Bromion, he pulls his own hair. The entire scene is dominated by a giant eye, which stares accusingly out of a cloudy face.

Accompanying the illustration's motif of punishment are suggestions of an archaic sexuality, whose focus is the anus rather than the genitals. Not only is the couple back to back, but Blake's composition emphasises straining backs and buttocks. The dangling ring of Oothoon's manacle hangs directly beneath Bromion and, echoed by a shadowy ring, visually associates the chain-circles with his buttocks and suggests a radical connection between the sadistically employed chains and the anal zone. In one version of this illustration, the manacle is a visual extension of Bromion's body hanging funnel-like over the black water beneath. In the context, Theotormon's posture also suggests anal reminiscences; he crouches over a black fissure in the rock, which leads down to the surrounding water.

The illustration and text thus suggest that both impotent suffering and its opposite, sadistic cruelty, are emotionally linked with anal experiences, both the bodily function of excretion and the power-struggle around it. Oothoon's rhetoric suggests that through rebellion and free love Theotormon can escape both masochistic suffering and sadistic cruelty. As in *Marriage*, filial rebellion becomes justified as a righteous struggle against oppression.

The implication is that if, instead of rebelling, Theotormon identifies with Bromion, he will become sadistic, just as in *Island* Sipsop decided to become a surgeon like his father. Oothoon illustrates this possibility by asking Theotormon's eagles to tear her breast. In effect, Oothoon is inviting Theotormon to repeat Bromion's rape. The illustration conveys both sensuality and punishment (*VDA* 3, *IB* 131 – Illus. 16); Oothoon lies backward voluptuously on a cloud resembling a cross while a huge eagle touches her belly with his beak. In its sadistic conception of sex, the illustration echoes Blake's sketch in *Island* where the 'beast' Corruption rapes Flesh, and their frustrated child, Surgery, turns his crooked knife – the equivalent of claws and beak – against his mother. Here however, Blake both expands the connection between sadistic sex and dirty or polluting sex and, through Oothoon, repudiates both of

And none but Bromion can hear my lamentations.

With what sense is it that the chicken shuns the ravenous hawk
With what sense does the tame pigeon measure out the expanse?
With what sense does the bee form cells? have not the mouse & frog
Eyes and ears and sense of touch? yet are their habitations.
And their pursuits, as different as their forms and as their joys:
Ask the wild ass why he refuses burdens: and the meek camel
Why he loves man: is it because of eye ear mouth or skin
Or breathing nostrils? No. for these the wolf and tyger have.
Ask the blind worm the secrets of the grave, and why her spires
Love to curl round the bones of death: and ask the ravnous snake
Where she gets poison: & the wing'd eagle why he loves the sun
And then tell me the thoughts of man, that have been hid of old.

Silent I hover all the night. and all day could be silent.
If Theotormon once would turn his loved eyes upon me:
How can I be defil'd when I reflect thy image pure?   (woe
Sweetest the fruit that the worm feeds on. & the soul prey'd on by
The new wash'd lamb ting'd with the village smoke & the bright swan
By the red earth of our immortal river: I bathe my wings,
And I am white and pure to hover round Theotormons breast.

Then Theotormon broke his silence. and he answered.

Tell me what is the night or day to one oerflowd with woe?
Tell me what is a thought? & of what substance is it made?
Tell me what is a joy? & in what gardens do joys grow?
And in what rivers swim the sorrows, and upon what mountains

Illus. 16   *Visions of the Daughters of Albion*, plate 3

these disturbing ideas. Theotormon complains obsessively that Oothoon has been dirtied by sex: she is 'a clear spring mudded with feet of beasts' (*VDA* 2:19, E 45). It is ostensibly to appease this feeling in him that she suggests the radical surgery of the eagle, which will expose his pure image under her sullied flesh. However, her acceptance both of such masochistic gratification and of his view of sex as filthy is only momentary. She rallies, and throughout the rest of the poem tries to raise him to another way of seeing, in which the oppositions between dirty and clean, powerful and impotent, are superseded.

A difficulty in moving from obsessed impotence to a sexuality seen as clean and creative is sexuality's connection with ideas of murder and incest. Theotormon is unconscious of incestuous wishes, although his love for Oothoon, a woman bound to an older rival, enacts them. Oothoon, much like a psychoanalyst, strives to make Theotormon conscious of his wishes, but unlike an analyst she also urges him to act on them. She begins by presenting an image of sadistic cruelty transformed into inspiration: the eagle returns from his prey and 'lifts his golden beak to the pure east' (*VDA* 2:26, E 46). Oothoon then begins to undermine the paternal ethic that limits both imaginative and sexual freedom. With the rhetoric of *Marriage* she compares the rational–moral and the imaginative modes of perception. The natural philosophy of the rationalist, limited by the five senses, is linked with constrictive moral attitudes like the Angel's in *Marriage*. What concerns Oothoon (and Blake) is that both the rational and the moral modes exclude imagination and, with it, forbidden fantasies. Under the domination of moral vision, the pleasurable sun of morning becomes the 'bright shadow, like an eye' (*VDA* 2:35, E 46) of the frontispiece illustration – the eye of conscience.

In order to make Theotormon acknowledge and act on his repressed desires, Oothoon asks rhetorical questions about individual differences, leading to the climactic question, 'tell me the thoughts of man, that have been hid of old' (*VDA* 3:13, E 46). The dangerous and forbidden nature of these thoughts is suggested by Oothoon's preceding description of worm and snake. The blind worm knows 'the secrets of the grave' and 'her spires / Love to curl round the bones of death' (*VDA* 3:10–11, E 46). Phallic 'knowing' and destructive incorporation are linked here, as they were in *Thel*. But here the second idea is stronger and includes the suggestion of a mother enveloping her bone–child. The snake, both 'rav'nous' and poisonous, is equally fearsome. Both creatures, although phallic in form, are female and suggest a dangerous archaic mother with a male organ. And both are earthbound, thus contrasting with the upward flying male eagle. This contrast reflects a dichotomy between dirty and clean sexuality: dirty, dangerous females and pure eagle. Theotormon's hidden fears of woman and her sexuality – shared at some level by Blake – contribute to his impotence.

Oothoon approaches the repelling aspect of her 'impurity' from two directions. First, she suggests that being slightly dirty or used, like the apple penetrated by the worm or the sooty lamb, is attractive. But, more important, the dirt is only superficial; it can be washed off: 'I bathe my wings. / And I am white and pure' (*VDA* 3:19–20, E 46). Renewed purity, like the flower that grows again, suggests a perpetual virginity, an idea made explicit in later work. Oothoon's assertion also functions within the clean–dirty dichotomy to defend both her purity and her own incestuous fantasy in her relations with Theotormon.[5]

When Theotormon answers Oothoon, he bypasses her talk of purity and responds to her earlier question about man's hidden thoughts with his own question, 'Tell me what is a thought? & of what substance is it made?' (*VDA* 3:23, E 46). His intellectual interest in substance defends against awareness of his hidden thoughts and their present reality for him. However, his imagery connects thought with joys and evokes the original paradisal garden: 'Tell me . . . in what gardens do joys grow?' (*VDA* 3:24, E 46). The thought of joyful desire leads him immediately to his own frustration. His question, 'And in what rivers swim the sorrows' (*VDA* 3:25, E 46) links his fishlike sorrows with the 'jealous dolphins' surrounding Bromion and Oothoon. Theotormon seems to be approaching a realisation that his allegory refers to his own emotions when he asks, 'and in what houses dwell the wretched / Drunken with woe forgotten' (*VDA* 4:1–2, E 47). The line suggests some earlier torment of jealousy that his present emotions echo, and his next question refers more clearly to childhood's lost loves and joys:

> Tell me where dwell the thoughts forgotten till thou call them
> forth
> Tell me where dwell the joys of old! & where the ancient loves?
> And when will they renew again. . . .
>
> (*VDA* 4:3–5, E 47)

His subsequent question suggests both that he knows the joys and loves are within him and that he is afraid to recall them because of the corresponding tortures of jealousy:

> Where goest thou O thought? to what remote land is thy flight?
> If thou returnest to the present moment of affliction
> Wilt thou bring comforts on thy wings. and dews and honey and
>   balm;
> Or poison from the desart wilds, from the eyes of the envier.
>   (*VDA* 4:8–11, E 47)

He seems to be wondering whether, if he lets himself 'remember' ancient loves, gratification (dews, honey, balm) or frustration and envy will be uppermost in his thoughts. The contrasting feelings of comfort and envy are projected in typical Blakean fashion so that they, particularly the envy, seem to come from external sources like the poisonous eyes, which Blake had earlier associated specifically with the paternal tyrant, Tiriel. In the accompanying illustration (*VDA* 4, *IB* 132), Theotormon sits rigidly, hands over his face, choosing not to see Oothoon, who hovers naked above him in a huge, black wave-flame. The similar colours of the wave and the surrounding 'black jealous waters' suggest that her image is contaminated by his jealous rage.

Now, as Theotormon struggles with his jealous desire, Bromion tauntingly asks him how he will gratify 'senses unknown' when he cannot even name what he wants. Philosophically, we return to *Marriage*'s debate between perception or experience and imagination; psychologically, however, Bromion's remark functions as a further clamp on Theotormon's already repressed wishes. Bromion goes on to question the existence of joys and sorrows that are caused by passion rather than by money or its lack. Bromion appears to be trying to divert Theotormon's attention from sexual wishes to an anal preoccupation with money: should Theotormon continue recalling forbidden joys, Bromion hints at future punishment: 'And is there not eternal fire, and eternal chains?' (*VDA* 4:23, E 47).

Theotormon subsides after this attack, leaving Oothoon to continue her argument. Bromion assumes that riches are man's only joy. ('And are there other joys, beside the joys of riches and ease?' – *VDA* 4:21, E 47.) Implicit in this assumption is the idea that this one joy has absorbed earlier 'forgotten' joys and loves. Oothoon, therefore, renews her attempt to liberate Theotormon by vigorously attacking the thought that individual joys are interchangeable.

> How can one joy absorb another? are not different joys
> Holy, eternal, infinite! and each joy is a Love.
> > > (*VDA* 5:5–6, E 47)

Unlike modern psychoanalytic theory, which suggests that desires or joys change and absorb each other as an individual matures, Oothoon's rhetoric asserts an intactness and coexistence difficult to imagine in practice. Oothoon's argument implies that past joys or fantasies cannot be forgotten or replaced by Bromion's love of riches. To strengthen her argument, she associates past implicitly sexual joys with qualities of generosity and creativity. In arguing this way, she – and Blake – bypass the problematic nature of her 'joy', which caused it to be forgotten, and direct our attention to the baseness of Bromion's anal model of retentive hoarding. Using body-imagery, she concretely illustrates the difference between generous openness and narrow meanness that mocks creative efforts: 'Does not the great mouth laugh at a gift? & the narrow eyelids mock / At the labour that is above payment' (*VDA* 5:7–8, E 47). The mouth that opens wide and laughs freely at a gift (whether in pleasure or rejection is not clear) contrasts with the squeezed eyelids that suggest Bromion's tight retentiveness and his malicious inability to 'see' the value of work that, like Blake's, gets no monetary reward. Through his subtle rhetoric, Blake elicits our approval for generosity and unselfish creativity and extends it to the associated forgotten joys.

Having contrasted generosity and envious tightness, Oothoon questions our setting up as authorities men lacking the qualities of generous imagination: 'and wilt thou take the ape / For thy councellor? or the dog, for a schoolmaster to thy children?' (*VDA* 5:8–9, E 47). Succeeding lines compare the prolific 'giver of gifts' with the profit-seeking merchant. The underlying contrast of retention and generosity becomes more sinister with the introduction of the hired soldier: 'Who buys whole corn fields into wastes, and sings upon the heath' (*VDA* 5:15, E 47). Through his syntactical association with the profiteer,[6] the soldier becomes a merchant of destruction whose activities, like those of the merchant proper, seem negatively excremental; 'wastes' puns on the transformation of the farmer's corn into useless dirt. The soldier's sterile fatness mocks the farmer's provision of nourishment just as his 'hollow drum' and drill tunes parody the poet's song. From envy and mockery, it seems only a short step to destroying others' goods while waxing fat oneself.

The idea of denying to another what one then appropriates provides the subsequent transition from economics to sexuality. The parson is the transitional figure. Taking the farmer's labour, the parson builds an exclusive pleasure-palace for kings and priests. Images of theft and exclusion echo the imagery of *Marriage*'s 'Preludium' and lead into Oothoon's description of explicitly sexual exclusiveness: 'Till she who burns with youth. and knows no fixed lot; is bound / In spells of law to one she loaths . . . to bear the wintry rage / Of a harsh terror driv'n to madness' (*VDA* 5:21–5, E 48). Observation of paternal brutality makes the son of this sadistic union choose a similarly antagonistic partner and, like Theotormon, view his own sexuality with revulsion:

> Till the child dwell with one he hates. and do the deed he
>   loaths
> And the impure scourge force his seed into its unripe birth
> E'er yet his eyelids can behold the arrows of the day.
> (VDA 5:30–2, E 48)

These ambiguous final lines, together with the illustrations that follow (*VDA* 5, 6, *IB* 133–4), suggest a sado-masochistic masturbation fantasy in which the child imagines himself scourged by the father and, like the mother, forced to respond sexually: the scourge forces out the youth's immature seed. Another possible reading is that the father's phallus as scourge intrudes into the womb itself and beats the child 'E'er yet his eyelids can behold the arrows of the day'.

The illustration presents what seems to be a complementary female fantasy. A half-naked woman lies embracing her pillow. Although the pillow alludes visually to plate 1's phallic cloud-mount, the pillow's trailing horse-tail suggests sadistic ideas of phallus as whip. This hint of sadism is reinforced by Blake's visual focus on the woman's bared back and streaming black hair, which is analogous to strands of tail or whip. The idea of whipping becomes explicit in the next plate (*VDA* 6, *IB* 134 – Illus. 17) when Blake returns to Theotormon and shows him scourging himself with a cat-o'-nine-tails while clutching his head. His 'cat' is linked visually with both

6

And a palace of eternity in the jaws of the hungry grave
Over his porch these words are written. Take thy bliss O Man!
And sweet shall be thy taste & sweet thy infant joys renew!

Infancy, fearless, lustful, happy! nestling for delight
In laps of pleasure; Innocence! honest, open, seeking
The vigorous joys of morning light; open to virgin bliss.
Who taught thee modesty, subtil modesty! child of night & sleep
When thou awakest, wilt thou dissemble all thy secret joys
Or wert thou not awake when all this mystery was disclos'd!
Then cam'st thou forth a modest virgin knowing to dissemble
With nets found under thy night pillow, to catch virgin joy,
And brand it with the name of whore: & sell it in the night,
In silence, ev'n without a whisper, and in seeming sleep.
Religious dreams and holy vespers, light thy smoky fires:
Once were thy fires lighted by the eyes of honest morn
And does my Theotormon seek this hypocrite modesty!
This knowing, artful, secret, fearful, cautious, trembling hypocrite.
Then is Oothoon a whore indeed! and all the virgin joys
Of life are harlots: and Theotormon is a sick mans dream
And Oothoon is the crafty slave of selfish holiness.

But Oothoon is not so, a virgin fill'd with virgin fancies
Open to joy and to delight, where ever beauty appears
If in the morning sun I find it: there my eyes are fix'd

Illus. 17   *Visions of the Daughters of Albion*, plate 6

the horse-tail of plate 5 and the phallic curves of the marigold on plate 1 (here flowerlike whip-heads replace the original flowers). The text and illustrations suggest that, for Blake, sexual desire when frustrated regresses to sado-masochistic fantasy. It would follow that gratified sexuality, in Blake's view clearly incestuous, would defend one against anal–sadistic fantasy and masturbation.

After the illustration of a dreaming woman, Oothoon urges Theotormon to escape from self-torturing fantasy and accept his desire for her. After illustrating the ways various predators satisfy their hunger, she concludes with the earthworm, who tells Theotormon how to satisfy his.

> Over his porch these words are written. Take thy bliss O Man!
> And sweet shall be thy taste & sweet thy infant joys renew!
> (*VDA* 6:2–3, E 48)

Oothoon attempts here to counter Theotormon's guilt and to encourage open enjoyment of the mother's body, but, significantly, the imagery suggests Blake's underlying anxieties about infantile greed and maternal retaliation which would interfere with pleasure. Like *Marriage*'s eagle-men, the worm builds a 'palace of eternity', erecting his phallic pillar in the grave's 'hungry' jaws. But, whereas the eagles' palaces suggested an independent re-creation of the maternal womb, the worm actually builds in the body and hollows it by eating it. The ideas of devouring present in the images of hungry grave and defiant grave-worm exert an inhibiting force counterbalancing Oothoon's positive rhetoric. Oothoon, however, ignores the darker implications of her imagery, presenting an idealised picture of unrepressed infantile sexuality.

> Infancy, fearless, lustful, happy! nestling for delight
> In laps of pleasure; Innocence! honest, open, seeking
> The vigorous joys of morning light; open to virgin bliss,
> Who taught thee modesty, subtil modesty! child of night &
>   sleep
> When thou awakest. wilt thou dissemble all thy secret joys
> Or wert thou not, awake when all this mystery was disclos'd!
> Then coms't thou forth a modest virgin knowing to dissemble
> With nets found under thy night pillow, to catch virgin joy
> And brand it with the name of whore; & sell it in the night,

> In silence, ev'n without a whisper, and in seeming sleep:
> . . . .
> And does my Theotormon seek this hypocrite modesty!
> . . . . . : . . . .
> Then is Oothoon a whore indeed! . . .
>
> (*VDA* 6:4–18, E 48)

The mystery disclosed in the night to the child is characteristically ambiguous. It suggests the religious teachings which, inducing guilt, make the child a hypocrite. But it also refers to the mysterious disclosure of sexuality. Oothoon's asking whether the child was awake during the disclosure suggests, more specifically, the observation of parental sex by a child perhaps feigning sleep. What connects the child's observation of (or fantasies about) puzzling parental sex and the concept of mystery as religion is Blake's intuition that religion is used by the father to exclude the child from acts the father does with the mother. Blake makes the connection between paternal religion and paternal sexual monopoly explicit in his later prophecies, where he uses 'mystery' specifically to refer to the lovemaking of the father–priest Urizen. Not only does Oothoon allude to the sexual mystery and the religious teachings which keep the child from participating in it, but her rhetoric suggests two possible ways of viewing the mother's sexuality. She sets up opposing views of herself (and woman in general) as whore or as virgin who remains unsullied. Blake's insistence on Oothoon's virginity – when she is literally not a virgin – by redefining virgin to mean one who innocently joys in sex reinforces his theme that sex is good, but it also, on another level, defends against the equally present idea that Oothoon (mother) is a whore. If she is thought of as a virgin, one does not have to think of her embraced by the father. She can be embraced by the son. Oothoon in her impassioned final speech urges such active fulfilment of desire on Theotormon.

> The moment of desire! the moment of desire! The virgin
> That pines for man; shall awaken her womb to enormous joys
> In the secret shadows of her chamber; the youth shut up from
> The lustful joy. shall forget to generate. & create an amorous
>   image
> In the shadows of his curtains and in the folds of his silent
>   pillow.

Are not these the places of religion? the rewards of continence?
The self enjoyings of self denial? Why dost thou seek religion?
Is it because acts are not lovely, that thou seekest solitude,
Where the horrible darkness is impressed with reflections
   of desire.
Father of Jealousy. be thou accursed from the earth!
Why hast thou taught my Theotormon this accursed thing?
(VDA 7:3–13, E 49)

In contrast to the possessiveness of the patriarchal 'Father of
Jealousy' and the jealousy of Theotormon, Oothoon promises to
catch and bring her lover 'girls of mild silver, or of furious gold'
(*VDA* 7:24, E 49).[7] Although put in Oothoon's mouth, this is a
masculine fantasy of incestuous gratification; Oothoon replaces the
repressive or frustrating mother with an ideally gratifying figure who
will not only satisfy her youthful lover herself but will find him
substitutes and, free of jealousy, will benignly observe their lovemaking:

> I'll lie beside thee on a bank & view their wanton play
> In lovely copulation bliss on bliss with Theotormon.
(*VDA* 7:25–6, E 49)

Blake's picture of 'free love' here was supposedly influenced by
Mary Wollstonecraft's *Vindication of the Rights of Woman*: Schorer
calls it a 'perfectly direct allegory of Mary Wollstonecraft's doctrines',[8] and Erdman accepts the connection.[9] Here, psychological
insight can be very helpful. If we look at the controlling fantasies
behind *Visions*, it becomes clear that the emotional forces of the two
works are entirely different. Blake releases woman from the tyrant
father only to make her totally available for the son's sexual pleasure.
The man who said that woman lives by light reflected from the male
would have been repelled by the feminist idea that a woman's first
duty is to herself, to develop her mind and particularly her reason.
But Wollstonecraft felt that 'the end, the grand end, of [women's]
exertions should be to unfold their own faculties'.[10] Far from seeing
woman as devoted to 'happy, happy Love' (*VDA* 7:16, E 49), she
wanted to substitute equality based on reason for woman's 'sexual
character' as a gratifier of man.

I cannot discover why, unless they are mortal, females should always be degraded by being made subservient to *love* or lust. . . . [Love] should not be allowed to dethrone superior powers, or to usurp the sceptre which the understanding should ever coolly wield.[11]

One of the few matters on which Blake and Mary Wollstonecraft would have agreed is the evil of coquetry and false modesty. But even here the reasons are different. Blake objected to their sexually frustrating results; Wollstonecraft objected to the demeaning effect of seeing oneself as a sexual object instead of a rational companion of man.[12]

Oothoon's 'free' sexuality modulates into a distinction echoing the earlier ones between generous giving and hoarding. 'Does the sun walk in glorious raiment. on the secret floor / Where the cold miser spreads his gold?' (*VDA* 7:30, 8:1, E 49). The sun's freely given gold contrasts with the miser's hidden reserves, and the image of secretly spreading the gold suggests the parallel act of defecation. Blake seems to be evoking here the crucial dilemma of an early developmental stage: whether to give or hold onto body-products. Blake's imagery associates retention with hostility; thus Oothoon opposes sunlike, giving virtues (which include pity) with examples of secretiveness and destructiveness. Oothoon's speech suggests Blake's insight on some level into the interconnection between early problems over control and giving and late ones over sexuality, and his awareness that later conflicts repeat essentially the same pattern in different terms. Oothoon's speech, however, ends on a positive note of exhortation to the still-paralysed Theotormon.

> Arise you little glancing wings, and sing your infant joy!
> Arise and drink your bliss, for everything that lives is holy!
> (*VDA* 8:9–10, E 50)

In *Visions* Blake for the first time gives the mother-imago a prominent place in the struggle between father and sons. Oothoon has two roles. She expresses Blake's social ideas – his opposition to economic oppression and slavery as well as his thoughts about himself as artist – and she is the fantasied, permissive mother urging her lover–son to overcome his jealous rage and his masochistic wishes and share her with the father. Blake's championship of impulse and free love appears to defend against masochistic and homosexual wishes, which are amply embodied in images of dirt, blackness, greed, tearing and beating. Bromion and Theotormon form a sado-masochistic pair, and Oothoon's task, on both overt and deeper levels, is to release Theotormon. She fails and Blake, alternating between optimism and despair, replaces Theotormon with the powerful young rebel Orc in his next work, *America*.

AMERICA A PROPHECY

America a Prophecy, printed in 1793, shares with *Marriage* a central struggle between fathers and sons. In *America*, the fathers are represented by King George and his Angel, and the sons by the rebels and the demonic Orc. But *America* has closer connections with *Visions*. In *America* the son is transformed from the weak Theotormon of *Visions* into the virile Orc, and Oothoon's role in *Visions* as 'the soft soul of America' here becomes that of a passive object of desire to be fought over, raped, or liberated by the hero. The American patriots' struggle against King George may seem unconnected to Theotormon's failure to possess Oothoon and his impotent observation of her rape by Bromion, but in the added 'Preludium' to *America* Orc reverses that failure by the rape, now explicitly incestuous, of his sister. The illustration to the 'Preludium' (*A* 1, *IB* 139 – Illus. 18), showing a naked man hunched miserably beneath tree-roots that resemble copulating bodies, strikingly echoes Theotormon's impotent despair at seeing Oothoon and Bromion together. Above ground, Orc is spreadeagled and chained beneath a tree. His position recalls Blake's engraving of a racked slave (see Erdman's commentary, *IB* 139), again evoking *Visions*' link between impotent son and tortured slave. Blake completes his representation of the Oedipal triangle by picturing Orc's mother turning toward him in grief, hands over her face, while his father, hands raised, looks at Orc in anger or horror. The crystal-clear, beautifully drawn illustrations of defeat and punishment are countered by the text's description of Orc breaking loose to commit the forbidden act. Speaking to his sister, Orc explains how, although chained by Urthona (who will be clearly identified as their father Los in *Urizen* and *The Four Zoas*), in fantasy he participates in rebellions everywhere. His serpentine

Illus. 18   *America a Prophecy*, plate 1

'folding / Around' Urthona's pillars and his sister's 'dark limbs' specifically echoes Theotormon's jealous 'folding' around the adulterate pair in *Visions*.

In his portrayal of Orc's shadowy sister, however, Blake deals not only with anger against the sexually unfaithful mother, as he did in *Visions*, but also with anger against an earlier bad nurturer, who is perceived as cold, masculine and pestilential. The 'shadowy' female assumes the role of a depriving mother; she feeds Orc from cold containers of iron. She herself is invulnerably armoured and helmeted and carries 'a bow like that of night, / When pestilence is shot from heaven' (*A* 1:5–6, E 50). For the human infant, the mother's face (and breast) is the most important thing in his world, and Blake powerfully evokes the infant's rage at being denied the beloved face. Orc howls joyfully when his sister brings him food, but her face and smile are inaccessible:

> my red eyes seek to behold thy face
> In vain! these clouds roll to & fro, & hide thee from my sight.
> Silent as despairing love, and strong as jealousy.
> (A 1:19–20, 2:1, E 50)

It is this rage against the withdrawn nurturer that precipitates and allows Blake to justify the punishing rape. His imagery emphasises its punitive quality by recalling Bromion's earlier cruel rape of Oothoon: 'O what limb rending pains I feel. . . . in furrows by thy lightnings rent' (*A* 2:15–16, E 51).

Through this incest Blake imagines Orc engendering himself (without paternal aid), and the illustration (*A* 4, *IB* 140) shows his joyous birth from a 'furrow'. However, the lines Blake etched beneath the illustration, although almost immediately masked, suggest anxiety and guilt aroused by the clear expression of such an aggressive sexual fantasy.

> The stern Bard ceas'd *asham'd of his own song*; enrag'd he
> swung
> His harp aloft sounding, then dash'd its shining frame against
> A ruin'd pillar in glittring fragments; silent he turn'd away.
> (A 2:18–20, E 51; emphasis added)

There is ample evidence that this pattern of exaltation followed by shame, rage and self-mutilating impulses occurred in Blake independently of political circumstances.[13] For example, in a letter to Butts, he describes a similar pattern following elation:

> Then my verse I dishonour, My pictures despise,
> My person degrade & my temper chastise;
> And the pen is my terror, *the pencil my shame*;
> All my Talents I bury and dead is my Fame.[14]

The king's initial confrontation with the rebels (plate 3) complements Orc's violent reaction to maternal deprivation in the 'Preludium'. There is no woman present in the body of the poem, but the rebels, who are shown to be in danger of enslavement, torture and penetration, struggle against feelings of passion and vulnerability. The patriots respond to the king's 'piercing' fires by showing their own virile powers (they 'rise in silent night' – *A* 3:3, E 51). Washington spurs them on by describing in intensely masochistic images what will happen to them if the king wins. Blake's imagery suggests that defeat in battle is an emotional equivalent of homosexual submission. The weak and depressed rebels are imaged not only as pierced and bleeding, but also as furrowed by the king's whip – just as the shadowy female was by Orc's lightnings. Thus, the 'Preludium' actively presents in the rape of the sister what is feared and desired from the father.

The 'dragon form' (*A* 3:15, E 51) in which the king challenges the rebels accords with a child's fantasy of forced submission to a brutal, all-powerful father. With marvellous insight, Blake illustrates changes in the child's perceptions and the parallel historical development of moral consciousness. First, in plate 4's top illustration (*A* 4, *IB* 142 – Illus. 19), King George appears as a dragon with human hands. Next, the dragon is metamorphosed into the biblical Jehovah, the father of later childhood – a white-bearded moral arbiter with sceptre, book, and a remnant of dragon-tail. In the bottom illustration, Jehovah is succeeded by a threatened, mortal father–king, crouching in terror beside a sea-monster, as power passes to the son. In an earlier version, the king's shape-changing depended on changes of role – at home or council – rather than suggesting a sequence of developing perceptions of him. In this early version too, the rebels' attack on the king resembled rape, revolutionary terrors rend the meeting-house. In rewriting, the idea of rending the father's 'dark

Illus. 19   *America a Prophecy*, plate 4

house' becomes Orc's rape of his sister's 'dark limbs'. Blake's first attempt, then, at representing an alternative to Theotormon's passivity, identification with the mother, and openness to sexual attack by the father involved activity directed towards the father – attack– rape. In the final version, homosexual impulses are denied altogether by making the activity a rape of the sister.

The text accompanying this illustration describes Orc's third mythic birth as a naked 'Human fire'. Orc's birth from the Atlantic reverses the impotence of Theotormon's waters in *Visions*, giving them a volcanic power – they swell, heave and belch – previously associated with Bromion's lust. Moreover, the idea of a hero born adolescent and ready to attack the father–king successfully denies infantile weakness.

In the following illustration (*A* 5, *IB* 143), the king is tied by three adolescent rebels and, it is suggested, is decapitated as judgement (an act foreshadowed by the king's hair-pulling on plate 4). Although Blake insists on the act's righteousness – one rebel holds scales of justice – its aggressive and sexual aspects are also clear. A penetrating or decapitating sword appears between a second rebel's legs like a burning phallus, countering the king's piercing fires, and a third rebel hurls the king down into the coils of a waiting serpent that recalls Orc's aggressive wreathing around his father's pillars in the 'Preludium' (as well as the devouring 'Serpents not sons. wreathing around the bones of Tiriel' – *T* 1:21, E 273). On the serpent's left is another image of decapitation: a figure lies clutching its head.

Thus, Blake's prophecy of the king's trial and death in *America* is linked with an attempt to master trauma by inflicting on the father what was once suffered or imagined by the child. In the text of plate 5, the moralistic Angel is forced to watch as Orc, in the guise of a serpent, pollutes his temple. 'The Spectre glowd his horrid length staining the temple long / With beams of blood' (*A* 5:6–7, E 52). The serpent's entry and pollution of the father-figure's holy place may be a retaliation for the father–priest's presumed sexual 'attacks' on the mother. (In 'Infant Sorrow' the father appears specifically as a serpent to steal a beloved woman from the son.) Orc's admixture of ruby brightness and slime suggests the mixed feelings of fascination and disgust evoked by the scene.

In an apparently earlier version of plate 5 (*c* – Illus. 20), in contrast, the king has both power and beauty; he metaphorically contemplates Orc's death: 'like an aged King in arms of gold, / Who wept over a den, in which his only son outstretch'd / By rebels hands was slain' (E 58). Blake's fusion here of Orc with Absalom, a king's son and rebel-leader, points up the dynamic identity of Orc's personal struggle against his 'father stern abhorr'd' (*A* 1:11, E 50) with that of the patriots against King George. In addition, the cancelled plate illustrates the way Blake struggled against maso-

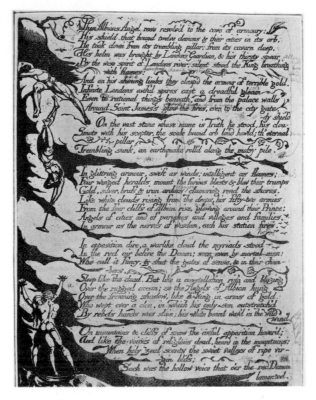

Illus. 20   *America a Prophecy*, place c

chistic fantasies by turning passivity into triumphant activity. The plate's emphasis was on the rebel's punishment by a harsh paternal 'apparition' or externalised conscience. In the rewritten text of plate 5, the apparition is no longer the father but the triumphant Orcian Spectre.

The Spectre's 'voice' announces the awakening of 'the bones of death' in plate 6. The traditionally Christian imagery functions here specifically to deny fantasies of bodily injury and slavery. The risen dead are like 'redeemed captives'. Their liberation and exuberant physical movement as they spring from their graves banishes Washington's earlier depressed image of the patriots enslaved with 'Heads deprest, voices weak, eyes downcast' (*A* 3:10, E 51). The accompanying illustration (*A* 6, *IB* 144 – Illus. 21) of a triumphant, naked youth sitting on a grave-mound is redrawn from *Marriage* (*MHH* 21, *IB* 118), with genitals more strongly outlined and the

Illus. 21   *America a Prophecy*, plate 6

youth's foot more clearly in earth's cleft than before. Here, too, as the trial and decapitation sequence suggests, life for the son is possible only after the father–king's death.

These visual and poetic images of freedom for those in despair are all the more moving when one realises their source in Blake's struggle with his own masochistic impulses and depression. Blake's mother had died in 1792; although we know little about their relationship, he appears to have grieved and longed for a reunion. His Notebook shows evidence of depression and preoccupation with death at this time, particularly in his sketches of death-beds and of reunited families. Here, the image of the prisoner 'Whose face has never seen a smile in thirty weary years' (*A* 6:9, E 52) at last united with his loving family is particularly suggestive of depression and its imagined antidote. Certainly, the absent smile recalls Orc's despair, in the 'Preludium', when he is deprived of the smiling face of his nurturer.

Continuing with wishful prophecy, the next illustration (*A* 7, *IB* 145) depicts a sleeping girl, boy and sheep beneath a paradisal tree. Although reminiscent of Blake's early sketch of Tiriel with the children Har and Heva (1788), the tyrant here has been removed. However, Paradise reigns only momentarily. The poem continues oscillating between imaginatively desired events and guilt, which pumps new life into the figure of the accusing Angel. Wrathfully counterpointing the sensuous paradisal vision, Albion's Angel, in the text, accuses Orc of being Antichrist, a serpent son who devours his mother's children.

Orc's dialogue with Albion becomes increasingly aggressive, moving from liberating images that deny masochistic fears to direct violence against the paternal moralist pictured on plate 8 (*A* 8, *IB* 146), brooding in the clouds. Orc is this god's traditional adversary, the satanic serpent 'wreath'd round the accursed tree' (*A* 8:1, *E* 52). The image gains power here through its association with earlier images of aggressive serpentine 'foldings' around paternal 'pillars' or bodies.

Succeeding images follow the pattern of 'A Song of Liberty', where freedom entails the destruction of God and moral code. Orc releases 'fiery joy' by bursting the enclosing roof of conscience, 'stamp[s] to dust' the Ten Commandments, and scatters religion like a torn book. The father's book, like *Marriage*'s ancestral 'bones of the dead', rots, is consumed, and fertilises the new Paradise. After this destruction–absorption of the father, Orc frees woman from the 'religious letchery' of father–priests. Liberated, she achieves a perpetual virginity, which 'can never be defil'd'. Man is also redeemed and liberated. The 'lustful fires' do not consume him as they did the father's book and law; instead, he becomes a precious, enduring object, 'breast and head like gold'. In Blake's brilliant use of the Book of Daniel, the redeemed son, like the men Nebuchadnezzar cast into his fiery furnace, not only escapes death but outdoes the father–tyrant's dream of glory. Nebuchadnezzar dreamed of a gold-headed statue with a silver breast and vulnerable clay feet. Blake's man has a gold head and breast, and its feet are strong brass.

On plate 9, an ominous voice takes the centre, sounding 'war-trumpets'. The paradisal vision recedes, appearing only in the ambiguous illustration (*A* 9, *IB* 147) of a child asleep or dead

beneath golden wheat. Blake progresses here primarily by association. Thus, the image of the endangered child calls up its opposite, a
greedy, destructive infant, just as it did in *Tiriel*: Albion's Angel
accuses Orc – in Tiriel's language – of being a·'Devourer of thy
parent' (*A* 9:20, E 53). In line with Blake's massive struggle against
passivity, Orc appears as a grown serpent without the infantile
trauma depicted in *Tiriel*, where 'milk / Is cut off from the weeping
mouth with difficulty & pain' (*T* 14–15, E 281–2). Albion, using
similar language, wishes Orc had childhood's vulnerability: 'where is
the weeping mouth? / And where the mothers milk? / instead . . .
parched lips drop with fresh gore' (*A* 9:22–4, E 53).[15] As in *Tiriel*,
Blake deals with guilt and rage by putting accusations in an enemy's
(Albion's) mouth, thus permitting us to discount them. Simultaneously, Blake denigrates the king as a devourer of the earth's
'fatness', who makes men impotent by subduing 'the plow and spade'
and who takes exclusive possession of the maternal city and castles
(*A* 9:5–7, E 53). In *America*, however, unlike in *Tiriel*, Blake con-
ceives the father–son conflict archetypically. Thus, previous rebels
against God are reborn in Orc and his rape of his sister reenacts an
ancient rape of the heavens by the 'Eternal Viper self-renew'd'
(*A* 9:15, E 53).

Plate 9's opposing images of helpless and destructive infants are
succeeded in plate 10's illustration (*A* 10, *IB* 148) by Orc, powerfully
rising from the flames Blake associates with desire. The desire's
specifically incestuous nature and its relation to rebellion are under-
scored by the fact that the rebels confer in a palace built by Ariston
for his stolen bride – an allusion to the original incestuous act. And
Ariston's mountains are also the place from which, Blake tells us in
the Notebook, his own visions emanate:

> . . . above Times troubled Fountains
> On the Great Atlantic Mountains
> In my Golden House on high.
> (E 472)

On plate 11, almost three-quarters through the work, Blake offers
us some narrative action. However, even at the historical centre of
the poem, the confrontation between George and the patriots, Blake
seems more concerned with the pattern of paternal accusation and
filial denial than with the events that represent it. The whole of plate

11 is a speech by Boston's Angel justifying the revolutionary violence of the following plates.[16] Here, as in *Marriage*, the non-aggressive, good man faces a moralistic hypocrite who appropriates sexual joys and who makes the honest man feel guilty. Boston's Angel denies murderous impulses against the king, along with allegations of guilt, concentrating primarily on his deprivation, by hypocritical rulers, of nourishment and sexual freedom. The vigorous illustrations (*A* 11, *IB* 149 – Illus. 22) convey sexuality's strength and innocence as Blake wishes us to see it and counter Albion's Angel's accusations of aggression by linking sexual fulfilment with brotherly concern. At the top, in an image that links *Vision*'s flying phallic mount with the creative power of the pen, a naked patriot riding a long-necked swan cries the words of the text to his fellows. At the bottom, three naked children ride a phallic serpent. The bigger boy reaches out a helping hand to the smaller one, suggesting that fraternal rivalries can be overcome through shared gratification.

The succeeding revolutionary action flaunts youthful sexuality in the king's face: the thirteen colonial angels strip and expose 'naked and flaming' bodies to the demon king before flashing across the country in destructive fires. Although Blake insists that their action is a reaction to the king's threats and is not spontaneously aggressive, the accompanying illustration (*A* 12, *IB* 150) of an old man entering death's door reveals the connection between the son's liberation and the father's death.

Blake's portrayal of outright revolutionary violence on the following plate has many disturbing sadomasochistic elements. Washington had feared entrapment by George's 'iron chain'; now the vanquished governors shake their 'mental' chains and fall at Washington's feet; what threatened the sons is visited on the fathers. Moreover, the victims' capitulation is described in language with overtones of sexual excitement, reminiscent of Blake's description of Oothoon after her rape; the prostrate governors 'grovel on the sand and writhing lie' (*A* 13:5, *E* 55). This similarity suggests that when a man loses a battle he becomes like a woman, vulnerable to penetration (an idea that occurs throughout Blake's poetry). The accompanying illustrations (*A* 13, *IB* 151) give further evidence of the sadomasochistic quality of Blake's fantasy here. The top illustration, a striking variation of Oothoon's fantasy in *Visions*, shows a bloody winged eagle tearing and devouring the belly of a naked female. The bottom illustration depicts a man lying under the Atlantic Sea, his legs chained by a sea-serpent, completely vulnerable to the jagged teeth of approaching fish.

Albion's Angel, enraged at his governors' overthrow, unleashes Pestilence. But, whereas Tiriel's parallel invocation of the pestilential

Illus. 22 *America a Prophecy*, plate 11

queen destroyed his rebel sons, this time the rebels refuse to accept their guilt. Rage overcomes terror and they hurl Albion's curses back at him, 'Fury! rage! madness! in a wind swept through America' (*A* 14:10, *E* 55). Orc's flames fold round the shores suggesting an angry phallic claiming of the motherland – he is like a 'wedge / Of iron heated in the furnace' – and contrasting with Theotormon's impotent folding round his rival Bromion and Oothoon. But, while describing the rebel victory, Blake also depicts possibilities of failure in images suggestive of rape and castration. The plague threatens to 'cut off' the patriots as blight does the tender corn, and individuals respond defensively by closing books (so that they cannot be 'rent') and locking chests. The writer and the builder, figures of importance to the later Blake, panic and throw down their tools, at once giving up creative power and potency. But, although each is individually afraid, all are saved by joining together as brothers against the tyrannical father.

The text portrays paternal threats; the illustration (*A* 14, *IB* 152 – Illus. 23) associates these with the tyrant's consort, the pestilential mother. Under a 'monster tree' (see Erdman's comments, *IB* 152) – visually representing the father's protection – a sibylline figure with a serpent between her thighs instructs a praying youth. Her hand, stretching toward him, measures his life-span (and perhaps also the inadequacy of his sexual organs). This female figure is related to other Blakean images of women. For example, the cowled figure with coiling serpent is a variant of *The Gates of Paradise* 16 (*IB* 276), which bears the inscription 'I have said to the Worm thou art my mother & my sister.' This inscription, in turn, recalls images in *Visions* of poisonous or devouring females with phallic shapes (the blind worm and 'rav'nous' serpent). Approached from another direction, the figure, juxtaposed as she is with Albion's invocation of Pestilence, must also be related to the pestilential queen invoked by Tiriel. As Blake developed the image of a plague-bearing queen he frequently added the phallic serpent. The evil queens of France and England have serpents beneath their robes, and in a Notebook poem Blake joins syphilitic plague and serpent in a metaphor: 'The Queen of France just touchd this Globe / And the Pestilence darted from her robe' (*E* 491).

The illustration presents the threat and attraction of this fascinating but deadly mother, under the father's aegis, but the text shows the defence, with its violent assertion of masculinity and brotherly

Illus. 23   *America a Prophecy*, plate 14

strength. The rushing together of males in the night suggests sexual union or fusion. United, the rebels force back the deforming plagues, and the 'shame' of venereal disease, against the king. Syphilis is a perfect physical expression of castration fears. And the insanity associated with the disease evokes *America*'s decapitation-theme as well as George's madness. Blake's stricken Albion suggests both madness and sexually pleasurable torment.

> Albions Guardian writhed in torment on the eastern sky
> Pale quivring toward the brain his glimmering eyes, teeth chattering
> Howling & shuddering his legs quivering; convuls'd each muscle & sinew.
>
> (*A* 15:6–8, E 55)

The father's punishment is followed by his enslaved females' liberation. This is not only a social by-product of revolution, as some critics suggest, but also a defence of the incestuous act at the heart of Blake's Revolution. Females previously enchained, like Oothoon, by the father–tyrant are released to the son Orc. They 'Run from their fetters reddening, & . . . They feel the nerves of youth renew, and desires of ancient times' (*A* 15:24–5, E 56). The marginal illustrations (*A* 15, *IB* 153) show despair overcome by incestuous passion. Beneath a depressed figure (upper left), a small boy hands a pointed flame to his mother. Although her feet are still rooted, she turns toward the flame and tries to move forward, feeling her nerves 'renew'. Beneath her a female soars through flames next to grapes representing ecstasy.

But Blake does not end his poem with desire's fulfilment. In the final plate (16) he pictures the lull between the American and French revolutions as a counterattack by the Urizenic father–god. Here, as elsewhere, Blake makes historical events fit his own distinctive fantasies of triumph being repeatedly blasted by fear and guilt. Urizen's vengeful 'cold mists' are reminiscent of *Tiriel*'s earlier wrathful rain and fog. And, although the later rebels repel the pestilence that killed Tiriel's sons, they are frozen by the guilt generated by the defeated Urizen's icy tears. A future thaw is suggested, however, by an illustration (*A* 16, *IB* 155) of a weeping, praying form – in despair but covered with hopeful figures making love and music.

Blake's poem concludes with Orc's sensual fire still burning as other European monarchies fasten the gates 'of their law-built heaven' (*A* 16:19, E 56). Evoking and expanding his image of the paternal serpent bursting the hinges of the chapel-door in 'I saw a chapel', Blake provides a final image of fulfilled incestuous desire: forbidden entry is enlarged to cosmic dimensions as Orc burns and the gates of heaven are 'consum'd, & their bolts and hinges melted' (*A* 16:22, E 56).[17]

Blake uses historical events in *America* primarily as vehicles for his own meditation and fantasy, and as a result the poem has an eddying, non-narrative quality,[18] in which images of impotence and successful rebellion alternate continually. The poem's frontispiece of Orc manacled is juxtaposed, for example, with the description of rape; similarly, a concluding image of the paralysed rebels is followed by Orc entering heaven's gates. Throughout the poem Blake presents variants of the central fantasy of incest and parricide. He uses this reiteration skilfully to analyse different emotional components of his fantasy. Orc's rape of his sister presents the basic incestuous idea. Orc's serpent pollution of the temple while Albion's Angel watches additionally suggests an attempt to master experiences or fantasies of a primal scene. In the final image of heaven's burning gates, sexuality and aggression have been projected on a cosmic screen.

In so far as the poem progresses, it does so because Blake has succeeded in resisting underlying masochistic ideas. That is, he everywhere attempts to replace images of submissive defeat with images of successful rebellion. The nature of the psychic struggle is such, however, that there can be no permanent victory for the rebel – in spite of Blake's defensive attempt to justify him by asserting his innocence, generosity and goodness – because success will always be followed by guilt and imagined punishment. Thus, in his next poem, *Europe*, Blake returns to a depiction of impotence, this time setting problems of helplessness in the psychologically illuminating context of a child's relationship to an overwhelming mother.

EUROPE A PROPHECY

Europe a Prophecy, one of the most difficult of Blake's early poems, continues the history begun in *America*, treating the period leading to England's declaration of war against France.[19] Though images of father–son conflict recur, *Europe*, as we have noted, emphasises a new, and developmentally earlier, conflict with the mother. Blake condenses previous images of pernicious females to create sky-queen Enitharmon, who wants to dally sexually with her son Orc as long as he, like Samson, is bound and helpless. Strong sibling-rivalry develops around mother Enitharmon as Blake distinguishes between the elder brothers, Rintrah and Palamabron, whom she controls and who control history, and the uncontrollable Orc, who brings the whole mother-dominated structure down.

Blake orchestrates these themes on several levels. His mythical frame begins with Jesus's birth and ends with Apocalypse, moving in psychological terms from the infant helplessly in his mother's power to the revolutionary adolescent who breaks free and avenges himself.[20] The historical period between these cosmic events appears as man's infancy, dominated by mother, repressive father and sycophantic elder brothers. Blake fits contemporary political events into a pattern of sibling-rivalry through his opening illustrations, which show the arch-conservative Burke as an assassin waiting to kill an innocent young pilgrim (*E* 1, *IB* 159), and the warmongering minister Pitt strangling rivals with a clear family-resemblance (*E* 2, *IB* 160). Significantly, as the mother and brothers become more malevolent, Blake's appreciation of positive elements in the paternal image seemingly increases, manifested most strikingly in *Europe*'s frontispiece of Urizen creating the universe (*E* i, *IB* 156 – Illus. 24*a*).

This illustration faces an energic serpent on the title-page. Although Urizen does not directly bind the grown serpent, his circumscribing of universal energy is associated with the question of parental domination over Orc's infant energies. After Orc's birth his mother asks, 'And who shall bind the infinite with an eternal band? / To *compass* it with swaddling bands' (*E* 2:13–14, *E* 60; emphasis added); the words pun on the previous visual image of compasses. The infant's repressive swaddling projected onto the cosmos becomes binding of the infinite. Physical compassing is also associated with conscience's circumscribing effects. Urizen's image appeared to Blake as a haunting presence hovering over his stair-

Illus. 24(*a*)   *Europe a Prophecy*, plate i

Illus. 24(*b*)   *Europe a Prophecy*, plate ii a

case – its function as an embodiment of conscience is suggested by its similarity to Blake's earlier incarnation of conscience, the hovering, gleaming king in *America*. Notwithstanding the negative connotations of Urizen's power – repressive binding, restrictive conscience, hovering images of guilt – the illustration itself idealises Urizen as solitary creator. Its significance for Blake is suggested by his purported colouring of a copy of it on his death-bed. Here he achieved a balance between love and hate, and between admiration and envy of paternal generative power.[21]

To understand this balance, we must consider not only what Blake included but also what he left out. Early sketches indicate the degrading sadomasochistic fantasies he struggled with before creating the triumphant final image. In a discarded version of the frontispiece (*IB* 396 – Illus. 24*b*), aesthetic distance and sublimity give way to hostile fantasy; Urizen is an old man absurdly scribbling laws while riding the energic serpent. An accompanying sketch of Blake's father (or brother) is probably not a coincidence. In one sketch the ironic image of Urizen riding the serpent is transmuted into an image of sexually suggestive struggle: an aged face with a serpent body is entangled with a falling manacled youth; the serpent face's position next to the youth's genitals suggests both perversion and devouring.

Blake later separated the figures who appear on plate 1 of *Europe* (*IB* 159 – Illus. 25) as falling manacled youth and a despairing patriot. These figures, together with revolutionary France's dagger-wielding accuser at the top of the plate, not only follow Blake's usual justificatory pattern – the rebels are innocent; the authority-figure is a malevolent fiend – but also illustrate the process of depression that Blake is trying to halt. The patriot and youth fall into depression by accepting the assassin's accusation – which the serpent title-page (plate ii) suggests is that they are devouring serpent–sons. The serpentine intestine-folds surrounding the patriot suggest that an aspect of his punishment is to be devoured by his own rage, now self-directed. At the same time, the fact that Blake gives the patriot the face of his sketch's anguished old man suggests that despair, like creativity, is a state shared by father and son. When the patriot is depressed, he sees himself (or Blake sees him) in the image of a weak, despised father. The assassin, on the other hand, suggests the father as murderous devourer. The assassin's dagger recalls the dagger-teeth of *Tiriel*'s enviers and visually parallels the open-

Illus. 25   *Europe a Prophecy*, plate 1

mouthed form of Urizen's compasses and the serpent's guillotine tongue in a version of plate ii (*IB* 398). In the final facing plates of creator and serpent, however, direct physical conflict is removed, and we can see their opposition more broadly as a tension between opposites such as reason and desire or control and impulse. Blake achieved this effect partially by removing some of Urizen's negative or sado-masochistic associations and transferring them to other figures, such as the assassin and the strangler.

The maternal principle also undergoes a split into the purely malevolent sky-queen Enitharmon and the fecund, suffering, shadowy female. In the 'Preludium', this female's complaint that her rival sons devour each other ends with the birth of Orc, the 'secret child' who will not be devoured by his brothers or bound by the father–God. Blake portrays the shadowy female as a soft victim of perpetual motherhood. But, in expressing her agony, she also shows threatening qualities associated with the pestilential mother: she brandishes her snaky hair and her roots like spears and wraps her 'lab'ring head' in a turban of clouds (recalling the serpent-possessing sybil in *America* and the devouring worm mother of *Gates*). The imagery suggests that Blake perceived birth as a trauma to the female body, arousing a feeling of counteraggression against the child: the plate 3 illustration (*IB* 161) shows what appears to be Orc's mother, ominously shaking her hair over a burning infant still enclosed in a womblike globe. Her sullen meteoric child recalls the abhorred rejected infants in *Visions* that 'live a pestilence & die a meteor' (*VDA* 5:29, E 48). The Urizenic father is blamed for maternal torment in both cases, and, in this fantasy, rebellion includes avenging her.

Although Blake bases his nativity-story on Milton's 'On the Morning of Christ's Nativity', he introduces many negative emotions, which Milton left out, into Christ's story. Christ's birth, as Blake portrays it, is accompanied by maternal resentment and fraternal rivalry, and, far from imposing peace, as Jesus's birth does in Milton's poem begins a warfare that can only be ended by apocalyptic violence. Blake's illustration of murderous siblings (plate 2) links competition between brothers (touched off by the birth of a new one) with contemporary struggles for political power. The conservative Pitt appears strangling his brothers; their contortions recall the Notebook sketch of father–serpent and falling youth. The question seems still to be who will devour whom.

The prophecy proper begins on plate 3 with the Saviour's birth, which is used metaphorically to describe the domination of every infant, rebel or saviour, by his mother. Los (Enitharmon's consort) reacts to the birth with pleasure and a desire to rest that parodies the trustful sleep of infants in *Songs of Innocence*. But for Los this passivity is a regressive abdication of his adult masculinity and poetic task. Moreover, it is dangerous because Enitharmon resembles Delilah and will be receptive to Los's enemy, Urizen. With psychological acuteness, Blake frees Urizen from his bonds just when Los, through regression, has become newly vulnerable. Los's reference to himself as 'strong Urthona' is a delusion, like Samson's confidence of strength that Blake's Delila[h] skilfully manipulates in 'Samson' (E 435). If Los were really strong, he would not be defined in relation to Enitharmon, but she in relation to him.[22]

Los's directing his sons to strike the elemental strings while he rests suggests a wish to enjoy two states at once: the masculine creativity later associated with Eden, and the nurturing passivity associated with Beulah. In Eden, contests of ideas or songs are life-enhancing, but here the challenging music of awakened thunder elicits an oppressive counterstrain from Urizen's sons. Envious, they want to appropriate Los's pleasures and perhaps even drink his blood.

> Bind all the nourishing sweets of earth
> To give us bliss, that we may drink the sparkling wine of Los.
> (*E* 4:5–6, E 60)

Blake describes the stormy music of fraternal envy, the human emotions that explain why Jesus's birth brought wars not lasting peace – a direct reversal of Milton's description of Jesus's birth quieting nature's ravings.[23] As an analysis of the political situation, counter-revolution appears motivated as much by envy of the rebel's supposed libidinous freedom as by fear of him. In terms of the poem itself, the imagery of storm and fraternal violence echoes the visual motifs of rivalry presented in the 'Preludium'. The objects of jealousy, 'bliss' and 'the nourishing sweets of earth', are mockingly evoked when, after Urizen's sons' envious reaction,[24] Enitharmon crowns Orc with 'the ruddy vine', tormenting her bound son with the sensuality and oral pleasure outside his grasp.

Plate 4's illustration (*E* 4, *IB* 162 – Illus. 26) complements the suggestive ambiguity of the text: Enitharmon's desire and sexual curiosity are manifested as she uncovers Orc's naked body. But her desire, connected as it is with binding and mocking, is destructive. Even if, as Michael J. Tolley suggests, she is contemplating incest,

Illus. 26 *Europe a Prophecy*, plate 4

what was imagined as liberating in *Visions* suggests here a further
humiliating binding to the mother.[25] Two of the tiny background
figures echo *Vision*'s illustration of Oothoon and Bromion after the
rape, suggesting perhaps that Enitharmon's sadism is motivated by
vengeance for violence against her sex.[26]

Exulting in her control over Orc, Enitharmon asks his two older
brothers to help her dominate mankind as a whole, thus amplifying
the theme of rivalry in the 'Preludium'.[27] This configuration of three
brothers, as we have seen, comes to *Europe* from *Island in the Moon*,
where it was based on Blake's family and friends, via the *Tiriel*
illustrations. In *Europe* Orc receives the sensual Bacchic vine of
Tiriel's third son. Rintrah assumes the kingly crown of Tiriel's eldest,
and Palamabron becomes a priest usurping the place of *Tiriel*'s
laurel-crowned visionary poet. Plate 5's illustration (*IB* 163) shows
Rintrah as a 'furious king' standing unhappily between two queens
apparently pleading that woman 'may have dominion' (*E* 6:3, E 61).
In the political allegory, they are the queens of England and France,
and Rintrah is Pitt, viewed as the son who wants to replace the
father–king.[28] The queens' doctrine, enunciated by Enitharmon, that
'Womans love is Sin' (*E* 6:5, E 61) effectively castrates their male
children while maintaining their own independence and power. The
binding imagery associated with both repressive father and teasing
mother is now extended to the sexual nets which little girls will set in
the path of the boys' sexuality ('from her childhood shall the little
female / Spread nets in every secret path' – *E* 6:8–9, E 61). And the
sons are bribed to accept sexual restraint by ideas of Heaven and an
'Eternal life' propagated by organised religion.

The illustrations following Enitharmon's forecast of female
domination depict not only the famine and pestilence resulting from
her wars, but fantasies about a pestilential mother. In *Tiriel* the greed
of the serpent sons was answered murderously by Pestilence. On
Europe's plate 6 (*IB* 164 – Illus. 27), the mother, not the son, is
clearly the devourer: a woman waits for a cauldron to boil in order to
cook the naked infant lying beside her. Here, as elsewhere, a
fantasy-core is brilliantly adapted to social criticism. The devouring
mother is richly dressed, while across from her a humbler woman
crouches despairingly. Thus, with the weight of his own suffering
behind his images, Blake makes us see the rich as devourers of the
poor.

On the facing page, plate 7 (*IB* 165), three youthful sufferers

Illus. 27   *Europe a Prophecy*, plate 6

succumb like Tiriel's children to the plague. War and its cruelties appear as the punitive acts of angry parent–gods against their children. Beside a door closed on plague-victims and inscribed with the motto 'The Lord have mercy on us', a girl raises her arms in anguish as though pleading with an absent, unmerciful God. Another girl expires, held by a youth, while a gloomy bellman, eyes averted, passes, ringing for a death-cart. The illustration draws much of its power from this aloof figure's conjunction with the dying children.[29]

The illustration recalls Tiriel's wish for his children's solitary death, but its visual antecedents suggest the devouring parent. In the original Notebook sketch, the central dying girl was held by a woman seated in a doorway.[30] The configuration relates her to the sibylline worm mother and her posture and clutching fingers suggest a possibility of devouring which becomes explicit in the sketch's final version, where the woman is transformed into Ugolino in prison about to devour his children (*IB* 274). This illustration's development suggests that cannibalism and poisoning by hostile substances are not just random examples of war's miseries but are dynamically linked parts of fantasies about a murderous parent. These fantasy-elements occur in a context of fixing blame. In plate 6 it is the rich who are at fault; in plate 7 the warmongers and the punishing God behind them; and finally, in the Ugolino engraving, Blake definitively shifts blame for murderous impulses from the parent to the God who forces him to eat his children as punishment.

The illustrations on plates 8 and 9 (*IB* 166 and 167) show punishment recoiling on the father as Blake reworks *Tiriel*'s images of father–son conflict. Plate 8 (Illus. 28) reverses the significance of an earlier illustration of Tiriel cursing his children, making it show an old man fending off the rebel sons' invasion. The picture's judgemental aspect becomes clearer in plate 9, where Albion's Angel is stricken retributively by his own plagues, released by two vigorous nudes through their curling trumpets.

Taken as a sequence, the illustrations on plates 6, 7, 8 and 9 first suggest the murderous effects of parental rage and then show an instance of its recoil against the father–king. Mother Enitharmon is not similarly punished; she seems, rather, to gain from father–son or fraternal conflict. And the text on plates 8 and 9 shows her continued domination. After ordering her sons Rintrah and Palamabron to implement her plans, Enitharmon falls asleep; man's eighteen-hundred-year history is her 'female dream', which only Orc's apoca-

Illus. 28   *Europe a Prophecy*, plate 8

lyptic violence can end. As the years draw to a close, Albion's plague-stricken Angel makes a counter-revolutionary recovery.

After rising from his hall's ruins, Albion's Angel approaches his Druid temple (plate 10). This serpent temple is an extension of the Angel's body. Its covering of England echoes the rape-imagery of 'I saw a chapel' as the serpent 'stretches out its shady length along the Island white' (*E* 10:3, *E* 62). The phallic paternal pillars threatened by Orc in *America* are here incorporated into the Druid temple's structure and are seemingly invulnerable: 'form'd of massy stones,

uncut' (*E* 10:7, E 62). The pillars' twelve-coloured stones (an allusion to Aaron's priestly breastplate) are a variant of the image of
gold-armoured paternal moralism in *America*. Through a further
allusion to Bacon, Blake identifies the temple as a whole with an
empirically viewed nature. The temple, with all it represents, is seen
as a massive serpent polluting or raping mother England. Blake has
fused here a set of moral and scientific ideas injurious to self-esteem
with the emotional impact on the child of the father's sexual
possession of the mother.

Attempting to explain how the Angel and his temple gained power
over man, Blake seemingly denies his earlier insight into adult power
and infant helplessness by explaining the Angel's domination as the
result of the fall of an originally powerful being. Paradoxically, the
fall appears to be a punishment for a crime against a paternal
principle not yet presumed to exist. It is described as a diminution in
the expansive powers of the senses, which become confined in the
newly created sense organs. Blake's description of man's senses
before the fall suggests a time when the body was experienced as
fused with the outside world. According to analytic studies, the
human infant gradually learns to distinguish his body from the
outside world through his senses, beginning with visual individuation
of familiar faces.[31] But Blake's description of the hardening and
rounding of the eye, for example, pictures these early experiences of
the separateness of things as a trauma inflicted on the organ itself.
Perceptual distinctions bring about a change in self-image, which
seems to shrink from a fluid self containing the whole world to a self
whose contact is limited to discrete organs. Infinite energy, once
shared by the whole body-world, is also portrayed as contracting
into the generative organs: 'Thought chang'd the infinite to a serpent'
(*E* 10:16, E 62). And this change in turn leads to generational sexual
rivalry and conflict; paternal pity becomes 'a devouring flame', and
Adam is expelled from Paradise.

Blake's anguish over the conflict seemingly inherent in sexual
definition and separateness becomes part of his philosophical outrage at Newton's universe of discrete particles and at scientific
attempts further to define, delimit and measure reality in relation to
the separating categories of space and time. The infant's early
world-experience is not governed by time or space, and Blake, like
many other thinkers, tried to transcend their confines. Early experiences of timeless wholeness become models for Blake's adult im-

agination as it creates images of gratified desire. His illustration (*E* 10, *IB* 168) shows an angry serpent caught up in coils of time and hissing in protest.

Returning to his narrative, Blake now shows the tyrant Angel approaching the head of the temple–body. ('Now arriv'd the ancient Guardian at . . . the Stone of Night' – *E* 10:24–6, E 62.) As in *America*, rebellious attack is followed by the retaliations of the paternal figure acting both in his own right and as an externalised conscience, symbolised by the Angel's entering the head. Blake maintains, however, that this head, 'the Stone of Night', was not always the place of torturing guilt. The brain, like the perceptual organs, was once fluid and 'open to the heavens'. Now it is in itself a miniature temple, roofed in by the rocky skull and shifted in position from the 'sweet south' to the 'attractive north'. Using guilt as its weapon, the altered brain enforces the supremacy of the paternal body–temple with its aggressively protruding porches and phallic pillars.

Blake's conception of religious institutions and laws as extensions and protective coverings of the father's body is expressed visually on plate 11 (*IB* 169 – Illus. 29). A bloated, bat-winged moralist sits in clouds holding his book on his knees. The text, indicated by two angel queens, describes the expansion of Urizen's laws through priests and kings. The temple as body is first suggested by the moralist's robes, which, embroidered with saints, join in the middle of his body like church doors. The cathedral throne behind him visually echoes his tiered papal crown, emphasising his head-centred control. The linking of aggressive head and rear parts is suggested by the figure's resemblance to buttocks with fat, full cheeks. His opaque, black wings and the cloud enclosing the heads of his angel queens effectively block off access to heaven and further suggest the linking of destructive power with anality. And, although the queens, allegorically the reactionary queens of England and France, bow lovely angelic heads to the king above, the serpents beneath their robes associate them with the pestilential, phallus-possessing mother.

Blake's historical narrative continues on plate 12 with the king's counter-revolutionary activities. The Angel involves England in 'grey mist' paralleling the 'icy tears' that stopped the rebels in *America*. The king's self-pity effectively generates guilt in the young rebels, who are brought by their parents to hear him preach 'canting'. Their enforced attention parallels Tiriel's insistence, using their mother's

Illus. 29　*Europe a Prophecy*, plate 11

corpse as text, that his sons hear his accusations. Here too, accusation inspires rebellion not submission: the English youth respond with a vision of England's pollution or rape and Orc's reactive burning anger: 'They saw the Serpent temple lifted above, shadowing the Island white: / They heard the voice of Albions Angel howling in flames of Orc' (*E* 12:11–12, *E* 63).

Blake links this archetypal image of the father punished to a specific political example: the downfall of conservative Judge Thurlow, 'Guardian of the secret codes' (*E* 12:15, *E* 63). In *America*, the

vanquished governors grovelled and abased themselves; Blake repeats the sado-masochistic imagery here, adding the idea that
Thurlow's official robes and wig fuse with his body causing him
acute torment.[32]

Orc delights at the howling of minister and king, since it means not
only that they are punished but also that the body's original
expansive consciousness will return. But his joy is threatened by his
brothers, who attack him in the familiar metaphors of penetration
and hovering anger:

> But Palamabron shot his lightnings trenching down his
>   wide back
> And Rintrah hung with all his legions in the nether deep
> (E 12:23–4, E 63)

and, in the illustration on plate 12, by a giant spider approaching a
bound and shrunken human victim (*IB* 170).[33] This image in the
context of Blake's description of woman's triumph in terms of a
bound figure in a locked-up house evokes the mother's original
power over her helpless infant. The text, furthermore, suggests
maternal repression of her infant (which takes place in the home)
while simultaneously describing man's continued victimisation by an
over-harsh conscience.

> Enitharmon laugh'd in her sleep to see (O womans triumph)
> Every house a den, every man bound; the shadows are filld
> With spectres, and the windows wove over with curses of iron:
> Over the doors Thou shalt not; & over the chimneys Fear is
>   written:
> With bands of iron round their necks fasten'd into the walls.
> (E 12:25–9, E 63)

Woman's triumph here depends on using the father's code and image
to frighten the child–man. The spectres filling the shadows are the
same hovering ghosts of conscience discussed earlier, and, just as in
America, where the zealous voice interfered with Orc's enjoyment of
the sweet virgin valleys, these spectres guard all openings of the
maternal house. The repression of sexuality begun in infancy turns
the female matrix into a prison. The life-giving cord becomes a
strangling bond of iron, and the soft bones natural to a growing

embryo are signs of starvation and degeneration in the adult man. This is Blake's clearest and most pessimistic picture of the mother's wish to inhibit her son's growth. Her wish is juxtaposed with Blake's denial of her success: the adolescent Orc's flames and the apocalyptic trump of doom.

Newton's blowing of the trumpet is commonly thought to suggest how his world view led to the materialistic and deistic errors of Blake's time. However, since Newton's blast shatters the moralistic angelic hosts, the image also suggests the shattering effects of science on institutional religion, effects similar to those produced by Rousseau and Voltaire in Blake's *The French Revolution*. There, reason's voice sends religious spectres crying from their abbeys to fall and shatter. Newton's trump similarly precipitates the angelic hosts through wintry skies 'in howling and lamentation' (*E* 13:8, *E* 64), stripped of armour and flesh. The imagined destruction of kings is counterposed on plate 13 (*IB* 171 – Illus. 30) with an image of man enthralled: a chained prisoner throws up his hands in horror as he looks at the scaly rear of his departing jailer, which seems to afford a revelation to the prisoner of the jailer's nature (see commentary, *IB* 171).

The illustration, occurring in the context of Newton's trumpet-blast, again links scientific or moralistic mind with cruel impulses which are in turn linked to early feelings about the backside and its products. This is a striking insight on Blake's part into the development of the adult's relationship to power from his early experiences with his body. Blake's connection of cruelty with the rear and anality, while accurate, may also serve, by seeing the process as disgusting, to exorcise the desire for domination and cruelty. His work and marginalia suggest that Blake was often overcome by cruel impulses, which at least in one instance, a satirical lyric on a rival poet, Klopstock, he spontaneously connected with the bowels.

This scatological verse reads like a parody of parts of *Europe*. 'Terrible Orc', rearing his snaky head, is replaced by 'terrible Blake' uprising 'in his pride' to exhibit himself with his pants down. Orc's rising in *Europe* is associated with fleeing stars and a fiery glowing sun. In 'Klopstock', stars flee and the moon blushes red observing Blake's nakedness, and perhaps his production, as he rises after defecation. Rising, Blake performs magical revolutions that constrict his enemy's bowels and lock his soul in his body, where it will remain until trumpeted out as flatus at the Last Judgement. Blake's magical

The red limbd Angel siezd in horror and torment;
The Trump of the last doom; but he could not blow the iron tube!
Thrice he assayd presumptuous to awake the dead to Judgment.

A mighty Spirit leapd from the land of Albion,
Namd Newton; he siezd the Trump, & blow'd the enormous blast!
Yellow as leaves of Autumn the myriads of Angelic hosts,
Fell thro' the wintry skies seeking their graves;
Rattling their hollow bones in howling and lamentation.

Then Enitharmon woke nor knew that she had slept
And eighteen hundred years were fled
As if they had not been
She calld her sons & daughters
To the sports of night,
Within her crystal house;
And thus her song proceeds.

Arise Ethinthus! tho' the earth-worm call;
Let him call in vain;
Till the night of holy shadows
And human solitude is past!

Illus. 30   *Europe a Prophecy*, plate 13

movements are only a slightly distanced representation of the movement of his bowels perceived as a powerful weapon against the rival poet. Anal trumpeting which signifies the final humiliation of a rival appears in more heroic form in Newton's trumpet-blast signalling the downfall of the Angelic hosts. Newton's ability to blow the trump depends on his words' power. Blake implies that Newton's ideas are responsible for the sadistic exercise of power imaged in the prisons, a conclusion which seems influenced by the emotional associations of Newton's emphasis on matter and force rather than the objective effects of his science. In 'Klopstock', he associates word-power with magical triumph over an enemy using the body and its products.

If Blake could do this when he rose up from shite
What might he not do if he sat down to write.

(E 492)

Newton's trump awakens Enitharmon, who, unaware that the time of man's dependent infancy is past, continues to call up her children, visualised as small insects, to help her dominate man. The seductive beauty of Enitharmon's daughters offers only a counterfeit gratification; they are cold and poisonous. Her sons, in addition to counterfeiting sexual fulfilment with 'flames of soft delusion' and 'pearly dew', represent the male under maternal control. Manathu-Vorcyon burns in his mother's halls, and Enitharmon asks her second son, 'O Antamon, why wilt thou leave thy mother Enitharmon?' (*E* 14:16, E 64). The last-mentioned sons, Sotha and Thiralatha, escape her domination only to lose themselves in dreams. And, as Damon notes, the end-result of sexuality's retreat to dreams is the outbreak of war,[34] as Orc explodes in the 'vineyards of red France' (*E* 15:2, E 65).

Pictorially, as Erdman notes, these vineyards resemble the ruins of Troy (*E* 15, *IB* 173 – Illus. 31), with Los rescuing his wife and child from the flames. However, hostility is present as well as care. Los carries a faceless (perhaps dead) wife like a sack over his shoulder and drags along an equally faceless child;[35] if this is a rescue of the females, it is also a reassertion of male power over them. The impression of aggressive sexuality is strengthened by the figure's muscular body and clearly drawn penis (unnaturally elongated in copy G).[36] The aggressively phallic nature of the figure's assertion is similarly suggested in the text by Los's snaky hair and an emblematic naked acorn, echoing the penis, that is placed next to Los's final call 'to the strife of blood'. Thus *Europe* culminates in bloodshed that will end maternal domination, along with the rule of kings and priests, and will result in a purified society of brothers. Man has come of age. The poem, which began with creation and birth, ends with apocalyptic violence, but within its frame Blake sketches an ideal of harmony that preceded conflict and that, presumably, will replace it.

This harmony depends on a return to a global consciousness in which the senses are dominant and the boundaries of the self are fluid. Ideas of fusion and omnipotence, themselves regressive, come into conflict with Blake's own analysis of the regressive anal–sadistic

Illus. 31   *Europe a Prophecy*, plate 15

base of oppressive social cruelty and moralism. Whereas in *Visions*
Blake suggests incest as a way of escaping the compulsive struggle to
control others through gratified sexuality, here his emphasis is on
revolutionary violence, and he no longer sees the female as a means
of redemption. Instead, he concentrates on wrenching free from her
to unite with a band of brothers whose harmony is a dynamic
replacement for the lost harmony of infant and mother world.

NOTEBOOK POEMS

Blake's Notebook poems,[37] including drafts of *Songs of Experience*, show him, at a slightly earlier stage than *Europe*, still working on the idea of redemption through incestuous union. Redemption is hindered here not only by the familiar father–rival but by the frustrating woman herself. The personal, bitter anger of the Notebook poems, however, suggests a crisis in Blake's life at the time of writing that may have influenced his subsequent turning away from woman as the chief agent of salvation. His fantasy of a totally permissive mother–wife could have led him to suggest introducing a concubine into his household, as legend has it;[38] but, whatever the current conflict with his wife, it evoked memories of past angers against an earlier figure. His imagery, correspondingly, evokes the frustrating mother along with her generous opposite.

Blake begins his Notebook poems with a lyric in which a woman rejects her faithful lover:

> A flower was offerd to me
> Such a flower as may never bore
> But I said Ive a pretty rose tree
> And I passed the sweet flower oer
> Then I went to my pretty rose tree
> In the silent of the night ⎤
> But my rose was turned from me ⎦ *first draft*
> And her thorns were my only delight.
>   (N 115)

The poem, in its final form in the *Songs of Experience*, is connected through its illustration (*SE* 43, *IB* 85 – Illus. 32*c*) both with the emblems, which help us understand many of Blake's visualisations of *Songs*, and with 'The Angel', another of the *Songs of Experience*. The rose woman shown in the illustration to 'My Pretty Rose Tree', reclining on one elbow and looking away from her mourning lover, closely resembles the mother rejecting her cupid–son in the emblem series (*N* 65 – Illus. 32*a*). Blake used variants of this rejecting figure in three different contexts in which he deals with the pain of rejection and attempts to modify its hopelessness. In the emblem sketch, the child pathetically tries to grasp his mother's arm as she pushes him away. Her hand spans his face in a gesture suggesting that he is too small to alleviate her depression or to satisfy her.[39] When Blake uses the figure of his emblem sketch to illustrate 'The Angel' (*SE* 41, *IB* 83 – Illus. 32*b*), the situation changes. The rejected cupid–angel has his bittersweet revenge when the mother, now a 'maiden Queen', realises her desire too late to satisfy it:

Illus. 32(*a*)   Notebook, p. 65

Illus. 32(*b*)   *Songs of Experience,*
plate 41

Illus. 32(*c*)   *Songs of Experience,*
plate 43

> For the time of youth was fled
> And grey hairs were on my head.
> (15–16, E 24)

In 'My Pretty Rose Tree', the lover is no longer portrayed as a child, the woman is mistress not mother, and his failure is one of nerve not size or age. Moreover, the jealousy of adult potency inherent in the child's position is transferred to the rejecting woman. She now suffers because of the supernaturally beautiful flower, 'Such . . . as May never bore', which is beyond *her* power to duplicate. If he had acted vigorously, Blake suggests, the lover could and should have enjoyed both the Rose and the sweet flower. For Blake, the lover's restraint is a form of self-castration, which leaves him vulnerable to the female.[40] Blake's images of this phallic woman – whether as a persona, a sibyl, an armoured virgin, or a partial attribute, such as thorns, sharp tongues, or the sharp-toothed comb in the illustration to 'Nurse's Song' (*SE* 38, *IB* 80) – suggest that, unlike the male phallus, which is inescapably linked with his creativity, the imagined female phallus can only be threatening.[41] Blake's ideal woman, in contrast, has neither phallic attributes nor intellectual power but an overflowing maternal and sexual generosity.

The cruel Rose's opposite is split into two figures, the masochistically pliable Clod and the receptive, virginal Lilly. In the Notebook the Clod follows the Rose and is contrasted both with her and with the self-delighting Pebble.

> Love seeketh not itself to please
> Nor for itself hath any care
> But for another gives its ease
> And builds a heaven in hells despair
>
> So sung a little clod of clay
> Trodden with the cattles feet.
> (*N* 115)

The Clod's prototype is the maternal Clod in *Thel*, who died nourishing the infant worm. Blake's illustration to 'The Clod & the Pebble' (*SE* 32, *IB* 74) suggests a similar fantasy of devouring the maternal body: sheep and cattle eat and drink while they trample the Clod underfoot. Although Blake does not assign a sex to either Clod or Pebble, the Clod has a clear female prototype, and the Pebble's alternative view of love ('Love seeketh only self to please' – N 115) resembles the Little Boy Lost's statement that 'Nought loves another as itself / Nor venerates another so' (N 106). Blake vehemently defends this little boy's stubborn honesty even though he seems to love his parents primarily as nurturers. In the Pebble's case, the negative connotations of his selfishness seem balanced by the illustration, which shows a variety of energic forms – frogs leaping, a duck swimming, and fleshy, tripartite leaves – that surround the Pebble's text. The appreciation of one's own energy and the right to take what is needed for growth without the bonds of obligation may seem at first to apply to both sexes. After all, in poems like 'A Little Girl Lost' and *Visions of the Daughters of Albion*, Blake defends woman's right to love freely; but on closer look, as we saw, this eloquent plea rests on a fantasy of male gratification.

The Lilly, the frustrating Rose's counterpart, has the white piquancy of eternal virginity, yet she is unarmoured and thinks only of giving herself in love.

> While the lilly white shall in love delight
> Nor a thorn nor a threat stain her beauty bright.
> (N 109)

The ideal Lilly grows out of the poet's suffering at rejection or exclusion, which continues in the Notebook poem 'Never seek to tell thy Love' (N 115) and reaches a climax in 'I went to the garden of love' and 'I saw a chapel', two Notebook poems of deprivation and trauma. In 'I went to the garden', the speaker is not rejected by a maternal figure but is kept from love by father–priests who have built a private chapel where the child 'used to play on the green'. The reference to a past in which the child freely played and implicitly enjoyed love's 'flowers' suggests that the primary prohibition is against incestuous love.

> And the gates of this chapel were shut
> And thou shalt not writ over the door
>
> So I turnd to the garden of love
> That so many sweet flowers bore
> And I saw it was filled with graves
> And tomb-stones where flowers should be

> And priests in black gounds were walking their rounds
> And binding with briars my joys & desires.
>
> (N 115)

The illustration for this poem in *Songs* (*SE* 44, *IB* 86) suggests that priestly prohibitions make both the child's Edenic first love, the mother, and her later substitutes appear horrible and frightening: a priest-guarded hole and briar-crossed body instead of the flowers of infantile desire. The red worms that wriggle through the text, which is the earth-grave, also suggest a destruction of the loved but withheld body. A similar movement occurs in *Island*, where the surgeon, frustrated at the breast, tries to kill his mother and later marries a corpse, substituting a dead body for the living desire.

In the Notebook, 'I went to the garden of love' is paired with the lyric, not included in *Songs*, 'I saw a chapel'. In it, the frustrated speaker of 'I went to the garden' is forced to observe the mother–chapel's rape by the paternal serpent:

> I saw a serpent rise between
> The white pillars of the door
> And he forcd & forcd & forcd
> Down the golden hinges tore.
>
> (N 115)

The speaker, feeling his own impotence, turns from the chapel to a pigsty and lies 'among the swine'.

The Notebook drafts of 'Infant Sorrow' (N 113) also deal with the father's sexual gratification and the son's impotent rage. This poem is Blake's most direct statement of this rage and the trauma of observing the father's lovemaking. It follows a sequence from birth to patricide. At the poem's opening, the infant, looking like 'a fiend hid in a cloud', is repressively swaddled and forced by his helplessness to pretend compliance.

> When I saw that rage was vain
> And to suck (sulk) would nothing gain
> I began to soothe & smile (soile).
>
> (N 113)

The infant's frustration at the breast gives way to the adolescent's discovery of sexual beauty in 'lovely flower and tree'. But gratification is forbidden by the father with his 'holy book'. Repeating the act of restrictive swaddling, he binds his son 'in a mirtle shade', where he is forced to observe his father's embraces:

> Like a serpent in the night
> He embracd my mirtle bright. ⎤ *cancelled lines*
>
> (*N* 113)

Blake's characteristic distortion of the Oedipal triangle here is similar to that in *Visions*, where the father is a rapist–thief who takes what rightly belongs to the son, his Oothoon's flower (his 'mirtle'). But, unlike Theotormon, who was paralysed by the rape, this son breaks free and murders his father.

> So I smote him (them) & his (their) gore
> Staind the roots my mirtle bore.
>
> (*N* 113)

Blake retained only the first stanzas of 'Infant Sorrow' in *Songs of Experience*, but his illustration (*SE* 48, *IB* 90 – Illus. 33) suggests the trauma symbolically described in the deleted passages: a naked, angry infant turns violently away from his mother's arms toward his parents' bed, which is shown with curtains suggestively drawn back to reveal the pillow.

At some point during revision of 'Infant Sorrow', Blake began another poem, about a youth bound under a mirtle (*N* 111). This poem has no traumatic observation of intercourse, and, although the youth still kills his father, he does so only because his father has restricted his sexuality, binding him in marriage:

> To a lovely mirtle bound] *cancelled line*
> . . . .
> O how sick & weary I
> Underneath my mirtle lie
> Like to dung upon the ground.
>
> (*N* 111)

The feelings of defiled impotence felt by the speaker of 'I saw a chapel' are still there but attributed to another cause. Direct anger against the father's sexual privilege extends into criticism of social restrictions that, unlike the father's right to the mother, can be challenged successfully.

Illus. 33   *Songs of Innocence and of Experience*, plate 48

This shift of emphasis also occurs in 'Earth's Answer', a lyric thematically connected with 'in a mirtle shade' and written on the same page (*N* 111). Here, Blake's criticism of restricted sexuality is structured by a rescue fantasy: the earth-mother, held captive by the jealous father, longs for a Perseus to 'Break this heavy chain . . . that free love with bondage bound'. The illustration in *Songs* (*SE* 31, *IB* 73), which shows a hissing serpent straining toward grapes just out of reach, links Earth to the traumatised youth in 'Infant Sorrow'. In deciding to use 'Earth's Answer' to begin his *Songs*, however, Blake presents a more hopeful version of his personal myth than he did in 'Infant Sorrow': mother, not son, is bound and may be released. The redemptive suggestions are strengthened by juxtaposing Mother Earth with her rescuer son as Bard in the 'Introduction' to *Songs*.

Blake's use of the Bard in *Songs* as sexual and spiritual liberator suggests the possibility of escape from sexual jealousy. In the early emblem series, he had a similar role in mediating the release of the caged cupid–son.[42] Perhaps because this view of the Bard is based on a fantasy of incest, however, Blake removed this figure from the emblems, which increasingly denied incestuous attraction. Many emblem elements – cupid, parental death, and liberating vision – reappear in Blake's opening sequence of *Songs*. The frontispiece, for example, depicts the once-caged cupid haloed and perched on the piper's head (*SE* 28, *IB* 70). Identical colouring makes the boy's naked groin seem to merge with the piper's forehead, strengthening suggestions of a redemptive union between phallic and poetic powers.[43] This joyful frontispiece is followed on the title-page by an image of death derived from emblem 37. Above the dead parents laid out on a bier and mourned by their children, Blake has added a dancing boy and girl, who suggest liberation not only from grief but from parental restrictions as well (*SE* 29, *IB* 71). The following 'Introduction', where the Bard calls on Earth to awake and she answers, reworks motifs both of paternal binding and of maternal rejection into a pattern suggesting the possibility of fulfilment. Our knowledge of the specific visual configuration expressing rejection – the reclining woman with averted head – gives an added poignancy to the Bard's plea to Earth, 'Turn away no more: / Why wilt thou turn away.'

The image of tempting woman sequestered by a jealous father merges in several Notebook lyrics with the image of forbidden fruit. Three of these poems, 'The Human Image' ('The Human Abstract'), 'Infant Sorrow' and 'Christian forbearance' ('A Poison Tree'), form a sequence in many copies of *Songs*, but the thematic link between them and the sexual nature of the temptation is obscured when Blake drastically cuts 'Infant Sorrow'. In the drafts, the forbidden tree is the body of the woman kept from the son and enjoyed by the father. The Notebook introduces the theme of forbidden fruit by a lyric that begins 'I asked a thief to steal me a peach' (*N* 114). Round, ripe fruit is a traditional symbol of the breast, and Blake joins a humorous description of the speaker's thwarted desire for it with his parallel failure to get sexual satisfaction from the lady. He is outmatched by his Angel rival, just as the thirsty poet of the early sketch was by the contented 'others' or Theotormon by Bromion. The Angel's amusing coolness suggests in the context a child's perception of the ease with which his rivals – siblings, father – seem to get what the child so passionately wants.

   In 'The Human Abstract', the final version of 'The Human Image', Blake accuses the paternal deity – the illustration identifies him with Urizen – of baiting a trap for man with a fruit, like the peach, 'ruddy and sweet to eat' (18, E 27). This deity seems cruel as well as deceitful because he must know that man's irresistible urge toward what has been forbidden him will lead to his expulsion from Paradise. In 'A Poison Tree', the speaker identifies with this tormenting father. The lines describing the fruit by its shine:

> And my foe beheld it shine.
> And he knew that it was mine.
>
> And into my garden stole,
> When the night had veild the pole
>   (11–14, E 28)

evoke in a wonderfully condensed way the gleam of the forbidden and the awakening need to steal it. In this poem, however, the fruit is not something loved and jealously guarded by the speaker, but is instead a product of his repressed anger. This idea is linked to the parable of forbidden fruit in such a way as to suggest that there need not be any 'forbidden fruit'; it is a purely mental growth whose root is 'in the Human Brain'.

   Blake's effort to eradicate the concept of 'forbidden' things seems to be an attempt to deny the early and, to him, difficult reality of the mother's exclusive sexual possession by the father. Blake's utopian vision continually sets itself against this reality by envisioning a life based on total sharing, including, according to Crabb Robinson, 'women in common'.[44] Such sharing would do away with the pity that arises from perceiving someone else's desire for what you already have. One form of this sharing is expressed in 'The Little Vagabond', where God shares with his ultimate rival, the Devil.

> And God like a father rejoicing to see,
> His children as pleasant and happy as he:

Would have no more quarrel with the Devil or the Barrel
But kiss him & give him both drink and apparel.

                                        (13–16, E 26)

Once we recognise the Oedipal fantasy underlying the opposition
between temptation and shared pleasure, we can see how Blake tends
to concentrate on it in *Songs*, although varying the juxtaposition of
individual poems.

But, whereas Blake suppressed the Notebook's most direct
accounts of sexual trauma, impotent rage and the accompanying
feelings of being 'like dung' find brilliant expression in those poems
in *Songs of Experience* about children injured and soiled by society
and their parents. Blake's empathy and compassion draw intensity
from his inner struggle: in the Notebook, his own fears and feelings
of degradation are expressed in similar images of stain and bondage.
His fears of being punished for his revolutionary ideas were probably
exaggerated because of their ties with fantasies of incest and patricide; he reproaches and tries to rouse himself from nervousness as
though he were a Theotormon.

> Tho born on the cheating banks of Thames
> Tho his waters bathed my infant limbs
> The Ohio shall wash his stains from me
> I was born a slave but I go to be free.

                                        (*N* 113)

These thoughts of fear, slavery, and contamination are absorbed and
transmitted in 'London' to form a moving portrait of the victims of
an oppressive society. Yet, no matter how accurate Blake's perception of society's sexual restraints and hypocrisies, the incestuous
fantasy-core of his thought remains to generate images of punishment and failure. And, in addition, Blake not only fears – and
creates – punishment for his desire, but he also fears what he desires:
the woman. She is alternately perceived as generous and good or
enormously wicked and all-powerful (an ambivalence that precludes
mature love). By the time of *Europe*, perhaps because of frustrations
in Blake's marriage, the negative view of woman was becoming
dominant. In his subsequent cosmological prophecies, Blake begins
to explore the earliest sources of anger against the female – the
trauma of original separation.

5   The Origins of Loss

THE BOOK OF URIZEN

Blake's *The Book of Urizen* is characterised by a repetitive patterning of events which replaces narrative progression and makes plot-summary impossible.[1] One way of viewing the poem's structure is to say that it revises the traditional Miltonic notion of man's fall. The fall, according to Blake, is not caused by Adam's sin but by the separation of Urizen, a parody of Milton's Jehovah, from the harmonious body of the Eternals.

The first part of *Urizen* deals with the effects of separation, the ensuing void and Urizen's desperate attempts to fill it with objects: the natural world and the Book of Law. Midway through the poem, the poet Los appears and binds Urizen within a limited human body, an act which, as we will see, is both an imitation of and a retaliation for God's punishment of Adam and Satan. Woman is born from Los's pity for his victim. She in turn gives birth to Orc, whom Los jealously chains to a rock. The poem ends as Urizen, awakened by Orc's cries, binds his suffering sons (and daughters) with the net of religion.

By making separation precipitate the fall, Blake offers an analysis of the human condition far more pessimistic than the one that sees the fall as the result of man's disobedience. For Blake, the very fact of having a separate identity means suffering and conflict. Urizen's experience of separation and emptiness, 'a soul-shudd'ring vacuum', refers to something more primal than the intellectualised Newtonian premise of void or Milton's view that God created the world by contraction.

According to psychoanalytic theory, when the infant first becomes

154

aware of himself as separate he experiences his mother's unavoidable absences as more or less catastrophic. It is this primary human experience that makes the concept of void so horrifying to Blake. Later, he connects it both to 'incoherent despair' and to hunger. In *The Four Zoas*, for example, Tharmas imagines himself 'starved upon the void'; in *Jerusalem*, the void is made of 'Doubt, despair Hunger Thirst and Sorrow'. Here Urizen experiences the Eternals' withdrawal as a cataclysmic event, leaving the self fragmented in the enveloping emptiness:

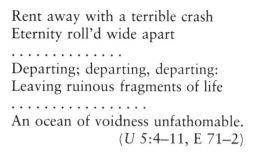

> Rent away with a terrible crash
> Eternity roll'd wide apart
> . . . .
> Departing; departing, departing:
> Leaving ruinous fragments of life
> . . . .
> An ocean of voidness unfathomable.
> (*U* 5:4–11, E 71–2)

The desire, fear and rage appropriate to one who has been abandoned appear projected in 'the flames of Eternal fury' that pour down on Urizen in the void and cause him to create a substitute for the lost matrix: 'And a roof, vast petrific around, / On all sides He fram'd: like a womb' (*U* 5:28–9, E 72). This is one of several versions in the poem of Urizen's creation of the material world as both a substitute for and a protection from the painful burning of the emotions. Urizen himself explains,

> I have sought for a joy without pain,
> For a solid without fluctuation
> Why will you die O Eternals?
> Why live in unquenchable burnings?
> (*U* 4:10–13, E 70)

Both quotations suggest that the creation of objects enables Urizen to escape both unbearable tension and emptiness. But by making him will his separateness and the ensuing void Blake denies the passive experiences of emptiness. Later, by shifting the perspective so that we empathise with Urizen, Blake is also able to describe vividly feelings of emptiness.

Urizen creates his world in a depressed state that Blake's images associate with anality. Depression is suggested initially because Urizen is 'rifted furious / By the black winds of perturbation', and the illustration (*U* 4, *IB* 186) shows him sitting, clutching his head under black rain. Urizen's organising productions attempt to cancel or deny the sensations of fragmentation and emptiness resulting from separation. They also turn Urizen's anger away from himself, channelling it into an attempt to control others. Urizen's religion controls men's desires while making him feel superior, 'set apart'. His Books of Laws similarly suppress desire while aggrandising Urizen as a hero

Illus. 34   *The Book of Urizen*, plate 1

Illus. 35   *The Book of Urizen*, plate 5

struggling against 'terrible monsters . . . Which the bosoms of all inhabit; / Seven deadly Sins of the soul' (*U* 4:28–30, E 71). Blake's title-page illustration (*U* 1, *IB* 183 – Illus. 34) shows Urizen blindly writing and engraving on what appears to be a stone coffin, suggesting that despite his efforts the products of his depression are sterile and dead. Contrasting moods of creative potency associated with freely expressed desire are shown in the illustrations (*U* 2, *IB* 184) of a naked cupid (a 'winged word') drawn through the air by his mother, and the illustration (*U* 3, *IB* 185) of a figure, presumably cupid in adolescence, running through fire. Blake, however, associates himself with both creative elation and Urizenic depression. Urizen is engaged in Blake's two activities, writing and engraving, and, as Erdman shows, a 'W' for William Blake appears on Urizen's book.

The anal nature of his enterprise is suggested by the black blobs and squiggles which replace words on the book's open page. The same meaningless dark shapes appear again on plate 5 (*IB* 187 – Illus. 35), dirtying a base of living colours of pink, blue and violet.[2] Moreover, Urizen approaches his book from the wrong end in the illustration on plate 1, squatting on it and pointing to the 'words' with his toe. Blake's association of Urizen's repressive writings with anality reminds us that the will to power derives from the small child's preoccupation with his faeces as symbols. According to psychoanalytic theory, he construes his faeces as a creative love-gift or child, as property, or as an aggressive weapon. Urizen's productions are primarily used aggressively to control or kill others. Blake's image of Urizen as warrior god, like his image of him as lawgiver, suggest the anal origins of Urizen's behaviour as he ranges 'his ten thousands of thunders' and prepares to loose a bombardment of 'stor'd snows' on his rebellious sons (*U* 3:27–32, E 70).

Urizen and his products, then, represent an attempt to cope with longing for the missing mother (he is presented as being without one) through the creation of substitute objects and through attempts to control others. Blake, however, alternately presents Urizen as traditional creator or tyrant and analyses the psychic origins of his behaviour. Thus, in chapter 1 (plate 3), Blake begins by describing Urizen's conflict psychologically as he fights with his passions and with hallucinatory 'shapes' bred from his isolation. At the end of the first chapter, however, he appears as the traditionally repressive warrior god preparing his thunders for war. Chapter 2 (plates 3 and 4) shows him enshrining himself 'in my holiness, / Hidden set apart in my stern councils', and recounting his creation of the world and his Book of Laws in a way designed to raise his self-esteem: he wrestles heroically with sin. Finally, at the beginning of chapter 3, Urizen appears as the father–god of the political prophecies, and Blake's description echoes the rhetoric of *America*:

> The voice ended, they saw his pale visage
> Emerge from the darkness; his hand
> On the rock of eternity unclasping
> The Book of brass. Rage seiz'd the strong.
> (*U* 4:41–4, E 71)

The 'enormous forms of energy' that attack Urizen at this point are a cosmological version of the Orcan flames that attack Albion's Angel in *America*.

In the earlier prophecies, this would be the moment when the tyrant's moral judgements and curses recoil. Blake effects the same thing here through Los's binding–creation of Urizen's body. Although logically Los's action makes little sense, since Urizen has already appeared as Jehovah, it makes imaginative sense in Blake's pattern of repression and retaliation. Los's binding of Urizen is part of the cycle of conflict which continues with Los's binding of his son. In so far as Urizen represents a paternal principle, Los's binding assumes a retaliatory significance similar to Orc's attacks on Albion in *America*.[3] The binding's retributive significance is masked by its being offered as part of the history of man's creation, a cosmological rather than a personal event. It is also more complex than Orc's retaliation in *America* because it involves a reversal of roles: Urizen, the father–god, becomes an infant, restrained by his creator, Los. In accordance with this role-reversal, Blake's imagery suggests that Urizen is guilty of self-abuse: he engages in 'silent activity' that is 'unprolific', 'unseen', and performed 'in tormenting passions'. Accusations of secret vice would ordinarily be made by father against son. Typically, Blake turns such accusations against the father–god Urizen: it is he, not the poet Los, who sins. The overall effect is to suggest the endlessness of the pattern of retaliation in which now one, now the other protagonist suffers. An important part of Blake's revisionism is to relocate blame for the fall, placing it on a father-figure who is then punished. Blake's illustrations offer traditional views of fall and punishment which his interpretations then replace. On plate 7 (*IB* 189), Los stares screaming (as Erdman notes, *IB* 189) at a vision of what Blake regards as the traditional view: a father punishing a son, both in a fall and in a crucifixion. The vision appears on plate 6 (*IB* 188), which depicts two head-clutching youths who fall through flames, entangled by the serpents of their father's threatening thought and potency. A third youth, Los, falls in a cruciform position. Meanwhile, in the text, Los's binding of Urizen functions both as a retaliation for the punishment the rebels suffer in the traditional view and as a repudiation of this view: it is the paternal principle Urizen who causes the fall by separating from Los; Los must then assume the father's role and punish or bind Urizen, as Jehovah traditionally punished man. In line with Blake's revision, the bound Urizen assumes the crucified position of Los in the plate 6 illustration.[4]

> He threw his right Arm to the north
> His left Arm to the south
> Shooting out in anguish deep.
> (*U* 13:13–15, E 75)

Text as well as illustrations shift blame and punishment from son-figure to father. Blake's revisionary intent is also evident in his use of identical phrases to describe the painful creation of Urizen's

body and the punishment, discussed earlier, of an accusing judge in
Europe. The creation's cruelty lies in awakening and thwarting desire
at the same time. For example, Urizen's earlier participation through
'all flexible senses' is reduced to jealous watching and, equally
painful, 'pangs of hope' when Los confines the senses to discrete
organs like the eyes. After the eyes are formed, two ears shoot out,
potential Jacob's ladders, but are immediately shunted back like
snails' horns 'petrified' in their shells. Other organs and body-parts
are similarly hardened cavities of desire waiting to be filled.

> In ghastly torment sick;
> Within his ribs bloated round,
> A craving Hungry Cavern;
> Thence arose his channeld Throat,
> And like a red flame a Tongue.
> Of thirst & of hunger appeard.
>   (*U* 13:4–9, E 75)

The newly created Urizen is like the struggling newborn of 'Infant
Sorrow', 'Enraged & stifled with torment . . . In trembling &
howling & dismay' (*U* 13:12, 17, E 75). The plate 22 illustration (*IB*
204) shows him weeping and submissive. Blake depicts him as a
shackled old man but simultaneously suggests vulnerable infancy by
using tender flesh-tones of pink and grey.

   Because of the aggression in Los's binding of Urizen, fears of
retaliation are inherent in the work of binding itself. The illustration
(*U* 10, *IB* 192 – Illus. 36) shows Los working, menaced by jagged
surrounding rocks imprinted with the features of his opponent
Urizen (see Erdman's commentary, *IB* 192). An enormous rock
directly above him blots out both his head and his hands, suggesting
the threatening possibilities of decapitation and mutilation. On the
following plate (*U* 11, *IB* 193 – Illus. 37), an anguished Los sits next
to Urizen's chained skeleton. A tower rises, seemingly from his groin,
and leans over Urizen. If the tower signifies Los's potency and
mastery, it is about to fail, or fall, and his hammer, although tightly
clasped, is not in use. In fact, the plate anticipates Los's ensuing
paralysis, which expresses both guilt for aggression against the father
and a subtler guilt over artistic creation that is contaminated by
aggression. Los's pity, like his paralysis, is a reaction to his cruelty
and comes about through an identification with his victim. Blake

Illus. 36   *The Book of Urizen*, plate 10

links Los's pity with his terror at the signs of Urizen's suffering: 'hurtlings & clashings & groans' (*U* 13:25, E 76). Thus, paralysing pity is seen as the other face of sadistic cruelty.

Los and Urizen alternately engage in acts of creation, which are also acts of power, and in reactions of pity. Urizen's pity, evoked by the sight of his bound children, is clearly connected with his bowels:

> Like a spiders web, moist, cold, & dim
> Drawing out from his sorrowing soul.
> (*U* 25:10–11, E 81)

Illus. 37   *The Book of Urizen*, plate 11

This excretion of pity, called 'a Female in embrio', is opposed to the phallic–creative 'wings of fire' that are trapped by it. Similarly, Los's pity, evoked by seeing Urizen bound, is described as the excretion of his life-fluids. The illustration (*U* 17, *IB* 199 – Illus. 38) shows Los bending over, squeezing a globe of matter from his head.

Enitharmon's birth – the birth of pity – involves several different fantasies. A fantasy of anal birth is suggested both by the illustration on plate 17 (where the curves of Los's head echo those of his buttocks, which in turn are connected to the globe by veins of blood) and by the analogous 'female' spun from Urizen's bowels. Once

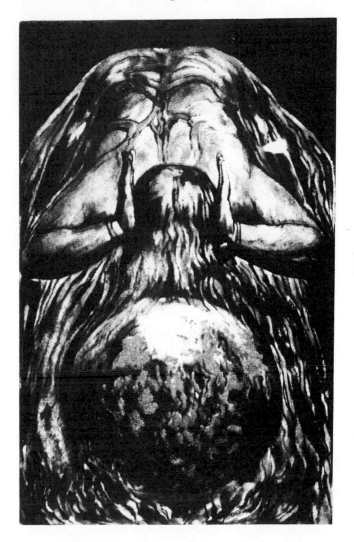

Illus. 38 *The Book of Urizen*, plate 17

born, Enitharmon is treated with the ambivalence characteristically accorded man's first product. She is both precious, composed of life-fluids, and disgusting when separated from Los's body. 'All Eternity shudderd at sight / Of the first female now separate' (*U* 18:9–10, E 77). Urizen's earlier differentiation from the Eternal body is similarly treated. Once he is separate, the Eternals experience him as alien and dead.

> . . . What is this? Death
> Urizen is a clod of clay.
> (*U* 6:9–10, E 73)

But there is more to the image of pity than a fantasy of anal birth. Pity, as an emotion, is central to Blake's analysis of human relations on a plane of sadistic power or mastery. Pity is represented here by a woman, Enitharmon, but as we have noted earlier, Blake fears that pity makes a man womanlike, helpless and impotent. It paralyses Los, and his hammer, the instrument of creative potency, falls from his hand. The illustration (*U* 18, *IB* 200) shows him standing as if crucified by his feeling of pity. In several copies, as Erdman notes, his right arm is distinctly withered. Although Urizen's form is strong in the final illustration (*U* 28, *IB* 210), pity, embodied in moral teachings, also immobilises him: he appears in Los's cruciform position, trapped within pity's net.

The struggle for power and the fears of submission exemplified in the binding motif in *Urizen* are by now familiar patterns in Blake. Another familiar and related theme is that of a son's traumatic observation of parental sexuality. In 'Infant Sorrow', this occurred after the son's binding. In *Urizen* the Eternals are similarly traumatised by observing Enitharmon's birth and copulation with Los. In Blake's illustration of the watching Eternals (*U* 15, *IB* 197), a Urizenic paternal figure and a youth are wrapped together in one robe, suggesting their harmony before the divisive event. The youth leans forward and is apparently curtaining off the disturbing sight. The other two Eternals – another old man and a boy – also form a father–son pair.

The Eternals shudder and flee at the sight of the woman's body, 'petrified' by conflicting emotions of veneration and fear. Then

> They began to weave curtains of darkness
> They erected large pillars round the Void
> With golden hooks fastend in the pillars
> With infinite labour the Eternals
> A woof wove, and called it Science.
> (*U* 19:5–9, E 77)

Here and in an earlier passage (plate 15) comparing the watching Eternals to planet-gazers, Blake suggests that scientific inquiry is related to sexual curiosity. Here the curtains of purportedly objective knowledge shut out or deny the original human events of birth and intercourse. The curtains themselves recall the curtains around the parental bed in 'Infant Sorrow', which could be drawn to hide parental lovemaking from the curious infant.

When the Eternals' tent is fully closed, Blake repeats the binding sequence, this time as a jealous retaliation for Oedipal desire. Blake's extraordinary illustration (*U* 21, *IB* 203 – Illus. 39) depicts Orc as a naked youth suggestively embracing his naked mother Enitharmon: his head is tilted back under her breast as though to kiss or suckle, and his body edges between her thighs. Los stands beside them

Illus. 39   *The Book of Urizen*, plate 21

looking sadly toward Enitharmon's breast, the chain of jealousy falling in bloody links to the ground. The accompanying text describes Orc's punishment:

> They took Orc to the top of a mountain.
> O how Enitharmon wept!
> They chain'd his young limbs to the rock
> With the Chain of Jealousy.
> Beneath Urizens deathful shadow.
> (U 20:21–5, E 79)

By making Orc's cries – the voice of repressed sexuality – waken Urizen and set him exploring, Blake suggests both the underlying motive force and the substitutive nature of science. Urizen is driven by hunger and 'the odours of Nature' (*U* 20:31, E 79). His quantifying manipulations of the earth's body substitute for Orc's pictured embrace. And his subsequent creation of a 'garden of fruits' symbolically re-creates the mother that Los has hidden from him. Urizen's forbidden fruit and iron laws derive, as Tiriel's did, from his deprivation. Urizen's pity for his sons, who cannot keep his laws 'one moment', is analogous to Los's guilty pity for him. It is also embodied in a female form: the net of religion, 'a female in embrio'. Again, the form that should unite men through love separates them because the thing that is most desired is forbidden: the mother's body.

Urizen's attempt to overcome the pain of desire through defensive moral and physical 'organisation' causes psychotic-like sensations of fragmentation and persecution by isolated body parts: he is 'annoy'd / By cruel enormities . . . similitudes / Of a foot, or a hand, or a head . . . Dread terrors! delighting in blood' (*U* 22:49–50, 23:4–7, E 80). The same bloodthirstiness characterises his deprived sons, who can satisfy themselves only at each other's expense. While one man eats, 'The Dog at the wintry door' (*U* 25:2, E 81) accuses another who is warm and fed inside. Blake's illustration (*U* 26, *IB* 208) of a small beggar boy and his hungry dog standing outside a closed door recalls the children of *Songs*, cruelly mistreated by parents and society.

Urizen ends with one son, Fuzon, attempting to free men from Urizen's oppression: he leads an exodus, but by now we know that the cycles of retaliation will continue.

In *Urizen* Blake has traced the conflict explored in the political prophecies back to its psychological beginnings in a primal separation. He analyses the separation's emotional legacy of depression and emptiness (described as physical properties of the new 'world') and shows how Urizen copes with his pain by creating matter and turning his depression, in which rage is directed inward, into oppressive attempts to control others and raise his self-esteem. Blake judges the products Urizen creates not in terms of the high ideals Urizen professes but in terms of their satisfaction of basic needs. Blake finds that these products are substitutes for primary desires – that is, for the attempt to satisfy basic needs – and that since desire is repressed or denied the creative force is primarily aggression: a will to control which Blake denigrates by associating it with anality. In Blake's myth, Urizen as moralist and Urizen as Newtonian scientist are joined as enemies of the primary worlds of wish and desire. Urizen as moralist is obviously committed to denying satisfaction of needs through repression. Moreover, Blake's implicit censure of Newton's world-view is relevant also because Blake finds that Newton offers no solution to the problem of separation. Newton's supposed concept of the universe as void alternating with solid masses insists that separateness is a basic fact of reality. Newton's world is drained of emotion, his masses act mechanically on each other and keep their distance.

Blake's attacks on repression and the scientific world view have been defended by modern thinkers such as Norman O. Brown, who argues that repression can and should be done away with and that men should not be conceptually separated from the rest of reality. We should understand, however, that for Blake the alternative to repression was incest, such as he portrayed between Orc and Enitharmon; and that even Blake, unwilling as his poetry suggests he was to relinquish Oedipal desire, seemed unable to picture incest without jealousy and retaliation: Los will not permit Orc the critical freedom and forcibly restrains him. Thus, at least in *Urizen*, incest as a way of resolving the problem of separation by entering the mother's body seems impossible without punishment.

Blake's attack on Urizen as scientific rationalist raises more problems. One of these is the problem of alienation – that is, the individual's sense that external reality is cold, unconnected to him, and meaningless. One traditional response to alienation is to see it as a function of a false or overly rationalistic scientific apprehension of reality. Blake suggests this approach by making Urizen will the fall. And scientific thought continues to insist on our fallen condition. However, Blake is not entirely unsympathetic to Urizen's plight; he is a protagonist in an emotional drama as well as a central figure in history. In this view the fall stems instead from some original experience of loss. If we connect Blake's images of separation in *Urizen* to his earlier images of abrupt weaning and deprivation (in *Tiriel*, for example), we come up with a picture of traumatic separation and disappointment at the mother's breast as the emotional factors leading to a sense of alienation.[5] Blake apparently felt this separation deeply to the point of sensing the outer world as dead and meaningless. He could not accept a solution such as Wordsworth's, which sees external reality as benign and nurturing because he did feel deprived. His insistent imagery of deprivation suggests a great emotional disappointment which Blake tried to heal by insisting that reality become totally human. Simultaneously, he tried to substitute for what had been lost by writing his vast systematic prophecies, which, like Urizen's creations, imposed Blake's will and his view of reality on other minds.

THE BOOK OF AHANIA

The Book of Ahania continues Urizen's story with the revolt of his youngest son, Fuzon. In the illustration on plate 24 of *Urizen* (*IB* 206), Fuzon and his brothers represent alternate ways of coping with a tyrannical father: Utha (water) and Grodna (earth) resemble the suicidal and depressed elemental figures of *Gates* and suggest rage turned inward against the self; Thiriel's red scarf links him with the poet Los, creator of the sun; and the fiery-faced Fuzon is the rebel.

As the book of filial rebellion, *Ahania* begins with Fuzon's violent attack on Urizen. The pattern resembles that of *Urizen* except that penetration has replaced binding as a central metaphor and the actors are now openly father and son. When Fuzon attacks and penetrates his father with his 'beam', Urizen retaliates by wounding and then crucifying him. Ahania, introduced lamenting over her son's 'living Corse', completes the Oedipal triangle. More important, Ahania invokes an ideal state of sexual sharing and harmony predating the sado-masochistic relations between father and son. In this ideal state, Urizen willingly shared Ahania with his sons just as she shared him with her daughters. Blake's myth suggests that only the permission to commit incest can prevent male warfare with its sadistic, substitutive gratifications.

As Blake develops his myth's details, he reinforces its structure with allusions emphasising the relationships between father, mother and son. Biblical and Miltonic allusions appropriately structure Fuzon's alternately submissive and dominant relations with his moralistic father, while allusions to a pagan mother goddess and slain son suggest the wished-for amoral relationship between mother and son. The opening allusions to Milton's Satan, for example, establish Fuzon's potency, while the title 'Demon of smoke' suggests his father's impotence. Fuzon's subsequent description of Urizen as a 'cloudy God seated on waters' (*Ah* 2:12, E 83) evokes the malevolent 'whore that sitteth on many waters' of Revelation.[6] Urizen, then, joins qualities of both impotent male and poisonous female. Fuzon's further title for Urizen, 'King of sorrow', associates impotence with Jesus and suggests Blake's ambivalence at this point toward the man who accepts passivity and suffering.

The poem's opening paradox is that, although rejecting Urizen's authority and suggesting his impotence, Fuzon identifies with Urizen's strength: Fuzon first appears as a Urizenic warrior, raging in his iron chariot. This problematic balance between liberating action and identification is central to Blake's view of Fuzon as a Moses or Robespierre – figures who began as liberators and ended as authoritarian tyrants.

The sexual nature of Fuzon's attack on Urizen clarifies the implications of the rebel attacks, penetrations, and 'rendings' of the king's 'house' that we noted in earlier poems. Now the attack is literally, not symbolically, on the father's body and genitals. As Fuzon hurls the globe of his condensed rage at his father, it lengthens into a 'hungry beam' that is both devouring and phallic. Urizen's opposing shield, forged in 'mills' of logic, functions, like the curtains of science in *Urizen*, to distance dangerous impulses by denying both hungry sexuality and aggression. But the mental shield fails; Fuzon's beam penetrates it and, 'keeping its direction', divides Urizen's 'cold loins' (*Ah* 2:28–9, E 83). Now Fuzon's aggressive attempt to castrate his father becomes fused with suggestions of rape. Urizen feels the penetration of Fuzon's weapon as pleasure: 'Dire shriek'd his invisible Lust' (*Ah* 2:30, E 83). This pleasure is immediately repudiated and, externalised, appears as Ahania: 'He seiz'd [her] on his mountains of Jealousy. / He groand anguishd & called her Sin' (*Ah* 2:33–4, E 83).

In so far as Blake is representing Urizen's inner conflict between reason and passion, it makes sense to have passion's 'attack' result in repression.[7] But Blake is also representing Oedipal conflict here in the form of the son's rape of his tyrannical father. The theme goes back at least as far as *Marriage*, where passivity and activity are central questions. In *Ahania*, active (sadistic) and passive (masochistic) tendencies are displayed alternately by Blake's characters. Fuzon is first actively cruel, identifying with his sadistic father, then passive; but it is Urizen who is made to feel the pleasure of being passively penetrated. His repression or denial of this pleasure leads to a counter-attack which gratifies desire sadistically.

Woman's position in this scheme is ambiguous. As in *Urizen*, Blake portrays her both as an object of love and as a part of the mind. Urizen's hiding and secretly kissing the 'invisible' Ahania suggests erotic activity with an 'amorous image'. Here, I think, Blake attributes to Urizen a struggle with masturbation stimulated by the incestuous image. Repudiated, Ahania generates the maternal 'moon' goddesses of primitive religion.[8] Ahania's role as the rejected maternal image is complemented by her other aspect as the female part of a man that draws him to other men. According to psychoanalytic theory, a boy's fear of castration eventually makes him give up his incestuous wishes and the masturbation that accompanies them. Sometimes, however, a boy will unconsciously resign himself to the idea of castration with the consoling fantasy of replacing his mother in intercourse with his father. If regression to a pregenital (anal) level takes place, this fantasy will be expressed as a wish to be sadistically beaten or tortured.[9]

Blake's descriptions of Urizen after he has repudiated Ahania suggest an individual regressed to the stage of sadistic anality, and using obsessional defence-mechanisms. Urizen's 'dire Contemplations' are particularly characteristic of the obsessive. Blake, correctly intuiting that this type of thought is related to the anal mode, expresses it through images recalling Theotormon's 'black flood'.

> . . . For his dire Contemplations
> Rush'd down like floods from his mountains
> In torrents of mud settling thick

> With Eggs of unnatural production
> Forthwith hatching . . . .
> (*Ah* 3:7–11, E 84)

Here, clearly, Urizen's mode of thought and its issue have an anal–sadistic quality. The birth of Urizen's egg follows Fuzon's 'rape', and when it hatches it becomes a second, degraded form of Fuzon – a 'poisonous horned' serpent. Urizen's obsessive thinking seemingly results in the return of the repressed desire: a 'lust form'd monster' approaches Urizen's knees, most probably to penetrate between them, but is killed and his backbone made into a murderous weapon.[10] Blake's imagery is predominantly anal: though the serpent is phallically horned, he is more important as a bearer of contamination. Accordingly, the rock that penetrates Fuzon is poisoned with the serpent's blood. The motif of penetrating poison in turn suggests regressive ideas of being impregnated by the father.[11] Blake directly connects phallus and poison: the serpent's poison is the blood issuing from Urizen's wounded genitals. The change from precious fluid to poison defends against a passive wish by transforming it into a feared punishment.

The poisoned rock enters Fuzon just as he imagines himself replacing his father: 'I am God. said he, eldest of things' (*Ah* 3:38, E 85). The rock symbolically deprives Fuzon of potency while satisfying his father's sadistic desire to penetrate him; on impact, Fuzon changes from a virile rebel into a 'beautiful' youth. Through an allusion to Absalom, the failed rebel, Blake emphasises Fuzon's shift in relation to his father, his change from defiant activity to an almost voluptuous vulnerability.

Urizen now crucifies Fuzon on the Tree of Mystery. What interests Blake most here is the psychic origin of Urizen's repressive institutions. By showing that such institutions derive from man's – here Urizen's – own frustrations and deprivations, Blake humanises Divine Authority and deprives it of much of its power to tyrannise. Urizen's crucifixion of Fuzon as a punishment for impulse points to the vulnerable spot in Christian myth: a beneficent God permits his beloved son's torture and death. Blake moreover suggests the source of the father's malice. The tree of temptation and death was nourished by Urizen's tears shed when he separated from the 'Eternal body'. That is, the tree is produced by the pain of his differentiation and the denial of his infant joys, his 'petrified' fancies:

> For when Urizen shrunk away
> From Eternals, he sat on a rock
> Barren; a rock which himself
> From redounding fancies had petrified
> Many tears fell on the rock,
> Many sparks of vegetation;
> Soon shot the pained root
> Of Mystery, under his heel:
> It grew a thick tree . . . .
> (*Ah* 3:55–63, E 85–6)

'Mystery' has a double meaning: religious mystery accessible only to priests, and sexual mystery accessible only to the father. On one level, the Tree of Mystery is the maternal body, which the father uses sadistically to tempt and then to punish the son. For this reason, the tree, like the net of religion, is related to the pestilential mother. It is the same entrapping and highly poisonous Upas-tree with which Blake once compared Queen Charlotte in his Notebook verse, and it grows malevolently around Urizen himself, appropriating his iron book of war.[12]

Blake continues to trace the origin of Urizen's murderous aggression, beyond Urizen's immediate conflict with Fuzon to the time when Urizen received a separate body. First Blake reworks his earlier image of 'nerves of Joy'[13] from *Urizen* and describes the nerves of Urizen's undifferentiated body in imagery suggesting orgasm and ejaculation; they melt, flow, and settle into a 'white Lake'. Urizen's as yet undifferentiated body seemingly existed in a state of constant sensual pleasure. Blake's language here is pseudo-scientific: the fluids of desire give off 'Effluvia' and, when a hard covering forms over the 'Lake' locking desire in, the excluded vapours turn into disease.

> Disease on disease, shape on shape,
> Winged screaming in blood & torment.
> (*Ah* 4:25–6, E 86)

In this sequence both disease and Urizen's poisonous cruelty originate in the frustrating diminishment of pleasure inherent in individuation. The effluvia produced by the contracting nerves suggest both desire's excess, which cannot be contained in discrete organs, and the rage felt at diminished satisfaction. As usual, Urizen deals with rage by directing it outward, but his attack on Fuzon indicates rage's connection, albeit distorted, with desire. Urizen's arrows, like the poison rock, both punish or castrate Fuzon and symbolically impregnate him.

The connection made in Blake's imagery between Urizen as punisher and Urizen as poisonous infector reflects the unconscious equation of infection with castration: fear of infection, particularly of venereal disease, is rationalised fear of castration. This equation explains why St Sebastian, Fuzon's prototype,[14] served as a talisman against infectious disease in the Middle Ages. The owner of a St Sebastian unconsciously asserts that he has already been castrated and does not need further punishment. Fuzon's other prototype, the brazen serpent Moses raised on a pole in the wilderness, served a similarly defensive purpose: the crucified serpent cured the Israelites of snakebite. Fuzon thus atones for his aggression by giving up his potency and becoming femalelike, but his 'infection' by Urizen's poison also represents a gratification of the passive wish to be impregnated. While representing ideas of passive gratification, Blake defends against them by presenting contrasting ideas of incest. In this view, being castrated does not lead to sex with the father but, by atoning in advance for sin, leads to the son's reunion with the mother. This is the psychological point of Blake's early sketch *The Couch of Death*, where after being pierced by God's poison arrows a youth dies smiling in his mother's arms.

In *Ahania*, Fuzon does not die in his mother's arms, but Ahania is none the less present, lamenting. Her description of the state of paradisal harmony before Oedipal conflict began embodies Blake's ideal of sexual sharing between father and son without 'cruel jealousy'. Ahania not only recalls Urizen's potency but specifically that he willingly gave her

> To the sons of eternal joy:
> When he took the daughters of life.
> Into my chambers of love.
> (*Ah* 5:16–18, E 88)

While the incestuous fantasy at the core of Edenic harmony becomes clearer, Blake's continuing investigation of homosexual desire suggests the fantasy's defensive nature; as in *Visions*, only incest can save the son from being locked into a love–hate struggle with the father.

Ahania, moreover, strongly suggests the possibility that Fuzon unconsciously wished to fail, since wounding and crucifixion signified receiving both punishment and love from the father. Blake relates Fuzon's failure to that of the revolutionary Robespierre: the illustration on the final plate (*Ah* 4, *IB* 213) depicts Robespierre, his bloody head severed by the guillotine. Fuzon–Robespierre's mistake would seem to have been his effort to replace his father's tyranny with his own. Blake explores the source of this perversion of energy in the son's identification with his father as aggressor. Such identification serves a defensive purpose. If Fuzon is in fact God, 'eldest of things', he need not fear punishment.[15] The alternative to such identification is victimhood. For Blake, no middle position existed, and thus there seemed no way out of the cycle.

But, in addition to this exploration of active and passive tendencies, Blake evokes in *Ahania* a paradisal state that clearly includes incest. In his open expression of incestuous desires at this time, Blake was in distinguished company. Incest often becomes a value in the writings of the French philosophers and is connected with a society of brothers in ways similar to Blake's. Diderot, for instance, imagines a Tahitian paradise where a visiting chaplain asks 'may a father sleep with his daughter, a mother with her son, a brother with his sister?' and is answered bluntly, 'Why not?'[16] Helvetius argues for total sexual freedom and the termination of all 'kinship bonds'. The Marquis de Sade took this idea to its logical conclusion, one startlingly close to Blake's ideal of sexual sharing between father and son: 'I would venture . . . that incest ought to be every government's law – every government whose basis is fraternity.' Although these ideas were never considered as plans for action, they tell a great deal about the emotional content of rebellion. Blake's poem deals with this inner content; it also suggests how unconscious wishes and fears can lead the rebel either into defensive tyranny or into self-destructive submission.

THE BOOK OF LOS

The action of *The Book of Los* intersects chapter 4 of *Urizen* and describes creation from a new viewpoint, that of Los. The book begins with a lament for a lost Paradise and describes Los's progress from a state of helpless desire through inner organisation and creative effort to a final confrontation with Urizen. The opening song by Eno, 'aged Mother', recalls 'Times remote' when greedy and selfish impulses were appeased, not suppressed:

> When Love & Joy were adoration:
> And none impure were deem'd.
> Not Eyeless Covet
> Nor Thin-lip'd Envy
> Nor Bristled Wrath
> Nor Curled Wantonness
>
> But Covet was poured full:
> Envy fed with fat of lambs:
> Wrath with lions gore:
> Wantonness lulld to sleep
> With the virgins lute,
> Or sated with her love.
>
> (*L* 3:8–19, E 89)

The images of feeding and lulling suggest an early state of harmony between the naturally greedy infant and his accepting mother. The images and tone of this paradisal state, lost because of Urizen's original separation, contrast totally with the description of the present: filled with raging 'flames of desire . . . arm'd / With destruction' (*L* 3:27–30, E 90).

Blake concentrates on Los's reactions to enforced separation. Frustrated and violently angry at being bound within the flames and forced to watch Urizen's shadow, Los pushes the flames away from him. The cold 'solid' that then encloses Los is the dead world of depression. It is a world of loss. Depression is described in Newtonian terms because, as noted earlier, Newton's concepts suggested the reality of a feared, inner world.

> Coldness, darkness, obstruction, a Solid
> Without fluctuation, hard as adamant
> Black as marble of Egypt; impenetrable
> Bound in the fierce raging Immortal.
>
> (*L* 4:4–7, E 90)

Los's subsequent rending of the rocky womb is a rebirth similar to that of the cupid hatching in *Gates*, which also follows images of despair. As an escape from depression, Los's breaking out is associated with freeing sexuality from repressive morality. Los's stamping the enclosing marble to dust recalls Orc's breaking and scattering the commandments in 'A Song of Liberty', although Los's act is perhaps less liberating because conflict here is perceived as internal. The rocky fragments of Los's despair become permanently embodied in Newtonian matter, the solid and, to Blake, frighteningly dead base of our world.

Los's rebirth also repeats the trauma of original separation, turning what was a passive experience in *Urizen* – 'Rent away with a terrible crash / Eternity roll'd wide apart' (*U* 5:4–5, E 71) – into active, willed repetition: 'impatience no longer could bear / The hard bondage, rent: rent, the vast solid / With a crash from immense to immense' (*L* 4:15–17, E 91). The fall that follows is, on one level, a punishment for refusing bondage, but it also leads to Los's birth as creator. Blake compares Los's helpless indignation at what is happening to him with the rage of a newborn infant forced to adjust to separate life.

> The Immortal revolving; indignant
> First in wrath threw his limbs, like the babe
> New born into our world . . .
> > (*L* 4:37–9, E 91)

This rage gives way to 'contemplative thoughts', which allow Los to reconsider his situation and to organise inner events, which are then reflected in the outside world.

> Incessant the falling Mind labour'd
> Organizing itself: till the Vacuum
> Became element, pliant to rise.
> > (*L* 4:49–51, E 92)

Blake's description of Los taking control of his fall purposely contrasts with and revises Milton's view of the fallen Satan's powerlessness.[17] And, although at length Satan, like Los, raises his head, it is through God's will, not through the power of thought.

Satan, when he does act, must do evil; but Los, although erring, has the creative power of a demiurge. His first creation is an airy element through which both he and light can move freely.

In *Urizen* Blake suggests a link between Urizen's creations and his struggle with loneliness and sexual impulses. Here Blake connects Los's development of the body with sensations of suffocating and drowning. It is no accident that the lungs are the first body-part organised by Los. Breath is associated with poetic inspiration, and disturbances in breathing can express anxiety.[18] Blake's imagery, as expressed in

> Sleep began: the Lungs heave on the wave
> Weary overweigh'd, sinking beneath
> In a stifling black fluid he woke
> > (*L* 4:60–2, E 92)

has a surrealistic, nightmare quality emphasised by the fact that suffocation takes place while Los is asleep: as a fearful nightmare experience, the lungs' plight resembles that of the drowning man in *Gates* who sinks in black waters. Even the representation of his strangely bloated belly is echoed in the 'dull and heavy' balloon of the lungs. Blake's image of suffocating lungs possibly originated in early, overwhelming feelings of anxiety over separation from the mother, repeated later in the poet's experience of lost inspiration. In *The Four Zoas* and *Jerusalem*, Blake develops the countering idea of a heavenly, in-spiring breath: 'the breath Divine' or 'breath of the Almighty' that uplifts Albion. But here Los must rely on himself. As he rises and falls, pipes form around his 'spent Lungs', which draw in 'The spawn of the waters' (*L* 4:70, E 92) in a manner suggesting both feeding and pregnancy. Enlarging in this way, Los grows into 'an immense Fibrous form' whose rage is responsible for his further organisation of the elements.

When Los's body was represented only by struggling lungs, it was surrounded by as-yet-unformed parts that 'crav'd repose'. This desire for rest is turned into fear, both through the disappointed anger of separation and through the association of rest with female weakness and death. Thus, Los reacts to the threat of suffocation first by growing and then by furious separation of the 'heavy' from the 'thin'. This separation mirrors the conflict between the lungs and the sleepy polypus surrounding the lungs by allowing the heavy to sink and join itself to 'the fragments of solid' and the thin to rise up and burn with a light that opposes Los's inner darkness.

Los turns from fighting female weakness to contemplate a new threat revealed by the light: Urizen's backbone whirling through space 'like an iron chain' (*L* 5:16, E 93). The whirling chain associates Urizen with Newton's principle of 'attraction', often characterised as a chain holding the planets in their places.[19] But equally important is the fact that Blake sees Newton's concept of a binding force in terms of his own fears of masochistic submission to a tyrannical father. This chain has the same function as the heavy 'iron chain' of *America* that descended from the sky to bind the rebel sons. Similarly, the spine's serpentine form here recalls the murderous serpent bow Urizen used against Fuzon. Los reacts to the threat posed by Urizen's backbone by 'upfolding his Fibres . . . / To a Form of impregnable strength' (*L* 5:18–19, E 93). That is, he asserts his phallic creative power, first by drawing himself erect, then by forming his tools – hammer and anvil – and finally by binding Urizen.

Simultaneously, Los binds the freely flowing light into an 'Orb' and chains it to Urizen's spine. Thus Los reverses the threat of Urizen–Newton's 'chain' and himself creates a power-focus, the sun, around which the other planets revolve. But Los's act is also a form of identification with Urizen. In fact, there seem to be two conflicting motives for Los's creation of the sun. One is defensive: seeing Urizen's threat, Los moves to counter-attack. And, indeed, the orb when bound to Urizen increases his 'fierce torments'.[20] This defensive, aggressive motivation is matched by a second, positive and redemptive motivation. The flowing light, before its condensation, opposes the black waters of anxiety and depression. But, whereas before, in 'Eternity', the whole body existed in a diffuse ecstatic state, now the desirable light is outside, and Los's problem is to get hold of it again. To do so, he forges a firmly defined orb of light and chains it to Urizen's spine so that his body will grow around it. This restorative act does not have the desired effect because it is contaminated by aggression. The energic orb is forced on Urizen against his need to deny or repress knowledge of it. Consequently, he feels its presence as torture, and his developing body sends out 'four rivers' to obscure it.

Throughout his Book, Los's awakening mind and creative energy struggle with his anger and despair, a struggle that finds its prototype in man's earliest reactions to separation. Margaret Mahler, a psychoanalyst, has studied in detail what she calls separation–individuation in infants.[21] Particularly interesting, in view of Blake's images of paralysing or suffocating despair, is her discovery that difficulties in the separation-process are connected with the development of depression. Mahler distinguishes several phases in the separation-process, which are experienced with increased pleasure in mastery or with despair and rage at losing unity with the mother. If experienced positively, the initial phase, in which the infant feels a symbiotic unity within 'an imaginary symbiotic membrane', is followed by a period of emerging self and joyful exploration and practising of motor skills. This phase is followed by a period in which the child has a dawning realisation of his helplessness and again draws near the mother.

In *Urizen*, in addition to his portrayal of pain and loss, Blake suggests the early 'love affair with the world' in Urizen's proud mastery of the elements. Early locomotor experiences are suggested by the muscular contractions and expansions prevalent in the text's illustrations as the naked Urizen balances, explores womblike openings, and paddles or swims through space (*U* 14, *IB* 196 – Illus. 40).[22] *The Book of Los*, as the name suggests, concentrates on the negative aspects of separation, viewed by the nostalgic poetic imagination. Eno's Paradise, where 'Covet is poured full', parallels Mahler's symbiotic phase where the mother rescues her child with care from potentially overwhelming tensions. But this Paradise is lost, and its loss precipitates rage and then depression. When Los separates a second time, his unity with the surrounding rocky womb is negative, coloured by depression, and his subsequent mental and physical organisation is defensive: if he had not started thinking, he would have kept falling through a void. According to Mahler, if an infant is not emotionally ready for differentiation, he may experience extreme organismic distress, even schizoid fragmentation of his ego. Manifestations of such distress are prominent in *The Book of Los*: Los first burns with desire, then is forcibly immobilised, then falls through a 'horrible vacuum' and suffocates under 'black fluid'. But, although Los suffers terribly after separation, Blake also presents attempts at mastery: Los's mind organises itself, and his body takes a form capable of autonomous effort.

One of the main problems in approaching the issue of separation in *The Book of Los* is that Blake's cosmology requires us to see Los's original separation from the 'Eternal Body' as a catastrophe and his

Illus. 40   *The Book of Urizen*, plate 14

later escape from the womblike solid as a positive act. Although intellectually the solid and the Eternal Body are opposites in meaning and value, Blake's use of the same imagery to describe separation from both of them suggests that he is describing opposite ways of feeling about the same thing. The mother–child unity is split into an Eternal Body, seen as male and 'good', and a womb, seen as female and 'bad'. Paradoxically, it is the longing for the lost mother that creates the negative image of Mother Nature, displacing all good onto the male body.

Three of the four illustrations of *The Book of Los* depict enclosing womblike shapes (see, for example, *L* 2, *IB* 214 – Illus. 41). In the third illustration (*IB* 215), Los's act of breaking free is suggested by an egg-shape worked around his name that opens out into a prophetic spiral. His liberation is contrasted with a trapped, spidery Urizen, who is seen crouching in the closed 'O' of LOS. His net of religion extends below, catching a naked male and female. These naked figures represent the evil mother and the morally restrictive father, who unite with each other and with matter itself in the rock womb.

As we have seen, Los, by breaking free of these oppressive elements, begins to turn passive suffering into active mastery. Similarly, his furious stamping of the rock to dust is an alternative – as tantrums were for Mahler's children – to feelings of loss, apathy or despair. The despair that lurks behind Los's anger is imaged in the heavy lungs that sink, like Bunyan's Pilgrim, in a slough. At the same time, disappointment transforms the longed-for mother's breast into the clinging white polypus, an oppressive inner weight. It would seem that the creative process is set in motion by loss or threat of loss and that, at least to Blake, the creative act involves attempts both to restore what was lost and to defend against losing more.

THE GATES OF PARADISE

Gates was engraved in 1793. Although it precedes the other works in this chapter, it is helpful to consider it now as a summary in visual form of Blake's major psychological themes: it begins with the question 'What is Man?' and ends with an emblem of his death. Blake selected the sixteen emblems from a series of seventy sketches in his Notebook. These, together with Blake's reorderings, are of

Illus. 41   *The Book of Los*, plate 2

considerable help to us in understanding the concerns that lie behind the final selections.[23] Often Blake's changes show him trying out alternate solutions to the basic problems we have been considering, such as the problem of dependence and depression. Blake's reordering counters ideas of need for and dependence on the mother by rearranging the emblems in ways suggesting man's spiritual freedom and divine, rather than natural, origins. Similarly, emblems that originally represented direct conflict with the father are modified, and orderings are introduced that suggest father and son are united in a common struggle against woman and their dependence on her.

Frontispiece

Blake begins his series directly with the infant's earliest experiences of passive dependence coupled with devouring hunger: a sweet-faced infant–chrysalis is juxtaposed to a greedily feeding caterpillar (*IB* 268 – Illus. 42). In the original sketch (*N* 68) the worm's greedy hunger for the mother's substance was combined with evocations of sexual hunger: the worm was crawling on a leaf whose shape suggested the female genitals with a gashlike stem in the centre.[24] Blake's juxtaposition of caterpillar and bound infant recalls the alternation, in works like *Tiriel*, between the infant as devourer and the infant as deprived and swaddled. But here Blake appears to transform fears of passivity into an image of confident waiting within a religious framework: the happy-faced chrysalis can be seen, as critics have noted, as the soul about to hatch as a butterfly from its mortal shell. In this context of spiritual potential and hope, feelings of infantile dependence become bearable.

Dependence also changes its object. The maternal leaf becomes only a way-station and the infant's dependence is not on it but on its own God-given nature. The maternal leaf, like her infant(s), has two aspects: a bright leaf which supports the chrysalis and a dark one which the worm eats and which hangs menacingly over the chrysalis, perhaps representing the punishment generated by greed. In any case

Illus. 42   *For Children: The Gates of Paradise*, frontispiece

the worm–infant's greed clearly generates the punishing image of emblem 16: a cowled grave-worm mother whose worm-part devours the corpses of men in the earth beneath her.

The ordering of the sequence in which the chrysalis/caterpillar appears was changed four times. Until the final selection for *Gates*, the emblems which followed the chrysalis/caterpillar reinforced painful aspects of infancy: for the chrysalis, bound helplessness; for the caterpillar, threats of retaliation for his greed. The chrysalis/ caterpillar is followed in the first ordering by a depressed figure struggling to break free from the surrounding earth (*N* 93);[25] in the second numbering it is followed by another image emphasising bondage, a chained giant form (*N* 85), and then by a devouring worm–mother (*N* 45) punishing the greedy caterpillar–infant. In the third and fourth numberings, the chrysalis/caterpillar is followed directly by the worm–mother and then by impotent, depressed, or suicidal figures. Finally, in *Gates*, Blake separated the chrysalis/ caterpillar both from the emblem of the punishing worm–mother which he used to conclude his series, and from images of painful bondage, thus permitting a more hopeful interpretation of its passive–swaddled state.

Gates 1: 'I found Him Beneath a Tree'

In the Notebook, the emblem of a mother uprooting a mandrake– infant (*N* 63), which became emblem 1, originally preceded the chrysalis–infant in a seemingly natural order of birth and swaddling– nursing. Blake's reordering for *Gates* reinforces the hopeful effect noted above because the infant man bearing his message of spiritual potential now comes first. Blake's change also de-emphasises the mother's importance, since it shows the infant being found by her rather than being born. The content of emblem 1 (*IB* 269 – Illus. 43) goes further and stresses the harm coming from her relation to her infant, who is imagined as an embodiment of sexual desire, a mandrake. The mandrake, a traditional promoter of fertility, was, moreover, associated with Reuben's desire for his mother Leah, to whom he gave mandrakes as a gift. As an expression of sexual desire, the mandrake–infant evokes his mother's threatening reaction toward him. Blake pictures her discovery of the infant (his birth) as a type of retaliatory castration: a fierce-faced mother pulls the infant up by his

Illus. 43

Illus. 43–56   *For Children: The Gates of Paradise*, emblems 1–14

long flamelike hair, with the implication that he will be shorn like his sibling(s) in her apron.

Maternal antagonism to the son's desire is more explicit in the succeeding Notebook emblem of a reclining woman repulsing a young cupid. Sometime before his final selection for *Gates*, Blake decided to use his rejected cupid to illustrate a song in which the mother gets rejected in turn: she admits her 'secret desire' for her Angel (the young cupid) only to find that she is now too old for his love. In the final selection for *Gates*, Blake removed the rejected cupid emblem and another emblem, an illustration of seizure or rape (*N* 60) which preceded the mandrake–infant emblem, and suggested a sequence of reciprocal violence between male and female. Blake's removal of these emblems, like his redrawing of the caterpillar's leaf, diminishes the theme of sexual desire for the mother and permits some readers to elaborate the emblems in terms of the philosophical or religious questions they raise. The original order, however, suggests that Blake's interest in these questions was the philosophical equivalent of desire, frustration, and the corresponding wish to deny the mother's importance.

Illus. 44   Illus. 45

Gates 2, 3, 4, 5: 'Water', 'Earth', 'Air' and 'Fire'

Images of infancy and birth are followed by emblems of the four elements composing man. Water sits despairingly at the edge of a pool under pouring rain (*IB* 269 – Illus. 44). Earth is a powerful figure protecting his head as he struggles upward under dark rocks (*IB* 270 – Illus. 45). Air clutches his head as he sits on a cloudy throne (*IB* 270 – Illus. 46), and Fire rises, armed, in flame (*IB* 271 – Illus. 47). The first three emblems represent states of anxiety and depression. In Water, the connection of the figure's depression with guilt is suggested by the similarity of the rain pouring down on him to the guilt-producing tears Urizen pours down on the rebels in *America*. In the Notebook motto for Water (*N* 95), Blake originally associated depression with the wish to ˙escape conflict through suicide by using Hamlet's words, 'Oh that the Everlasting had not fixd His canon gainst Self slaughter.' Coming after the depressed Water, Earth and Air figures, the Fire emblem shows the use of energy to alleviate depression by directing aggression outward with spear and shield. The sequence of the four elements together suggests man's innate nature: the found infant of emblem 1 is characterised by a propensity for depression and a tendency to use aggression as a solution.

The original Notebook sketches show that aggression was at first

Illus. 46   Illus. 47

directed specifically against the father. In these sketches there was a dynamic interaction between the figures later called Earth, Air and Fire: Earth and Air represented threatened father–kings and were preceded by a sketch of a fiery, youthful antagonist (N 91).[26] As father–king, Earth was linked with Shakespeare's analysis of Oedipal ambivalence by the motto 'Rest Rest, perturbed Spirit' – an adjuration to Hamlet's father's ghost. Moreover, as Erdman points out, the ghost king is a reference to the murdered king of France. Air is his forewarned brother king of England and Fire is the rebellious patriot.[27] This same rebel was apparently first conceived as a revisionist's Satan – one who triumphs. Blake drew the figure on a Notebook page following a sketch of Milton's Satan for Blake's illustrations of *Paradise Lost*, one point being that Blake the rebel was to be viewed as superior to his poetic father Milton. Thus the Notebook sketches show Oedipal conflict at a variety of levels. For *Gates*, Blake replaces the original dynamic of filial aggression and paternal impotence with images suggesting a mood-shift from depression to aggression. Perhaps Blake needed to break the connection between sexual rivalry and depression so that he could imagine it alleviated without guilt. At any rate, the final ordering suggest the utility of energy in turning depression-causing rage away from the

self. After Blake breaks the sequence of fiery rebel and defeated
kings, Fire takes on a defensive rather than an offensive function:
instead of coming first it follows and counters the emblems of
despair.

Gates 6: 'At length for hatching ripe he breaks the shell'

This emblem (*IB* 271 – Illus. 48) represents the post-depression
state: a young winged cupid emerges from his broken eggshell among
clouds. Looking at the emblem in the light of what we know about
Blake's characterisations of mental states, we can see that the egg
from which the cupid emerges is another image that connects
depression, matter and anality. All of the preceding depressed figures
squat or sit in ways suggesting Urizen's constricted anal mode, and
the egg which most commentators take to represent matter provides
a visual summary of the depressed figures' material surroundings.
Cupid's traditional association with love makes him an appropriate
representation of phallic sexuality as a means of 'rising above'
depressed impotence. His self-induced birth contrasts directly with
the maternal plucking of the mandrake infant, and suggests the
power of active sexuality and its mental equivalent, inspiration, to
combat both maternal threats and self-punishing depression.

Illus. 48   Illus. 49

Gates 7: 'Alas!'

In this emblem (*IB* 272 – Illus. 49) an eager curly-haired boy tries to catch or swat a small flying figure, presumably female, with his hat while another figure lies lifeless at his feet. The potentially redemptive sexuality of emblem 6 has turned here into mindless cruelty whose dire result is stressed by the contrast in the two fragile figures of exuberant upward flight and pitiful collapse. The male's attempt to reconcile his inner needs by substituting outward aggression for his inward despair is too successful: it transmits the conflict he felt within himself into a conflict with woman, and he martyrs her.

The contrast between the fallen and the joyously flying figure also suggests alternate moods of depression and sexual awakening with its attendant joy and inspiration. The emblem recalls similar imagery in the preface to *Europe*, where Blake catches a fairy in his hat. There, however, the flying fairy is not the sexual object but the power, both phallic and imaginative, that Blake must grasp in order to shake off depression and to see the material world as alive and joyous: the fairy promises to transform the dead material world for Blake only if he is fed on 'love thoughts'. What Blake seems to recall in *Europe*'s preface is a state of infantile depression, echoed by later states, in which one's waste-products are seen to be dead matter instead of the living creatures one lovingly imagined. This devaluation of one's first products is countered in the male by his discovery of the winged, magical phallus, which Blake clearly connects with inspiration. Blake takes the fairy to his bosom and together they commit the sexually symbolic and cruel act of plucking flowers, laughing like bad boys when the flowers whimper. Then, pen poised, Blake listens as his fairy dictates *Europe*.

Gates 8: 'My Son! My Son!'

Just as the youth's defensive sexuality leads him to rape or kill the female, he is also led to threaten the father. Pointing his raised spear against his father (*IB* 272 – Illus. 50), the youth condenses into one moment earlier images of father–son conflict. His nakedness, his phallic spear, and the caption's allusion to the story of David and Absalom, who wished to take his father's concubines as well as his place as king, suggest the sexual nature of the youth's rivalry.

Illus. 51

Illus. 50

Gates 9: 'I want! I want!'

The emblem which shows a youth climbing a ladder to the moon (*IB* 273 – Illus. 51) indicates the strength and insatiability of young desire, which the caption generalises but the ladder-climbing suggests is explicitly sexual. It is a foregone conclusion that the youth will fail, and the next emblem confirms this.

Gates 10: 'Help! Help!'

This emblem shows a figure drowning and calling for help (*IB* 273 – Illus. 52). We know that he has fallen from the ladder because the emblem originated in two Gilray cartoons showing a Whig patriot fallen into the Slough of Despond after trying to climb into the Paradise of Freedom on a ridiculously short ladder. The fall's symbolic significance is emphasised by the fact that the preceding emblems, from Fire on, all showed figures whose bodies were open and whose gestures expanded upward. The fallen, drowning figure represents the depression that attends the failure to gratify desire.

Blake's various reorderings of 'Help!' show other meanings it had for him. It seems to represent a depressed 'let-down' from an inspired state as well as from sexual desire, because in the unnumbered series it follows a bard on a cloud (*N* 57) fallen from visionary heights. It also shows that, for Blake, depression is the main alternative to aggression because 'Help!' replaces the emblem of a dagger-wielding assassin (*N* 97). A striking parallel to the alternation between dagger-wielder and depressed figure occurs in *Europe* (plate 1), where a picture of the assassin is followed by that of a depressed falling figure. Finally, Blake's orderings suggest the connection between depression and fears of retaliation for aggressive or sexual activities.

In his early ordering, Blake follows the drowner with the frightful image of Ugolino (*N* 59), the starving father who devours his sons; and, in subsequent orderings, with emblems of the stern mother plucking the mandrake–infant. In *Gates* the despairing figure is preceded by patricidal impulses ('My Son! My Son!') and desire ('I want!') and followed by images of retaliation: Aged Ignorance clips a youthful cupid's wings and Ugolino crouches among his sons (emblem 12).

Gates 11: 'Aged Ignorance'

In this emblem a white-bearded old man with a huge scissors clips the wings of a naked cupid who struggles to free himself and move toward the rising sun (*IB* 274 – Illus. 53). Although the figure of the

Illus. 52

Illus. 53

cupid evokes our sympathy, nevertheless the psychological significance of the emblem's presence here is that the cupid – or his
surrogate, the youth – has committed sexual and aggressive acts
which must inevitably incur punishment. The degree to which the
cupid is sympathetic is the degree to which Blake is ambivalent about
admitting guilt. Imagining oneself as an innocent, wrongly punished,
may also have served to alleviate depression. Blake's sympathetic
portrayal of the cupid and the negative political associations of the
old man have obscured the emblem's ambivalent significance and led
some critics to a total identification with the cupid as rebel: 'In this
oppressive world, all revolutionary thinkers are viciously tortured
and immured in dungeons by the King and Church.'[28]

Gates 12: 'Does thy God O Priest take such vengeance as this?'

In this emblem (*IB 274* – Illus. 54), Ugolino sits in prison starving,
surrounded by his sons. The motto blames Church and society for
forcing Ugolino to eat his progeny: both father and sons are victims.
Blake's first emblem-sketches were of a flying bearded devourer
holding a man in his mouth and threatening a traveller. The
devourer's hair and beard resemble Ugolino's, suggesting that he is a
transformation of the cannibal. The change from the monster's
willed attack to Ugolino's enforced devouring of his children represents a significant effort to escape from father–son conflict by uniting
against a common enemy, Church and priest. The punitive implications of Ugolino's act were suggested in an earlier ordering by placing
it after criminal acts of rape and fratricide. Subsequently, as though
working toward a lessening of fear, Blake preceded the Ugolino
emblem with a group of emblems of children punished and reconciled with· their parents. In the final selection, although cupid is
clipped, hostility toward the father is perhaps diminished by the fact
that the old man's action can be seen as the result of ignorance rather
than of murderous intent.

Gates 13: 'Fear & Hope are – Vision'

In the light of the sequence of filial aggression, desire, despair, and
punishment that precedes it, this emblem (*N 61; IB 275* – Illus. 55)
appears to be more complex – and less hopeful – than has been

Illus. 54

Illus. 55

supposed. Critics have emphasised the emblem's uplifting aspects, its assertion of the soul's immortality, but the appearance of a father's ghost has negative connotations as well. Such connotations are suggested, for example, if the ghost is seen as a visual allusion to the ghost of Hamlet's murdered father, invoked earlier in these emblems. Similarly, the image of hovering ghosts has negative connotations in *America*, where it is associated with a rebuking conscience. The white-bearded ghost of *Gates*, ascending from his corpse, is visually similar to previous Urizenic figures; moreover, the family's reaction to the father's pointing toward heaven is more startled than hopeful. The eldest son, in particular, shrinks back guiltily.

In Blake's reorderings of the Notebook emblems, the paternal ghost's relation to rebuking conscience was particularly stressed. Initially it followed an emblem of rape, making a juxtaposition like that in *America*, where an image of rape is accompanied by the rebuking voices of the dead. In subsequent numberings, Blake's ordering suggests that stirrings of conscience were provoked by ambivalence about the death of parents or siblings. Open death-wishes appear in the Notebook emblem of an armed man approaching the paternal sick-bed with clearly murderous intent (*N* 46). The related fear of a vengeful paternal ghost is expressed clearly in Blake's late numberings of the series, where the death-bed scene is followed directly by an evil spirit on a cloud pouring down rain (*N* 81). This spirit is the feared demonic father, and his icy rain recalls Urizen's guilt-producing rain in the prophecies. The demonic father is followed by the lurking assassin, also an image of the accusing father.

Blake's final caption for this emblem, 'Fear & Hope are – Vision', indicates the emblem's dual nature as well as the alternating states characteristic of the series; the original caption, 'what we hope, we see', was a simpler statement of vision as desire. The two emotions, which Blake says compose the visionary experience, were originally shown separately in the Notebook. Written next to a sketch showing the attack of a paternal serpent on a falling youth (*N* 75) is 'a vision of fear'. Hope is contrastingly associated with union. The motto 'a vision of hope' is placed suggestively near a Notebook sketch of parents embracing over a child (*N* 75). The sketch suggests both negative and positive emotions. The child's face is troubled, and he seems to be trying to push the mother away from the father. That the hope is of reunion with the mother, and that it is threatened by the father, is suggested by Blake's earliest emblem sketches, where fear was evoked by the sight of a flying paternal devourer and hope by an image of man's reunion with the mother as wife after death.

In *Gates* the placement of this emblem serves to mitigate fear in several ways, despite the ghost's rebuking posture. Thus Blake does not precede this emblem with images of the son's violence or with other death-scenes, as he had in the Notebook, but with images of punishment: cupid clipped and Ugolino imprisoned. In both emblems, particularly that of Ugolino, Blake attempts to shift fear and anger away from the father and onto an external enemy. At the same time, he represents the feared punishments of castration and devouring as having already occurred before the father's death. Consequently, the father's ghost is stern but his uplifted hand can even promise eventual relief from the cycles of retaliation – but only after death. In accordance with this shift, the images of evil conjurer and assassin no longer follow the death-bed scene. Instead, the traveller, reassured by the once threatening father, hastens to the grave.

Gates 14: 'The Traveller hasteth in the Evening'

The emblem shows the traveller with hat and staff walking vigorously toward death's door (*IB 275* – Illus. 56). Blake's first Notebook
sketches show death as a fearful punishment. Death was also, as we
shall see in connection with emblem 16, viewed as a union with the
mother. In his successive reorderings, Blake shifted from a direct
portrayal of a paternal figure as punisher to a modification of the
father's role so that while he still stands for a rebuking conscience he
also promises relief. The mother's role was changed simultaneously.
Blake de-emphasised her desirable qualities as an object of union and
emphasised instead her frightening and punitive qualities. For now
let us examine the traveller's relation to the father. The series
originally began with the traveller seemingly threatened by a flying
devourer in the margin (*N 15* – Illus. 57*a*). In the next plate (*N
16* – Illus. 57*b*) the devourer is clearly flying toward the traveller, a
naked body in his mouth. Blake developed the figure in the margins
of a third plate with frightening details of the monster's mouth and
teeth (*N 17* – Illus. 57*c*). When the traveller is moved toward the end
of the series in the first numbering, he is followed by a skeleton and
then by the emblem of Ugolino, which softens fear with pity for the
father–devourer. Nevertheless, the sequence is still one of fear and
despair, concluded by the drowning hand of 'Help!'. In the second
numbering, Blake breaks the latent connection between son and
devouring father by placing the Ugolino emblem before that of the

Illus. 56

Illus. 57(a)   Notebook, manuscript

father's ghost, so that the father's rising spirit and pointing finger
could suggest release from prison or spiritual starvation. Blake kept
this ordering in the third numbering although latent fears of punishment remained in the emblems of conjurer and assassin which
followed the father's ghost, but all the father's demonic aspects are
suppressed. As we shall see in discussing emblem 16, as the father
becomes less threatening, the son relinquishes claim to the mother.

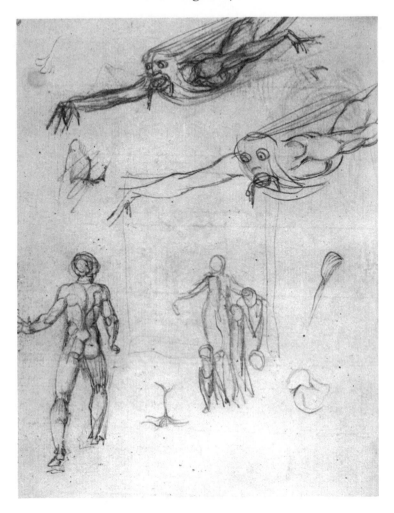

Illus. 57(*b*)   Notebook, manuscript

Gates 15: 'Death's Door'

In Blake's ordering of emblems for *Gates*, this emblem (*IB 276* – Illus. 58) immediately follows the traveller; as a consequence, it seems as if the traveller has suddenly aged. His assumption of an old man's identity has the effect of a reconciliation with the father; instead of sending him to his grave, both enter it together. On another level, however, the old man, who closely resembles *Gates'*

Illus. 57(c)   Notebook, manuscript

other explicitly paternal figures, still represents the father, but, though he would naturally precede the son to death, and the devouring worm–mother of the final emblem, there is no doubt that Blake identifies the son with the same fate.

Gates 16: 'I have said to the Worm: Thou art my mother and my sister'
In this emblem, a staring white-hooded figure, at once both female

Illus. 59

Illus. 58

Illus. 58–9   *For Children: The Gates of Paradise*, emblems 15–16

and of unspecified gender, sits beneath dark tree-roots, holding a
staff (*N* 45; *IB* 276 – Illus. 59). A large worm emerges from behind
her knees in the area of her lap and, coiling around her, enters the
ground next to two buried heads, one bearded. Presumably the worm
has been feeding on the bodies. The fate of father and son – of all
males – seems the same: woman – for 'mother and sister' implies all
women – eats both who came through death's door. The figure is
visually related to other images of the phallic mother, including the
serpent-possessing sibyl of *America*, who is controlling and threatening there and elsewhere. Moreover, the mood is one of depression,
recalling, with its dark surroundings and squatting figures, emblems
2, 3 and 4, but especially emblem 3, which, as we said earlier, suggests
anality as a depressed, regressive response to conflict. This depression,
which concludes *Gates*' exploration of man's sexual experience,
is that of the father and son, identified with each other. They are
depressed because their common fate is death and emasculation,
while competitive woman lives and possesses the worm–phallus.

   The concluding emblem strikingly recalls the frontispiece with
which *Gates* began, and thereby suggests the cyclical, non-redemp-
tive quality of the human condition. The ambiguities of the frontis-

piece are here resolved – finally and negatively. The infant–worm which fed on the dark mother has now been eaten by her; the punishment has been fashioned to fit the crime. The circle is closed in another way too: the further implication is that the son and mother partake of the same destructive nature. This belief is suggested by the androgynous nature of the cowled figure, whose image telescopes the threatening mother's image with that of the traveller in his shroud.

Through his early Notebook sketches and repositioning of the traveller and the worm–mother emblems, Blake tried to clarify relationships to both parental figures. And as we shall see, the more terrifying or anxiety-producing aspects of these relationships were suppressed in Blake's final selection. His initial sketch of the flying devourer (*N* 15 – Illus. *57a*) was accompanied by other sketches that suggest homosexual fears. One shows the naked legs and buttocks of a man struggling to walk with a serpent coiled around his leg (*N* 13). Another (*N* 16 – Illus. *57b*) shows the traveller naked in rear view accompanied by detailed sketches of his buttocks and anus. There are also suggestions of two ways to deal with these fears. The first is the way of the impotent child. On the same page as the initial sketch of the devourer Blake shows a urinating traveller and some helpless children. The juxtaposition of the traveller's act with the devourer's threat resembles Theotormon's reactive release of black floods when faced by paternal power in *Visions*. The fact that the traveller's response is the response of a child to fear or trauma is suggested by the accompanying sketches of defenceless children. A second way of dealing with fears, particularly of homosexual attack, is to commit incest. Accordingly, the frightening images are countered by juxtaposition with the figure of a mother with children, her arms open to receive the traveller (*N* 16). Images in others of Blake's works have suggested that confusion over sexual identity is related to observation or fantasies of a confusing primal scene. Another sketch and accompanying lyric relate aggressive and defensive sexuality to Blake's own marriage. The sketch shows a couple, presumably Blake and his wife Catherine, in bed. Above the sketch was Blake's first idea for a title for his emblem series, 'Ideas of Good and Evil' – good being union with the mother–wife, evil the threat of paternal attack. An accompanying lyric echoes the imagery of 'I saw a chapel', where the speaker witnessed the paternal serpent forcing open the chapel-door, and suggests that Blake experienced consummation as an identification with the aggressive father in a primal scene:

When a Man has Married a Wife
he finds out whether
Her knees & elbows are only
glued together.

(N 14)

The idea of imitating the father through incest precipitates ideas of
guilt and punishment; it means, as we have seen elsewhere, that one
is never free from the cycles of retaliation. If son and father are to be
reconciled, incest must seemingly be renounced. This in turn leads
Blake to an increasingly negative image of the mother. The traveller's
relation to the mother is complex and suggests love, fear, and sense
of rejection. In the first numbering, Blake drops the initial blissful
reunion between traveller and mother–wife, which now appears
strikingly in *Jerusalem*, in favour of an emblem of a skeleton–mother
who greets the traveller at the grave with scythe in hand. A
subsequent sequence of emblems suggests a child's feelings of
exclusion; the mother is shown repulsing cupid and, later, mourning
a dead infant. In the second numbering, two emblems of mothers
with dead infants (N 73; N 83) are joined by an emblem of parents
embracing over a troubled child (N 75). The group now suggests the
child's exclusion either because of a sibling's death or because of the
mother's union or reunion with the father. This group of emblems
now follows the emblem of the father's ghost, thus more securely
contrasting his death with a reunion troubling the son and with the
preoccupied mother's mourning for dead infants. While these
emblems primarily suggest sadness or loss, more fear-provoking
images appear in the reorderings of emblem 16, which make clear its
negative quality.

In the unnumbered Notebook series, the worm–mother emblem
follows Blake's emblem of the father on a bier in N 43. The emblem
preceding the bier (N 42), has never been properly explained, but
makes sense in the context of the threatening phallic mother: a large
spider dangles in front of an old man with a crutch, threatening or
pointing with its leg. This spider, like the devouring spider of *Europe*,
seems to be yet another version of the death-dealing mother.

In the first numbering, the worm–mother is preceded by and seems
to await Abel, murdered by his brother, Cain. The emblem of
'Death's Door' follows linking her both with a father's and a
brother's death. However, this order failed to satisfy Blake; in the

second numbering he moved her to the beginning of the series, linking her image with subtler states of passivity and despair. Here she follows the chrysalis–infant and enchained giant. This pairing emphasises binding or enclosing and suggests that death is similarly perceived as an enforced passivity. The suicide that follows in this numbering suggests a mistaken attempt to avoid coming to terms with this threat through self-destructive activity.

In the third numbering, Blake places the worm–mother directly after the chrysalis/infant–worm, forcing a connection between the infant who devours his mother and the mother who devours her child. Images of binding and depression now follow her and culminate in suicide. 'Death's Door' is widely separated from her in this ordering, since Blake is exploring instead the origins of fear. Finally, in *Gates* Blake again joins the worm–mother with the old man, this time joined at death's door by his traveller son.

The development of Blake's emblem series, with its diminution of sexual themes and its movement of son toward father in the final selection for *Gates*, strengthens our understanding of a similar shift from the vibrant sexuality of *Marriage* and *America* to the negative image of the female will in *Vala*. One way of dealing with depression which we observed earlier was through incestuous union with the mother, but this 'escape', as we have seen, started new waves of guilt. In *Urizen* and *The Book of Los* Blake imagines forms of work or creative world-building as ways out of depression, while simultaneously denying the need for the mother and hypothesising a primal unity of men. Here, in *Gates*, Blake prepares the ground for reunion with the father by denying incestuous wishes. This, however, involves an imaginative exploration of passivity and evokes deeper and earlier fears of an all-powerful threatening mother. The son draws closer to the father, not as a man who triumphantly possesses the mother but as a crippled or dying man about to be eaten. In this compounding of negatives, the ghost's uplifted finger promising release from the body in emblem 13 becomes the only bulwark against the regressively perceived worm–mother.

6 *Vala* and *The Four Zoas*

INTRODUCTION

Vala, later *The Four Zoas*, is perhaps the single most important work for those interested in Blake's development. Blake's work on the 132-page manuscript spanned the crucial years (1796–1807) of his troubles with Hayley and his experience of enlightenment or, possibly, conversion. It was neither finished nor definitively abandoned, but continued to grow by a process of accretion, moving from a mythic–dramatic core in the early Nights to a more abstract conclusion that is marked by a proliferation of Christian imagery. Margoliouth and Bentley have worked to disentangle early layers of text from later additions and critics have subsequently been more careful in distinguishing between the early negative view of man's condition and the later redemptive one.[1] I think it is possible, however, to be much more specific about the subjective components of both Blake's negative and positive attitudes toward the human condition.[2]

The core of the early, mythic *Vala* revolves around fantasies of a seductive but murderous phallic female and a feminised or hermaphroditic man. These fantasies not only are embodied in the text but also find graphic form in a series of remarkable and highly sexual illustrations. When the subjective side of the early *Vala* is clearly grasped, we see that it presents a view of man's position that is fearful enough to threaten sanity. Blake's heavy additions, as well as the concluding Christian Nights, can be seen as efforts to use 'positive' concepts – here, heavily Christian – to combat other, more archaic, 'negative' ones. For instance, the concept of Beulah and of the benign females in it combats fear of the murderous mother in very specific ways. But Blake's ideas and changes in symbolism and imagery do not develop in a linear fashion; each concept is part of a network of other concepts, images, and symbols. The murderous mother, for example, is not only bad for the individual male in relation to her but is also responsible for conflict between men themselves and thus becomes offered as the 'cause' of war and social evils. Similarly, Blake's vision of male harmony is dependent on access to the females of Beulah, who offer themselves undemandingly and then inconspicuously die.

NIGHT I

Night I's development illustrates the way in which Blake modified his most archaic fantasies to make them less frightening. An early fragment describes 'the struggling copulation. in fell writhing pangs' (E 764) of two hermaphrodites, Enion and Tharmas.[3] The male Tharmas is described as appearing from beneath his mother's controlling veil, without a penis:[4]

> Male formd the demon mild athletic force his shoulders spread
> And his bright feet firm as a brazen altar. but. the parts
> To love devoted. female, all astonishd stood the hosts
> Of heaven . . . .
>
> (E 764)

Paired with Tharmas is his necessary counterpart, the phallic woman: 'Female her form . . . but the parts of love / Male' (E 764). Such a female is depicted (*V* 22 – Illus. 60)[5] with clearly defined breasts and an erect penis.

It is impossible that such clear symbols as Blake's female male and male female are not highly significant. Yet they are dismissed as bizarre or 'strange' by a critic who none the less notes their recurring importance in *Jerusalem*.[6] Perhaps one reason for this kind of dismissal by critics is that Blake has expressed a fearful fantasy directly and without adding supportive intellectual meaning. Psychoanalysis of children has shown that they regularly imagine a phallic mother and worry about their own castration and that these early imaginings are usually repressed. As we follow the development of Night I, we shall see a process similar to repression in which the fantasies gradually become less fearful and are eventually replaced by

Illus. 60   From *Vala* manuscript

images of triumph: the male without a penis becomes the sexually potent male genius, and the powerful phallic woman becomes castrated and weak.

Blake uses a variant of the fragment's mating-scene to initiate Night I of *Vala*. Enion's rape by Tharmas (now no longer hermaphrodites but male and female) is followed by descriptions of the birth of twins, Los and Enitharmon, their infant greed and frustrated incestuous love as adolescents. During their courtship, Enitharmon relates how Man, whom Blake later named Albion, fell because of Luvah's greedy attempt to steal from Urizen. Urizen himself then appears to preside over Los and Enitharmon's marriage. The Night ends with a wedding-song and the lament of the children's exiled mother, Enion.

The text of Night I before additions is remarkably coherent in its thematic concern with the horrible consequences of attempting to satisfy basic human needs for food and sex. Blake characterises these needs as destructive, since they involve the absorption of one person (or part of him) by another. Consequently, rather than being satisfied, the characters receive a destructive reciprocal of the need itself: they are eaten, raped or castrated. Blake therefore views essential needs as dangerous not only because they leave the individual vulnerable to painful deprivation, but also because they are too excessive and too mixed with aggression, thus damaging those chosen to satisfy them. Enion's infants, for example, drain their mother. Such damage in turn brings about retaliation: Enion becomes a vortex to suck in her children. Retaliation at this point in *Vala* is not justified by any moral or religious standards but occurs naturally as part of the fallen human condition.

The Enion and Tharmas episode beginning *Vala*'s Night I forms a psychologically comprehensible unit in terms of the mutually destructive activities of mother and son. Enion initiates the pattern by destroying Tharmas's body in retaliation for his sexual possessiveness (he had hidden her in 'Jealous Despair'). Enion draws out and manipulates his 'nerve[s]', every 'vein & lacteal'. Reborn as Enion's woven child, Tharmas gets revenge by raping her. The rape itself suggests that sexuality is dangerous for the male: Tharmas's body fuses with Enion's during intercourse, creating a monstrous woman–serpent. This variation on the fragment's portrayal of a phallic woman adds the suggestion that the woman absorbs or appropriates the man's penis in intercourse. She also seems to appropriate the creativity that Blake associates with male sexuality: she acquires a poetic voice. Enion's first act after the rape is to sing, and Blake in revisions alternately gives her a warbling 'female voice' or a serpent's voice whose complaints suggest the absorbed male's protests.

Blake's subsequent development of the plot illustrates similar destructive consequences of need satisfaction with other partners. The infants, Los and Enitharmon, appear both vulnerable, lying exposed on the rocks, and destructively greedy. The illustration (*V* 8) shows them avidly sucking at Enion's breasts, 'drawing her Spectrous Life' (*FZ* 9:4, E 300). Verbal parallels suggest that this destructive greed is a punishment for Enion's earlier attack on Tharmas: the twins 'draw' out Enion's milk and life just as she 'drew' out Tharmas's veins and lacteals. Furthermore, the infants' sucking makes Enion 'melt' with love just as, we hear later, Man melted in Vala's embrace after giving up his seed. By making the infants' destructive sucking follow woman's mutilation of Tharmas and Man's fall, Blake lessens guilt over greedy impulses: the mother deserves punishment. As they grow older, Los and Enitharmon continue to consume their mother, and also consume their father: 'to make us happy let them weary their immortal powers / While we draw in their sweet delights' (*FZ* 10:3–4, E 301). Los and Enitharmon defend themselves against guilt for their actions by rationalising their scornful greed as necessary to produce love: 'for if we grateful prove / They will withhold sweet love, whose food is thorns & bitter roots' (*FZ* 10:5–6, E 301).[7]

The adolescent Enitharmon torments her brother Los not by draining his powers but by denying him sexual satisfaction. Her torment includes telling him the story of Man's fall, in which Luvah steals 'the Horses of Light' from Urizen, and Luvah's bride, Vala, sleeps with his rival, Man. Enitharmon's story suggests that the primal sin is aggression against the father, who retaliates by stealing the son's bride, thus setting off all the retaliatory cycles characteristic of fallen Man. Enitharmon identifies with Vala, the unfaithful consort, and, although she pretends sorrow over the fall, she is in fact involved in the subsequent punishment of sons – namely, Tharmas, Los and Luvah. For example, Enitharmon's marriage to Los weakens rather than gratifies him. Before the wedding, Urizen descends and exhibits his superior potency to Los: a sunset display and 'chariot of fire'. His descent itself repeats within the narrative action the rivalry between Luvah and Man (or his delegate Urizen) for Vala. During the wedding, Blake repeats the images of Enion's rape, suggesting that marriage is a civilised form of rape and can similarly weaken or destroy the male. The 'warbling' of the wedding-song echoes Enion's warbling, and her transformation into a serpent is recalled in the illustration (*V* 14) of a three-headed woman–serpent. The female's absorption of potency is further suggested by an illustration (*V* 13) of an exhausted male spirit trying to blow his horn. The male's depletion in marriage and the usurpation of his poetic voice result in warfare between the frustrated men; accordingly, the wedding-song is about sadistic slaughter.

In most of his additions and revisions, as well as in repetitive events in the initial plot, Blake tried to deal with the dire consequences of attempting to gratify one's needs. What interests him primarily is the danger to the male of feminisation or draining. He deals with this through a process of reversal that transfers power from the female to the male (what was once feared from her is now done to her). A parallel alternation in power occurs between mother and children. A second strategy that made Blake's perception of human nature more bearable to him was to introduce the concept of an outside will, Christ, directing events. Retaliatory acts, instead of being merely inevitable natural responses, become a necessary, if painful, part of a benign pattern of redemption. The first example of reversal occurs in the opening lines of Night I. Blake's song was originally to be the song of Eno, implicitly dictated to him by the Ancient Mother. His later changes suggest, on the contrary, that her song is an angry response to his potent verse. This 'long resounding strong heroic Verse' (*FZ* 3:2, E 297) is Blake's masculine weapon, analogous to Tharmas's 'masculine strength', and the song's opening lines suggest a rape enacted in terms of language with the fearful feminine landscape as victim. Blake's transference of potency to the male accords with his other changes. His rewritten *Vala – The Four Zoas* – involves the 'resurrection' or potent uprising not merely of one man but of 'Four Mighty Ones' – a seemingly unbeatable combination.

Blake began to modify the fragment's fantasy of a feminised male in Night I's initial scene by eliminating the hermaphrodites and making Enion female and Tharmas male. He next replaced the idea of castration with the idea of total body-destruction, an idea that is still very frightening but more susceptible to intellectual explanation:

Enion is Mother Nature turned man-destroyer by a primal sin. Blake's illustrative imagery supports the intellectual allegory while simultaneously allowing him to work out fantasies of mutilation. There has, however, been a defensive shift. Enion's destruction of Tharmas is only temporary. His woven shadow (made from his destroyed body) grows into an aggressive, narcissistic male who punishes her with rape.[8] In a first effort to deny Tharmas's feminisation, Blake went to the opposite extreme and made him a self-glorying, righteous bully who addressed Enion as 'my slave' and threatened to bring her 'to rigid strict account' for her sins (E 741). Later Blake deleted this direct and vengeful sadism.

Another revision that strengthens Tharmas and weakens Enion concerns Enion's motives for destroying Tharmas. In *Vala* Tharmas jealously hides Enion; the emphasis is on Tharmas's vulnerability and Enion's failure to understand or to 'pity'.[9] In *The Four Zoas*, it is Enion who is jealous, because Tharmas has harboured the fallen Zoas' female emanations.[10] This type of reversal is familiar in Blake; it parallels the shift from the Notebook emblems, where the cupid–son despairingly woos his mother, to the later song 'My Pretty Rose Tree', where jealousy and longing are transferred to the rose–maiden. Blake's transfer of jealousy from Tharmas to Enion results in a less degraded position for Tharmas but he still cannot evade maternal anger. Instead of trapping a girl for Tharmas as Oothoon offered to do for her love in *Visions*, Enion nets and kills her rival Enitharmon.

Blake not only transfers power from female to male but also changes the relative positions of mother and child. At birth, the infant twins are vulnerable, hungry and weeping. But, at their wedding, their exiled mother weeps 'upon the desolate wind' in dire hunger. Reversal is more complex here, however. Blake's imagery suggests that Los and Enitharmon still feel the results of earlier deprivation. Their longing for the breast is replaced by abstract pleasure in planetary revolutions and by sadistic pleasure in slaughter. Blake implies that the abstract and sadistic pleasures reflect frustrated desire for nurture by describing them in terms of round shapes that coldly or destructively imitate the breast: revolving heavenly bodies and wheeled 'chariots of the Slain'. Enion, for her part, having been drained and punished for depriving her children, becomes a spokesman for others who are deprived. As such, Blake identifies with her and gives her his voice. Her lament evokes the suffering children of *Songs of Experience*, here depicted as starving birds and beasts. The cornfields surrounding the birds' nests specifically link them with Enion's similarly encircled twins. Blake seems to be suggesting that the unwary child who trusts his parent will be slaughtered like the innocent lamb.

The Night originally ended with Enion's lament. Starting with Enion's destruction of Tharmas's original body, we have observed a series of destructive attempts to get satisfaction: man rapes woman, woman absorbs man's potency, infant drains mother, mother sucks in child with her vortex. One of Blake's most significant changes in Night I was the addition of the Daughters of Beulah, whose actions soften and deny woman's power to mutilate or kill man. Blake contrasts Enion's cruel treatment of Tharmas with an ideal state where Beulah's 'Females sleep the winter in soft silken veils / Woven by their own hands to hide them in the darksom grave / But Males immortal live renewd by female deaths' (*FZ* 5:1–3, E 298). Although the males do not actually kill these females, who reportedly 'delight' in self-immolation, this Eden seems created out of fear not love. The Beulians' weaving of their cocoon–coffins contrasts both with Enion's destructive drawing out of Tharmas's fibres and with her weaving of a tabernacle to hide her murdered rival, Enitharmon. Blake not only reverses the females' murderousness against themselves; he also distances and disguises the original threat by adding secondary meanings. Enion's drawing out of fibres becomes allegorised in revision as reason dissecting imagination. Thus, instead of unweaving Tharmas's body, Enion anatomises 'every little fibre of [his] soul' (*FZ* 4:29, E 298). The concept of Beulah as 'a Soft Moony Universe feminine lovely / Pure mild & Gentle' (*FZ* 5:30–1, E 299) denies both the original fear of bodily destruction and the secondary threat reason poses to the imagination: Beulah is a world both of gentle nurture and of unconscious logic, the language of imagination. The Daughters of Beulah follow sleepers in their dreams, apparently to protect them from their impulses' nightmarish aspects, thus creating protective spaces for the males. More specifically, they enclose Enion's 'Circle of Destiny' in a space called Ulro, which, since Christ is guiding them, makes the creation of matter part of Christ's redemptive work.

In spite of Blake's efforts to deal with fearful fantasies by creating a benign, self-immolating maternal ideal, his ambivalence keeps contaminating his portrayal of Beulah, making the Beulians appear sinister. Blake, for example, makes them close 'the Gate of the Tongue' against the rewoven Tharmas. At this point Tharmas is composed primarily of raging desire, and closing the gate signifies barring entry to male passion as well as shutting off a nurturing paradise. Moreover, the Daughters repress and constrict the passions by luring them with siren-songs and 'loving blandishments' into forms of vegetation so that they can be controlled. In a final confused addition, which elaborates the image of exclusion and desire, Man's fall appears as traumatic separation from the paradisal motherland. Falling into 'unknown' Space'

> Deep horrible without End. Separated from Beulah far beneath
> The Mans exteriors are become indefinite opend to pain
> In a fierce hungring void. . . .
>
> (FZ 18:38–41, E 308)

NIGHT II

In Night II, the 'Eternal Man', weakened by his encounter with Vala, gives control to Urizen, who then builds a world. In both this and the following Night, Urizen assumes prominence, illustrating ways of sublimating the dangerous impulses and desires explored in Night I. This sublimation is the intrapsychic meaning of his refining Luvah (love) in the furnaces to obtain building material for his golden world. On an intrapersonal level, however, Urizen enters the cycles of desire and retaliation illustrated in Night I: his rival, Luvah – having stolen the 'Horses of Light' that symbolise Urizen's potency – is destroyed and transformed into lights for Urizen's world.

This pairing of destruction with creativity, which becomes increasingly important in Blake's works, recalls Enion's earlier destruction and reweaving of Tharmas. The parallel events reveal Blake's disturbing belief that creativity is always closely tied to destruction and suggest a negative view of human development. Tharmas represents total body sensuality; Enion's destruction of him as she makes the world suggests a comparable psychological phenomenon: a developing infant's awareness of his separateness, which involves a loss of global consciousness and polymorphous sensuality. Urizen's destruction of Luvah's body similarly suggests the transformation of sexual libido into creativity.

What Urizen creates is a world akin to the fictional world of Blake's poem. Critics have often characterised Urizen's structuring of chaos as repressive and limiting; what critics have not noticed is Blake's share in Urizen's preoccupations, his emotional closeness to Urizen here. Urizen's actions and reactions in Night II are patterned on Los's actions and reactions in *Los*, and Los is a figure with whom Blake clearly identified. For example, Man's woman-induced weakness parallels Los's sinking under the polypus, while Urizen's defensive building echoes Los's forging of the sun. Both men's activities occur alongside fears of being weakened by the female and of becoming female themselves. Before Urizen starts building, Man is already weakened by Vala. After taking control, Urizen is terrified by Mother Enion's ravening hunger: 'Mighty was the draught of Voidness to draw Existence in' (*FZ* 24:1, E 309). The void draws in and absorbs one's existence here just as milk and sexual potency were drawn in in Night I. Blake shows Urizen, like Los, defending against fears of dissolution or castration by creating hard, permanent objects. Los creates solids; Urizen's first creations are all hard, clearly defined implements of labour: the anvil, loom, plough, harrow, compasses, quadrant and rule.

After Urizen's creation of instruments, Blake describes Vala tending the furnace enclosing Luvah. This episode illustrates graphically Urizen's reasons for fearing his impulses – they may lead to destruction – and suggests the impulses' incestuous nature. Vala tending her furnace, 'forgetful' of who Luvah is, illustrates maternal unfaithfulness and collaboration with the punishing, repressive father. Vala's own sufferings are, in part, a punishment for her betrayal of Luvah, first with Man and then with Urizen. Her failure to recognise Luvah is at best only a surface exoneration. Blake's illustration (*V* 32) suggests that she is basically false and far more sinister than Urizen: she appears naked, hiding her genitals with her hand, while a sister female hides a closed fist behind her back.

From within the furnace, Luvah describes his relationship with Vala. Vividly depicting fears of being drained and weakened by the female, he also indicates a desire to give birth (as Tharmas was to have done in the fragment). In a fantastic reversal of the natural situation, Luvah sees himself as a male mother whose resources are drained by Vala, a greedy female infant. Vala grows progressively more monstrous, draining all his world's sources of nourishment and forcing him to open 'all the floodgates of the heavens to quench her thirst' (*FZ* 26:14, E 311).

The similarities between being a mother drained by her infant and being a man drained by a woman's sexual demands is explored in the four marginal illustrations (*V* 26 – Illus. 61). The first sketch of a flying woman with butterfly wings developed eventually into the asexual Jerusalem, but here her whole body suggests a voracious sexual organ: her frizzy hairdo resembles pubic hair, and Blake gives her a huge (erased) vulva. In the next figure the wings have become those of a bat, and the woman rides a penis and scrotum (complete with pubic hair). Below her is a woman with a phallically dangerous beak, scaly tail, and clearly defined vulva. The woman, in fact, seems to be absorbing the man's penis and becoming a phallic woman or woman–serpent. This conclusion appears in the final illustration of a huge dragon with a woman's head, a serpent's neck, and bat wings.

Illus. 61   From *Vala* manuscript

She has three breasts, the last ambiguously placed on her lower abdomen, and a long scaly tail.[11]

In the conclusion of Luvah's speech, Vala as a dragon is mysteriously transformed into a 'weeping Infant'. Again Luvah nurtures her 'in [his] bosom', but this time she grows into a jealously guarded sexual object hid 'in soft gardens & in secret bowers' (*FZ* 27:5, E 311). The double view of Vala as insatiable monster and as vulnerable woman corresponds to Night I's double view of the infant twins. As in earlier poems, there is no middle ground, but a constant swing from tyrant to victim. This swing, which can also be seen as a split into all good and all bad images, expresses strong ambivalence. Luvah puts his finger on the problem when he speaks of the chaos-producing 'Discordant principles of Love & Hate' and describes his own painfully mixed emotions: 'I suffer affliction / Because I love. for I was love but hatred awakes in me' (*FZ* 27:13–14, E 311).

Luvah tries to rationalise his hatred toward 'Man' by seeing himself as a saviour rescuing men from the bondage of the human form. With the concept of collective brotherhood, rebellion no longer makes sense as it did against a tyrant father; now it becomes rebellion against a unified self. Although not elaborated here, Blake's view of rebellion has changed from his earlier prophetic endorsement of it to seeing it more traditionally as the original sin. Blake's developing solution to father–son conflict depended on men sharing as brothers, equally gratified. Luvah, however, continues to think in the old way, 'reasoning from the loins', and so his rebellious body is reduced to building material.

All of Blake's images of world-building, in fact, suggest the desiring body's concomitant containment or destruction. Enion's manipulation of Tharmas's body, for example, is replayed here by the 'weak' who spin the heavenly threads and draw out the cords. Blake's illustration (*V* 29) shows a naked woman holding a net to trap spirits and 'bind them, condensing the strong energies into little compass' (*FZ* 30:5, E 313) – a punishment for too much desire. In contrast to the bound spirits, the lovers Los and Enitharmon are still able, much to Urizen's envy, to contract or expand their 'all flexible senses'. Their other activities, however, reinforce the theme of murderous mother, with Enitharmon playing the rejecting mother and Los her frustrated son. Los, weak and abandoned ('poor forsaken Los'), is mocked by insect siblings while vainly trying to embrace the elusive Enitharmon. Refusing him her sustaining presence, Enitharmon taunts him with his rival Urizen, who possesses her, leaving Los only the unresponsive 'body of death'. At the same time, Enitharmon is furiously jealous of Los's desire for other women. To trick him, she takes the shape of Urizen's wife and of Los's mother Enion and then rebukes him for desiring them.[12]

The rich pageant of incestuous rivalries and loves is followed by Enitharmon's triumphant song, 'The joy of woman is the Death of her most best beloved / Who dies for Love of her' (*FZ* 34:63–4, E 317). The lyric's Romantic sadism contrasts with the sexual generosity of Blake's earlier heroine, Oothoon. Blake alludes to Oothoon by incorporating her climactic lines about 'infant joy' into Enitharmon's song.[13] The contrast between the two women is summed up in their reaction to rivals. Oothoon nets other girls for her lover's satisfaction; Enitharmon drives them away. The pale Lilly and reddening Rose, who defend Los against Enitharmon, echo the earlier girls of mild silver and furious gold netted by Oothoon.

Enion's lament and the illustration (*V* 35 – Illus. 62) that end the original Night show contrasting images of the innocent, afflicted and the castrating mother. The illustration shows the body-destroying mother: women pluck vegetated phalluses and put them in a basket. In contrast, Enion's lament, here as in Night I, shows the mother punished and suffering. Enion assumes blame for harming children and helping thieves instead. Her repentance allows a sympathetic merger between afflicted mother and suffering son and enables her to speak some of Blake's most profound and beautiful poetry:

> What is the price of Experience do men buy it for a song
> Or wisdom for a dance in the street? No it is bought with
>   the price
> Of all that a man hath his house his wife his children
> Wisdom is sold in the desolate market where none come to
>   buy
> And in the witherd field where the farmer plows for bread
>   in vain.
>
> (FZ 35:11–15, 318)

Blake's Christian and socio-political additions to Night II, although not as significant or as extensive as those to Night I, introduce similar explanatory and structuring concepts. His changes

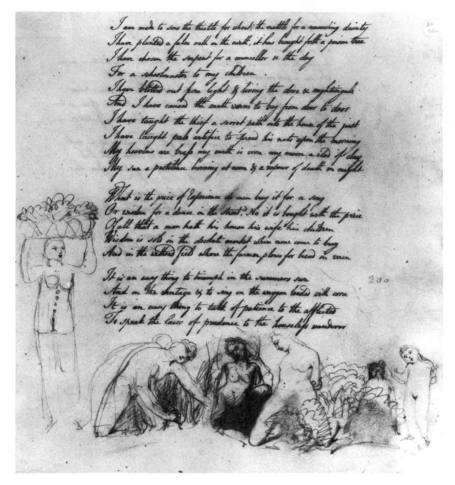

Illus. 62   From *Vala* manuscript

here, although satisfying his teleological needs, diminish Urizen's connections with the artist and make his character less complex and sympathetic. When Jesus is retrospectively introduced to justify Urizen's world-building as part of a redemptive scheme, Blake seemingly transfers Urizen's good qualities to Jesus, while simultaneously darkening his picture of Urizen's world, paralleling its structure to oppression in religion, industry, science and politics. Although Blake's social insights are often illuminating, I think he loses more than he gains by breaking down Urizen's complex portrait as anxious but creative builder of a golden world and remoulding him as a villain.[14]

NIGHT III

Night III begins after Urizen's world is built. By creating something hard, separate and ordered, Urizen exemplified one way of defending against fears of dissolution: he reinforced feelings of potency and control. Now, examining Urizen's way of coping more closely, Blake finds it ineffectual. Woman's destructiveness is not neutralised; if anything, she becomes most powerful when she seems most submissive. She undermines Urizen's system of tightly controlled impulse in two ways. First, she sets man against man as rivals for her favours; second, she directly drains man's power through the sexual act. She succeeds because Urizen's seeming sublimation of impulse in Night II was not a real transformation but a repression. Furthermore, Luvah's burning is motivated by hostility and fear. That Urizen's world rests on the destruction of a rival's body necessarily perpetuates the cycles of retaliation. Thus the first shadow in Urizen's world is the threatened retaliation of Luvah reborn as Orc. As in earlier books, fighting between son and father is seen as the mother's fault. Encouraging both sides, she persistently divides and weakens the males.

Critics have defended Urizen's consort, Ahania, and criticised Urizen for exiling her in Night III.[15] I would suggest, however, that Blake's ambivalent portrayal of her, joined with his striking visual illustration of female destructiveness, indicates that on some level Urizen's fears of Ahania are justified. At the outset of Night III, for example, Blake compares Ahania to the traitoress Delila[h]. Delila[h]'s speech, 'Thus, in false tears, she bath'd his feet . . . he seemed a mountain, his brow among the clouds; she seemed a silver stream, his feet embracing . . . "what shouldst thou [Samson] fear? Thy power is more than mortal, none can hurt thee"' (E 435) is strikingly similar to Ahania's opening lament:

> O Urizen look on Me. like a mournful stream
> I Embrace round thy knees & wet My bright hair with
>   my tears:
> Why sighs my Lord! are not the morning stars thy
>   obedient Sons
> Do they not bow their bright heads at thy voice?
> . . . .

Why wilt thou look upon futurity darkning present joy.
(*FZ* 37:2–10, E 319)

Although Ahania sounds dutiful and loving, the illustration (*V* 37) shows her tenuously controlled by Urizen, who presses a clawed foot on her neck. What Urizen fears is his wife's collaboration with the rebel son – 'O bright [Ahania] a Boy is born of the dark Ocean . . . & that Prophetic boy / Must grow up to command his Prince' (*FZ* 38:2–7, E 319–20) – and the rest of Blake's myth shows that he is correct.

The highly erased illustrations (*V* 38) visualise in sexual terms this conflict between Urizen and a threatening usurper. In the left margin Urizen appears as pure phallic power: he has a tubelike body with 'a pointed phallic tip to which a human head was somehow attached'.[16] In the large illustration (Illus. 63) Urizen appears in a bloated, effeminate form. He embraces Ahania from behind, apparently ejaculating; Ahania, instead of attending to Urizen, watches his rival, Orc, who is engaged in some activity (presumably sexual; the figure's genital and buttocks area is highly erased) of his own. Possibly Blake had a conscious allegorical meaning in mind here; nevertheless, it is difficult to deny the illustration's primitive sexuality.

In Blake's narrative, Ahania reacts to Urizen's fears of future usurpation by blaming him for giving his original rival, Luvah, control of 'the Horses of Light'.[17] After taunting him with their being out of control, she relates her version of Man's fall. Here, too, she notes Urizen's failures: he was asleep when Man, besieged by Vala, looked up for guidance. She describes the fall as the result of Man's succumbing to Vala's 'deluding dreams', but the illustration suggests instead a sexual act that drains potency. In the illustration, Vala is seated and Man, with a long hoselike phallus, crouches between her legs (*V* 39). Grant speculates that this might have been a scene of fellatio.[18] If so, it would unite earlier imagery of draining the breast with an explicit image of draining the phallus.

This Ur scene of woman weakening Man (*V* 39 – Illus. 64) is watched by the children, Los and Enitharmon. Enitharmon reacts with alarm and Los with an erection (which was subsequently erased). There is no need to speculate about this symbolising a primal scene and the young child's reaction, because Blake represents it with utmost clarity. The child's confused perception of the act – both his confusion about his parents' sexual identity and his idea that the

Illus. 63 From *Vala* manuscript

male has lost his penis – is suggested by Blake's drawing of an enormous phallic object with facial features and swellings, which could represent either scrotum or female breasts. As a phallic female, this figure is a bizarre variant of the female–dragon.[19]

Blake's subsequent illustration (*V* 40), which continues to relate Man's fall to the insatiable female who drains his power, also suggests how a child might have observed the penis's disappearance: Man, spurred on by a winged cupid, penetrates Vala from behind. Ahania's description of Man's fall evades the sexual facts but retains their consequences: Man, tired by his 'walks' with Vala, creates a watery (that is, a female or phallusless) semblance of himself, which he then worships. Illustration and description both portray the moral man as weak or castrated and religion as part of the female's plan to dominate him. And, although Ahania seems sympathetic to Man's

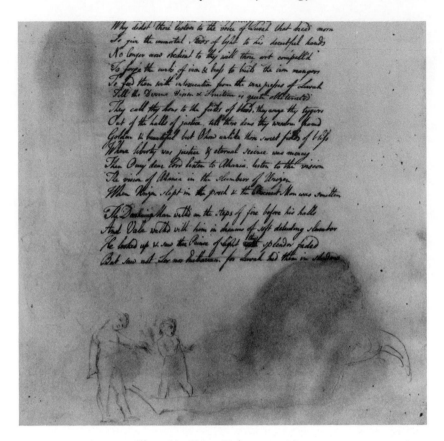

Illus. 64   From *Vala* manuscript

plight – she is 'astonished' to hear him declare his 'nothing-ness' – Blake continues to show woman as the weakening agent. The next illustration (*V* 41 – Illus. 65), for example, shows that the female is willing to destroy Man in order to obtain possession of the phallus. In this illustration Vala bends backward with a lascivious expression. She is being penetrated anally by a huge unattached phallus. Behind her is another man portrayed as a headless, limbless trunk whose phallus she is manipulating with her hands.[20] Grant suggests that Vala is also giving Man syphilis; lines suggesting syphilitic boils appear on the trunk's thighs.[21] There could not be a fuller portrayal of the pestilential mother seducing and destroying her son.

Blake's idea of morality as a symptom of the feminised man is familiar from his early work, but the corresponding idea of liberation

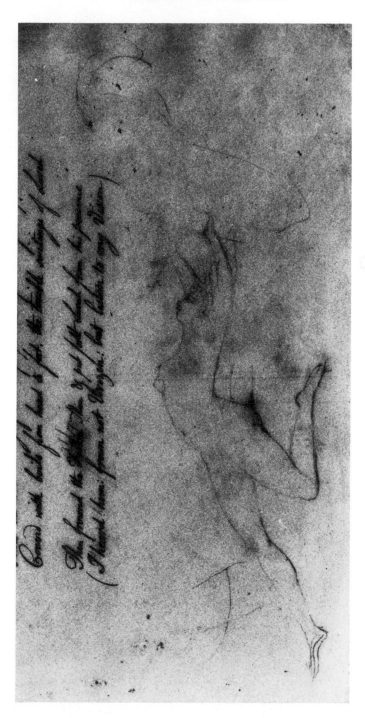

Illus. 65   From *Vala* manuscript

through sexuality has changed. Here it seems impossible because of the female's envious, destructive nature. The sexual urge has become Man's enemy, leading inevitably to disease or mutilation. But Urizen's defensive denial of sexuality is only a further sign of weakness. Attacked by Luvah, who represents both the rival son and Urizen's own desire for the dangerous Vala, Urizen retaliates and initiates a new cycle of conflict. The illustration (*V* 42 – Illus. 66) shows a large woman spanning or manipulating the young Luvah's penis, an action recalling the phallic sibyl's similar gesture in *America*. Here, as there, the action suggests both maternal lust and threat.

Illus. 66   From *Vala* manuscript

The 1797 version of Night III ended here. Blake's additions at first continue the theme of weakening through sex. Urizen accuses Ahania of being like Vala and of threatening him, as Vala did Man, with her 'feminine indolent bliss' and 'darkness of Death' (*FZ* 43:6–7, E 322). The underlying fantasy comes through so forcefully that one feels that Urizen is right and Ahania is insincere, a Delilah. At the same time, the allegorical meaning noted by critics suggests that, in rejecting Ahania, Urizen is mistakenly rejecting an inner component, whether femininity or intellectual passivity, that is necessary for creativity. The two viewpoints are difficult to reconcile and may be a reason for the poem's failure.

Asking himself how Ahania assumed power over him, Urizen answers with a sinister image in which wearying 'labor' symbolically replaces weakening sex. Tired by ploughing, he reposes in her 'deadly' cavern beside her 'dim waters' and wakes, as Los did in *Los*, in nightmare, sinking:

> And thou hast risen with thy moist locks into a watry image
> Reflecting all my indolence my weakness & my death
> To weigh me down beneath the grave into non Entity.
>   (*FZ* 43:17–19, E 322)

Ahania's watery image is a variant of the white polypus that suffocated Los in *The Book of Los* and reintroduces the theme of separation explored in that poem. Urizen, terrified by Ahania, rejects her, and they both fall. This time the fall is described not as a draining, but in terms of the despair of separation from a loved person. Blake suggests an original separation from the mother by making Tharmas, whose total body sensibility and vulnerability are characteristic of infancy, emerge as a result of Urizen's separation from Ahania. Tharmas tries desperately to assume a separate identity: 'Struggling to utter the voice of Man struggling to take the features of Man. . . . at length emerging' (*FZ* 44:18–19, E 323). His pains of individuation are precise verbal echoes of Los's, when in *Los* he separated from the enclosing womblike rock.

> *Los*:   . . . wrath, strug'ling for vent
>   . . . stamping furious to dust
>   And crumbling with bursting sobs . . .
>   (*L* 4:19–21, E 91)

> *Vala:*   . . . gnasshing in fierce dispair . . .
>   . . . bursting sobbing. deep despairing
>   stamping struggling.
>   (*FZ* 44:16–17, E 323)

But, whereas in *Los* Blake emphasised Los's power to deal with separation through creative work, here Tharmas despairs. The illustration (*V* 44) shows Tharmas sinking in the water, his hand raised like the drowning man in *Gates*; above is a crowned naked woman with a Gothic shrine in the place of her genitals. This illustration, in which an aloof woman withholds help from a suffering man, contrasts pointedly with the proofsheet of *Night Thoughts* that follows it, which shows Christ raising Lazarus. Christ, not woman, will be Man's saviour.

Night III's conclusion describes Tharmas's rage at separation from Enion, who vanishes like tears, re-enacting her original desertion. This scene, viewed in conjunction with Night III's other images of separation, suggests that Blake was trying to work through unconscious memories of a cataclysmic separation from the mother. *Los* defended against feelings of loss: by denying any longing for the mother, negatively symbolised as a polypus. In Night III's conclusion Blake goes behind the defences to express the original rage and anguish provoked by separation. Eventually, in his Christian additions to *Vala*, Blake denies the mother's importance definitively by defining the initial separation as not from the mother but from a unity of men. He simultaneously restores the image of a nurturing mother in the Beulians, whose nature is beneficient only because Blake completely transforms it to accord with his fantasy.

NIGHT IV

At the beginning of Night IV, Tharmas is in a near-schizophrenic state of rage against the depriving earth-mother Enion, expressed in terms of oral imagery: 'Like a famishd Eagle Eyeless raging in the vast expanse / Incessant tears are now my food' (*FZ* 47:10–11, E 325). His condition illustrates the woman-produced dissolution feared by Urizen. But, unlike Urizen, Tharmas admits his need and enlists the poet Los's aid to create 'some little semblance' of the lost Enion. In Tharmas's limited vision of a decaying universe, whose wasted inhabitants will mirror his own painful dissolution, death becomes an objective correlative of the original separation.

Tharmas, in his impotent rage, recalls Blake's other deprived and vulnerable infants; Los, in his arrogant behaviour, reminds us of Blake's narcissistic and greedy infants. Like Blake, whose upward spiraling curls he shares, Los is furiously proud. He boasts of having 'drunk up the Eternal Man', threatens Tharmas with his appetite ('Beware lest we also drink up thee rough demon' – FZ 48:14, E 325), and narcissistically maintains that, after Urizen's fall, 'Los remains God'.

Tharmas reacts to Los's threats by stealing Los's sister–wife Enitharmon, thus putting Los into a position exactly like his own. This new separation is described as the wrenching apart of a unified being, a re-enactment of the original dissolution of the mother–child unity, which causes a bleeding wound. Seen from this perspective, the blood spurting from Los's breast in the illustration (V 48) is, like Tharmas's tears, a masochistic substitute for the nourishing milk.[22]

Los's separation from Enitharmon also causes his personality to split into the Eternal Prophet and the Spectre. The ghostlike Spectre embodies individuation's devastating effect on infantile narcissism. He represents imagination that cannot be immediately gratified but must work through the real world.[23] For Blake, the necessity of compromise and delay represents a diminishment equivalent to physical castration. Thus the Spectre is described as depressed, 'blue, obscure & dismal', mutilated or 'bent'. The underlying equation – bent/impotent versus straight/potent – is made clearer by Tharmas's promise to the spectre that his 'spungy marrow' will harden if he will work to return Enitharmon to Los, the Spectre's prophetic alter ego.

Before beginning to work, the Spectre tells about an earlier time when Tharmas was heaven's 'mildest son' and Los was a potent, heavenly blacksmith. A war in heaven changed Tharmas into a hungry vortex. And, in a variation of the hermaphroditic birth, the Spectre's loins dissolved into a 'bloody mass' that became Enitharmon. Although the Spectre is not given female genitals, as Tharmas was in the fragment, he appears weakened or symbolically impotent. Moreover, the male who gives birth seems competitive with the child-bearing female: the Spectre finds himself *and* the newborn Enitharmon in Enion's body. Enion gives birth to Enitharmon and Los while the Spectre, unwilling to be born of woman, issues from Enion's nostrils. The Spectre now occupies the position of a slighted sibling, perhaps an older brother observing the younger getting coveted satisfactions. After hearing this story, Tharmas recognises the mutilated Spectre as his 'old friend' and promises him Enitharmon as his reward for helping Los bind their common enemy, Urizen.

Urizen, paternal denier of impulse, must be bound if Tharmas is to be reunited with Enion. The Spectre obediently forms a 'World' under Los's feet, and this brings back Enitharmon. The wish – exemplified by Tharmas – to restore unity with a mother–bride implicitly conflicts with Blake's developing ideal of a self-sufficient fourfold Man. Tharmas is accordingly presented as Man's enemy: 'The Eternal Man is seald never to be deliverd / I roll my floods over his body' (*FZ* 51:15–16, E 327). The watery 'monsters of the deep' and dreams 'of furious oceans cold' that plague Man echo Tharmas's depressed, watery state at the end of the last Night. And here, despite his declarations of omnipotence and his attempts at rebuilding, Tharmas is still caught in nightmare, striving 'Against the monstrous forms that breed among my silent waves' (*FZ* 51:28, E 328).

Reluctantly, Tharmas urges Los to continue binding Urizen.[24] Blake's description of Urizen's binding is repeated almost verbatim from *Urizen*. Los's motivation is clearer here, however: driven by frustrated desire, Tharmas, he is openly furious about Urizen's relations with Enitharmon.

> . . . absorbd in dire revenge he drank with joy the cries
> Of Enitharmon & the groans of Urizen fuel for his wrath.
> 　　　　　　　　　　　　　　　*(FZ* 53:12–13, E 329)

After the binding, here as in *Urizen* Los becomes paralysed by guilt; his hammer drops and his 'iron sinews bend like lead' (*FZ* 55:30, E 331). In *Urizen*, Los's pity for his victim resulted in Enitharmon's birth. The suggestion that she represented Los's female identification is strengthened by Blake's changes here. Now, instead of having Los give birth to Enitharmon (who already exists), Blake shows Los himself becoming feminised; his body does what Enitharmon's did in the earlier prophecy:

Urizen:　　Fibrous, writhing upon the winds;
　　　　. . . . .

... in tears & cries imbodied
A female form trembling and pale
Waves before his deathy face.
(U 18:3–8, E 77)

Vala: ... his muscular fibres writhing to & fro his pallid lips
Unwilling movd as Urizen howld his loins wavd
like the sea.
(FZ 55:24–5, E 331)

The connection between the two passages is stressed by Blake's marginal note to introduce the earlier Enitharmon passage at this point.[25]

Los's bodily mimicry and identification both with his weakened enemy and with Enitharmon suggest the seizures of a hysteric:

At Enitharmons shriek his knees each other smote & then he
   lookd
With stony Eyes on Urizen & then swift writhd his neck
Involuntary to the Couch where Enitharmon lay
The bones of Urizen hurtle on the wind the bones of Los
Twinge & his iron sinews bend like lead & fold
Into unusual forms dancing & howling stamping the Abyss.
(FZ 55:26–31, E 331)

To avoid guilt over murderous impulses, the hysteric often identifies with a father who is afflicted – like Urizen, bound and impotent.[26] Identification with the suffering mother is also possible and allows him to gratify homosexual impulses: his wish to be loved by the father.[27] Blake's illustration (*V* 56) suggests homosexual seduction: a demonic male figure draws a curly-haired youth forward between his knees.[28] The illustration appears equally suggestive of heterosexual seduction or violence; Grant, for example, thinks it represents Urizen's rape of Enitharmon.[29] Certainly Los's alternate mimicry of Urizen and Enitharmon suggests an involuntary re-enactment of such an event.

Los's identification with his victims also suggests a movement from his original cruel thoughts to feelings of pity. Here Blake presages psychoanalytic findings in which pity, whether merely a shaky reaction formation or a real transformation of the original sadism, is an identification with its object.[30]

In Night IV, then, the world is rebuilt by the desiring senses (Tharmas) and imagination (Los) in order to regain the lost mother. This project necessarily entails rendering 'the enemy' Urizen impotent. Vengeful hostility, in turn, brings Los a guilty identification with both his impotent rival and the faithless partner, Enitharmon. Thus the Night ends with a maddened, feminised Los. The Christian additions specifically combat the idea of feminisation. For, although joining Christ in guarding Man's vegetating body, the women of Beulah are no longer fearful but feeble, unable even to raise their eyes and look at Christ: 'for we are weak women & dare not lift / Our eyes to the Divine pavilions' (*FZ* 56:3–4, E 330). Additionally, Blake reminds us that the women will die periodically, in winter, while Man, like Lazarus, will be raised to new life. Finally, Christ himself intervenes to limit Man's dissolution:

> The Saviour mild & gentle bent over the corse of Death
> Saying If ye will Believe your Brother shall rise again
> And first he found the Limit of Opacity & namd it Satan
> In Albions bosom for in every human bosom these limits stand
> And next he found the Limit of Contraction & namd it
>   Adam.
>
> (FZ 56:17–21, E 331)

In this passage the Christian imagery clearly functions to stave off fear of identification with the female by presenting an alternate identification with the ideal figure of a risen Christ, combining an acceptable gentleness with masculine power.

NIGHT V

In Night V the cycles of retaliation continue, now explicitly connected with Oedipal rivalry and observation of a primal scene. Orc is born, lusts for his mother, and is bound by his father Los. Blake begins the Night with Los still in the seizure into which he was thrown by his observation of Urizen and Enitharmon. The sadistically perceived nature of what he observed is suggested by the *Night*

Thoughts illustration Blake chose as visual background for his text: a demonic Nimrod watches gloatingly as his dogs attack a naked youth bent voluptuously backward beneath them. A literal primal scene is depicted in a preliminary drawing for the illustration (*V* 58) of Orc intently watching his mother Enitharmon being mounted by Los. Orc's oddly elongated fingers held against his mouth suggest that he reacts with a regressive form of autoerotic activity. His other hand is secretively held behind his back, the gesture Blake used to denote a liar. Perhaps he will deny his nocturnal observations like *Visions'* youthful virgin. The psychological point of Blake's opening text and illustration is that man's fallen state arises from the archetypal parents' intercourse, which, arousing the observer's desire and fear, sets in motion a cycle of act and retaliation. Los's seizure imitates both the original act and the ensuing 'fall' with its spasmatic contractions of the world and Man's body. Blake structures events here by developing the various meanings of 'contraction' which are implicit in Los's contractive seizure:[31] contraction in the sense of restricting energy (as in Urizen's binding); contraction in the sense of limiting the body and senses; and contraction in the sense of birth-pains.

After the illustrated primal scene, Enitharmon gives birth, just as Enion did earlier after the rape. An accompanying demon song fixes responsibility for father–son violence on the seductive mother, Vala, to be reborn as pestilential virgin war-goddess. Blake's juxtaposition of the song with his *Night Thoughts* illustration of Christ pierced by nails suggests that, as castrating mother, she is responsible for the crucifixion too. The mother's responsibility (by merely existing) for Oedipal conflict and thus for her son's eventual mutilation is shown clearly in the next episode, which explicitly develops Orc's incestuous love for Enitharmon:

> But when fourteen summers & winters had revolved over
> Their solemn habitation Los beheld the ruddy boy
> Embracing his bright mother & beheld malignant fires
> In his young eyes discerning plain that Orc plotted his death.
> (*FZ* 60:6–9, E 334)

The illustration (*V* 60) shows Orc no longer a boy, as in *Urizen*, but a naked youth who kisses and embraces Enitharmon, entwining his legs with hers while Los kneels, bound by jealousy, and regards them desperately. A hole in his wrist links him as a victim of sexual jealousy to Christ crucified.[32]

Los reacts to his torment by nailing Orc down to a rock. Enitharmon clearly sides with her son (as Urizen feared Ahania would) and does not help repress him. Most of this is familiar from *Urizen*, but Blake adds a significant event: when his son is still too young to be a menace, Los attempts to forestall Oedipal conflict by building Golgonooza around Enitharmon to hide her. Golgonooza's inclusion of a symbolic replica of the female organs, Luban's gates,[33] suggests that the city of art, although developing from a wish for exclusive possession of the mother's body, eventually re-creates that body in a form that is under the creator's control.

Los fails to halt conflict, however, and Orc is bound. Blake clearly sympathises with Orc, and Orc's frustrated incestuous desire ('Storgous Appetite') stimulates a moving paean to the omnipotent imagination. Orc's imaginative power is clearly related to his frustrated impulses. It not only satisfies his basic needs for food and sensual pleasure 'to quell his ceaseless rage' but also permits him entry into Vala's 'hidden things'. In a sense, imagination duplicates the self-sufficient state of primal narcissism before the infant's separation from its mother: Orc's body is a complete world. Paradoxically, however, though imagination appears self-sufficient, its use leads to aggressive action in the world. Orc's invulnerable strength, symbolised by his 'adamant knees', is linked to armed spirits of war. Like Freud's id, Orc wants satisfaction at any cost.

Los, on the contrary, transforms or sublimates desire in accord with 'higher' values. Overcoming jealousy, he decides to free Orc and return him to Enitharmon 'Even if his own death resulted so much pity him paind' (*FZ* 62:20, E 335). Guilty identification with the victim seems to have moved to a higher plane: it leads to compassionate action, not paralysis. But Orc's release is impossible; the chain of jealousy has become part of Orc's body, allowing his energy to function only at certain allowed centres.[34]

Blake's attitude toward this incorporation of repressive strictures is highly ambiguous. On the one hand, Blake suggests, as he did in earlier prophecies, that energy should be free. He amplifies this idea cosmologically by identifying the restricting father with Newton's universal laws. His dual critique of a world of obedient 'forces' and repressed desires is distorted by the assumption that an unrestricted state is desirable or possible. On the other hand, as Blake himself sees, desire in its unfettered Orcian state would not be benevolent. Blake's illustrations, for example, show seemingly inescapable cycles of destructive Oedipal conflict. In one (V 62) Los and Enitharmon look at Orc splayed out on the ground. Fibres, or what Grant calls 'influence lines',[35] join them to him. A facing *Night Thoughts* illustration (V 63) shows the infant at his mother's bared breast, his body malevolently spanned by his paternal rival's hand. There seems no escape from this endless cycle without outside help. Los fails to release Orc; Urizen, Los's arch-enemy, wakes, and Vala too begins to reanimate within Enitharmon. That she does so now seems to emphasise woman's responsibility for Man's continuing torment.

When Urizen wakes he relates a new version of the fall in which he, like his rival Luvah, covets another male's power or possessions: Urizen gives Luvah the 'steeds of Light', which he has jealously refused 'the Lord', in exchange for 'wine of the Almighty'. The Oedipal triangle appears yet again in the illustration on V 64. Although Los has trapped an unwary 'fish' in his nets, his real quarry is free: behind Los's shoulders Orc kisses his mother, Enitharmon, who arches backward toward him, manipulating his large erect phallus. Seemingly, no matter how successfully the father binds the son or the son the father, incestuous desire continues to initiate new cycles of action.

NIGHT VI

In Night VI Urizen again takes the central position he had in Night II. Disturbed by Orc's libidinous struggle to break free, Urizen seeks reassurance by surveying his dens, which, unlike the earlier golden world, represent Blake's own eighteenth-century world. There, instead of reassurance, Urizen finds everywhere signs of conflict and alienation that suggest reason's failure to solve the problem of need-satisfaction. The action itself begins with a symbolic depiction of maternal deprivation: three threatening females refuse to let Urizen drink from their stream. By juxtaposing this event with his description of alienation in reason's world, Blake suggests a psychological explanation for it: man's alienation from himself and from nature is a result of earlier deprivation.[36] Possibly feelings or memories of deprivation influenced Blake's own ideas of a delusive and untrustworthy nature that seduces and disappoints. At any rate, both Tharmas (in Night IV) and Urizen have been hurt by female nature, but they react differently. Urizen becomes aloof or abstract, while Tharmas admits his need and, with Los, tries to recover the lost mother.[37] When Tharmas encounters Urizen in Night VI, he becomes desperate at Urizen's mode of coping and proposes mutual suicide. He will not allow his instinctive force to be drawn into defensive uses, 'food' for Urizen, because then he will not have a chance to recover Enion.

Urizen's primary defence not only against the frightening phantasms he sees in his survey but also against his own depression and objective social evils is to witness and record what he sees:

> But still his books he bore in his strong hands & his iron pen
> . . . .
> Time after time for such a journey none but iron pens
> Can write And adamantine leaves receive nor can the man
>   who goes
> The journey obstinate refuse to write time after time.
> (FZ 71:35–42, 72:1, E 342)

In obsessively recording painful visions, Urizen resembles Blake. In his subsequent fall and attempted organisation of the elements, Urizen also resembles Los, although Urizen is more passive and depends on a nurturing Christ. Blake indicates now that Urizen's world-construction fails to solve the problem of need-satisfaction. Ironically, the void and solid that he creates themselves correspond to psychological states of longing emptiness and fullness. Urizen cannot endure the alternation between them, just as he cannot endure intellectual uncertainty and spontaneous thought.

In fullness, Urizen is painfully aware of his dependence and involvement with his material (feminine) environment. He wants, on the contrary, to be 'self sustaining' and distanced, to have perspective. Plenitude is also unsatisfying because of Urizen's fear of the ensuing emptiness, symbolised by the fact that, wherever he starts from, he has always to climb upward, 'against futurity'. He resembles the man who must repeat his successes, feeling that satisfaction is just out of reach. His equally painful experience of the void repeats the original trauma of separation and fall: he falls through the void until he reaches a clay bosom provided by Christ and begins again as an infant. His real wish is to 'leave this world of Cumbrous wheels'

(*FZ* 72:22, E 342) and find a state of equilibrium 'where his life might meet repose' (*FZ* 72:21, E 342). He recalls, in an Edenic childhood, experiencing such a peaceful state, combining mental and sensual pleasure, 'Where joy sang in the trees . . . & sweet friendship met in palaces / And books & instruments of song' (*FZ* 72:39, 73:2–3, E 343). Nostalgia for the past stimulates him to form a new world 'better suited to obey / His will'. His suppressed need for security and care is transformed into a need to control others. Yet his web, later named 'Web of Religion', functions as the mother once did; it connects the voids and vortexes just as the mother (or her image) connects the child's experiences of emptiness and satiation to a single person. The web is accordingly defined (in *Urizen*) as the 'female in embrio'. Unlike the good mother, who makes tension bearable for the child by giving it memories of satisfaction, the web drains man's powers through guilt, just as Vala drained him physically. As Urizen's web grows, Man's eyes contract and his weblike eyelids block visions of eternity. Blake suggests that the web of guilt blocks both creativity and the sight of the primal scene; the eyes' anguished vibrations resemble Los's imitative fit and evoke the parents' quivering limbs once observed or imagined in intercourse.

Blake's image of a female Web of Religion meshes with images of the web of cold, Newtonian necessity. Both webs negatively replace experiences of joy and 'basic trust' that once unified the world. Urizen's memories of 'the once glorious heaven' evoke such experience. Blake, in describing them, reverses the evolution of mental constructs out of sensual experience; abstract nouns, like 'innocence' and 'laughter', become gambolling children. The pastoral world of play and relationship contrasts with Urizen's world of heroic posturing. The love that creates and binds relationships is missing. Sensing its lack, Urizen seeks instinctual 'food' from Tharmas and attempts to find Orc, the missing energy. But, having denied his basic needs for so long, he feels that desire, in both its infant and its adolescent forms, is his enemy. The night ends with an image of his search and his conflict: Tharmas and Los's hostile Spectre confront Urizen as he seeks Orc.

NIGHT VIIa

Having again shown reason's failure either to satisfy basic needs or to renounce satisfaction, Blake now confronts Urizen with his repressed desire: Urizen enters Orc's caves. What he sees suggests that repression of sexual need makes it break out in war:

> The plow of ages & the golden harrow wade thro fields
> Of goary blood the immortal seed is nourishd for the slaughter.
> (FZ 77:14–15, E 346)

Rebellion, although expressing desire destructively, yearns for satisfaction. Orc's spirit symbolically consummates incest by entering his mother's 'shrine'. Urizen reacts with jealousy and repressive laws, but he is also studiously curious about his enemy. He observes that Orc's physical torments are external manifestations of inner states of rage (fiery arrows) and depression (stifling waves). Urizen instructs Orc in denial, but he cannot help wondering what 'visions of delight' sustain Orc in the tortures of deprivation and rage and despair, visions

> . . . so lovely that they urge thy rage
> Tenfold with fierce desire to rend thy chain & howl in fury
> . . . .
> Or is thy joy founded on torment which others bear for thee.
> (FZ 78:38–41, E 347)

The coexistence of joy and pain evokes Urizen's contrary need for 'a joy without pain', a need that made him create a solid, mechanically organised universe. The illustration (V 78) suggests an equation between painful tension and sexual frustration: a naked man with large genitals lies rigidly, his back uncomfortably arched. The implication is that Urizen has accustomed himself to deprivation until he no longer feels desire, but sits 'grovelling . . . In tortures of dire coldness' (FZ 79:3–4, E 347). Like Orc he endures his torments obdurately, but takes refuge from them not in fantasy but in an increase of intellectual activity; he writes:

> Thundring & hail & frozen iron haild from the Element
> Rends thy white hair yet thou dost fixd obdurate brooding sit
> Writing thy books. . . .
> (FZ 79:9–11, E 347)

To enforce Orc's submission to his teachings, Urizen asks his daughters to deny Orc food. Blake effectively compares Urizen's attempt to control Orc through deprivation to the attempt by society's rulers to starve the poor into submission.[38] Blake's condemnation of Urizen's attitude is balanced by his unconscious understanding of Urizen's fear of being devoured himself. Urizen's speech links the hungry poor with the insatiable, devouring woman who causes perpetual conflict between men: he fears that Enitharmon's 'devouring appetite' for sex and power will force Los to 'ambitious fury' and, presumably, rebellion. But, with his increased focus in revision on social evils, Blake tends to diminish Urizen's inner complexity and make him a stereotypical villain somehow responsible for life's evils.

Possibly Blake's current problems with his patron, Hayley, who urged him to neglect his visions and work for money, influenced his negative revisions of Urizen's character. Blake first perceived Hayley as a nurturer, bearing wine and bread from heaven. Later, Blake saw him in the role of seductive mother professing sympathy while manipulating him through his basic needs. Urizen offers Orc correspondingly tainted food: bread kneaded on clouds which suggest the breast but offer icy rain instead of milk. Urizen assumes the coldness that is a key attribute of the rejecting mother. Urizen's 'cold attractive power' evokes the seductive force of Blake's various icy temptresses. Simultaneously, Newton's world-view with its impersonal forces is drawn into Blake's own complex of associations and given a strongly negative emotional charge.

Despite Blake's increasingly aggressive attack on Newton, however, the main issues continue to be psychological. Orc, weakened by his need, becomes meekly compliant: 'Like a worm I rise in peace unbound / From wrath' (FZ 80:29–30, E 349). But even as an obedient worm infant he recalls the alternative possibilities of rebellion and theft. Blake understands that anger makes it difficult to enjoy what has been stolen. Thus Orc's envious rage will not permit him to use Urizen's stolen light constructively: 'Despising Urizens light & turning it into flaming fire ... A Self consuming dark devourer' (FZ 80:45–8, E 349). Remembering his envious crime, Orc develops a serpent body. Urizen, standing in for the paternal god who created the original tempting situation in Eden, makes Orc climb the Tree of Mystery. There his mother Enitharmon's shadow weeps over him; in Blake's revisionism, incestuous love becomes the archetypal temptation.

Los's jealousy completes the story: Enitharmon is cold with him but 'ruddy as a morning' when she returns from her gratifying visits to his rival, presumably Orc. Los broods obsessively, as Urizen did in *The Book of Ahania* when threatened by Fuzon. In both cases, thinking is depicted as a type of anal birth, and there is a turn to sadistic cruelty. Failure or frustration of desire, whether of father or son, leads in this model to regression, first from thwarted sexuality to anal sadism and its corresponding intellectual manifestation – obsessive thought – and then to cannibalistic fantasies. Los's sexual frustration is expressed in imagery of oral deprivation and rage: his winged woes sit 'on barren rocks / And whet their beaks & snuff the air . . . And Shriek till at the smells of blood they stretch their boney wings' (*FZ* 82:11–13, E 350).[39]

There are many parallels in Night VII (as in earlier Nights) between the characters' repetitive actions and a developing child's repeated struggles to gain satisfaction. Orc, physically bound but omnipotent in thought, resembles the child or adolescent whose power is limited by his parents' will and his own body's capabilities. Orc's helplessness against Urizen's pressure suggests the child's emotional dependence: Orc's basic need for food and care enforces conformity. His rebellion and lust for his mother illustrate the child's Oedipal strivings repeated in adolescence. Finally, Los's jealousy not only shows the situation from the father's viewpoint but also suggests how failure in the Oedipal struggle leads to regression and sadism.

In keeping with Blake's revisionism, sexual rivalry now results in Man's fall. The shining fruit 'of many colours & of various poisonous qualities' (*FZ* 80:21, E 350) that appears as Orc climbs the tree suggests the pestilential mother – intoxicating perhaps, but deadly. Los's spectral alter ego distracts Enitharmon from her preoccupation with Orc by getting her to describe the original fall instead. Her words describing Man and Vala's intercourse substitute for her interrupted contact with Orc and are followed by the birth of a surrogate Vala. Enitharmon's story stresses woman's part in initiating hatred between the men. Vala's responsibility for Oedipal conflict is shown by having her generate both the repressive Urizen (as her son) and Luvah–Orc (as a split-off part of herself). Their fraternal union to bind their father is another variation of the primal crime.

Blake's constant fabrication of new genealogies enables each character to play different parts in the Oedipal conflict: sister, mother, son, father, brother, husband.[40] For example, Vala reborn from Enitharmon after her 'conversation' with the Spectre becomes Orc's sister and caretaker – Enitharmon's surrogate. The Night ends with Los again traumatised by a primal scene: Enitharmon gives birth to Vala while Los watches her, terrified and not understanding the cause of her spasmodic movements. In the final lines a new cycle begins as Vala takes charge of Orc.

In a long addition to this Night, Los draws closer to his Spectre, attempting to heal the woman-induced split between men. The Spectre, talking with Enitharmon, had already put her in her place, informing her that woman was once only a part of man, a source of pleasure, not trouble. Now, Los approaches the Spectre 'as a brother' or 'another Self' with whom he can share sexual rights: 'In Self abasement Giving up his Domineering lust' (FZ 85:29–31, E 353). But once again woman perversely exerts her will: Enitharmon flees to Los's rival, Urizen.

Unable to attain harmony, Los (like Blake) must now create a model of it through art; he constructs Golgonooza. Golgonooza, once begun as a fortress to seclude Enitharmon, now becomes a place where Los accepts her nurturing of others: he creates bodies for the dead, who then repose as infants on her bosom. This acceptance of infant rivals is a redemptive contrast to Los's binding of Orc and alleviates Orc's suffering. Los's new willingness to 'sacrifice' his desires makes creation of a body appear as a benevolent act instead of a vengeful punishment. Los's previous rage-filled creation of Urizen's body was equivalent to binding. Now, finding his enemy in his hands awaiting new form, 'he wondered that he felt love & not hate / His whole soul loved him he beheld him an infant' (FZ 90:65–7, E 357). Orc, too, gains benevolence through identification with the new Los: 'As the Eldest brother is the fathers image So Orc became / As Los a father to his brethren' (FZ 90:47–8, E 356). Blake recognises here that jealous hatred of one's brother (or son) at the breast and one's father is absolutely central to the human condition. Consequently, in order to achieve a state of harmony, Blake now feels that human nature itself must be changed through religious ideals of self-sacrifice, love and forgiveness. In this way Blake uses the Christian ideal of brotherhood to solve, at least imaginatively, problems of jealousy and envy.[41]

NIGHT VIIb

Night VIIb was written after VIIa and seems inferior to it imaginatively.[42] Its central events are Orc's rape of Vala and war with the repressive Urizen. Vala here vengefully leagues with the repressors and takes pleasure in the sight of father and son killing each other, smiling like the pestilential mother in *Tiriel*. The imagery of the rape itself, in which Orc mingles with Vala's 'dolorous members' and yet remains serpentine, echoes Enion's transformation into a serpent–woman in Night I. Although Blake still portrays male–female hostility here, he distances it, denying his most terrifying fears through a combination of allegorisation and revision. First of all, the female's absorption of the male is denied; Orc as proud serpent among Urizen's stars resembles the potent and boastful Tharmas *before* he rapes Enion. Admittedly, Orc loses something, but now it is the human form, not the phallus. The act itself becomes less sexual and frightening by being given greater allegorical weight, so that, for example, Vala can 'represent' Europe rent by war.[43] Similarly, Vala's vortex no longer directly represents the retaliating cannibalistic mother as it did with Enion, but is a representation and rejection of Descartes's mechanistic system.

It is hard to determine how much of Blake's rejection of scientific theory was based on a rational understanding of its defects and how much was based on his emotional apprehension of the theory as a threat to his and Man's omnipotence. But whatever lay behind the intellectual meanings Blake gives the central events and images, it is the emotional correspondences that tie together his narrative. The fact that Vala's rape is a variation of Enion's, even though the most fearful elements have been denied, generates the next episode: Tharmas appears and mistakes Vala for Enion. Vala tries to induce guilt (as she did earlier with Orc) and despair in order to tame Tharmas. She is at once a 'howling' woman and the representation of Tharmas's self-destructive feelings of betrayal. As oppressive melancholy or depression, Blake identifies Vala with the clinging polypus. Her effect is counteracted by the Daughters of Beulah, whose assertion of faith in man's resurrection ends the revised Night.

In the Night's earlier ordering, Urizen's megalomaniac idea that he is God defends against guilty melancholy.[44] Blake here suggests the defensive uses of authority: the more anxiously vulnerable Urizen becomes, the more he asserts his power over others and attempts to guard his sexual authority in a religion that excludes the worshippers from 'The hidden wonders allegoric of the Generations / Of secret lust' (FZ 96:4–5, E 393). Understandably, Urizen's attempts fail, and the Night ends as Los and Tharmas prepare for war.

NIGHT VIII

This Night, which was written very late, clearly aligns Christian concepts against threatening fantasy, particularly the fear of dissolution: God's Council sets a 'Limit of Contraction' beyond which man cannot fall. This limit, personified in Adam, reassures us that the male will not dissolve or be femalised. The female agent of dissolution is countered here by Christ pictured as the ideal mother: Man 'reposd / In the saviours arms, in the arms of tender mercy & loving kindness' (FZ 99:13–14, E 357). Blake's narrative makes it clear, however, that, while female nature exists unchanged, Man is in danger. Vala remains a threat. With 'sweet / Delusive cruelty' she seduces the 'dead' away from Beulah's good mothers into our world, Ulro.

Christ not only assumes the role of good mother; he also becomes the passionate but good son, appropriating Luvah's body. Blake accordingly makes Orc ever more negative, emphasising the fact that his 'badness' results from poisonous food fed him by the treacherous mother, Vala:

> . . . Still Orc devourd the food
> In raging hunger Still the pestilential food in gems & gold
> Exuded round his awful limbs Stretching to serpent length
> His human bulk. . . .
>
> (FZ 101:17–20, E 359)

Urizen also becomes a more negative figure – a warmonger and hypocrite. The extent to which Urizen's ghastly war-machines defend against fears of castration is suggested by his confrontation with Satan, whose hermaphroditism recalls the threat of feminisation symbolised by Tharmas as hermaphrodite.

> The Soldiers namd it Satan but he was yet unformed & vast
> Hermaphroditic it at length became hiding the Male

Within as in a Tabernacle Abominable Deadly.
                                    (*FZ* 101:35–7, E 359)

Urizen's reaction indicates failure effectively to counter such threats: in a paranoid escalation of conflict, he gives his war-machines life, in order to 'avert / His own despair even at the cost of everything that breathes' (*FZ* 102:21–2, E 360).

Simultaneously, Urizen continues writing repressive moral codes, and again repression plays into the hands of the female: Vala absorbs Urizen's codes and 'enormous Sciences', because they help her to subjugate Man.[45] Absorbing his ideals, Vala turns Urizen's own defensive strategies against him. She weighs down Urizen's net with 'tears', symbolising his guilt and depression, and traps him in a cycle of 'sorrow lust repentance' (*FZ* 103:31, E 361).

Now, when Urizen has in essence undergone the weakening feminisation he feared, Blake introduces Jerusalem, a 'Universal female form', as a neutralising counterpart to Vala. Christ appears as a lamb (that is, an innocent child) beneath Jerusalem's veil, just as Tharmas first appeared beneath Vala's (or Enion's). In an accompanying song by Eden's sons, Blake stresses the fact that this positive transformation, both of the nature of mother and son and of their relations, is impossible without external help: 'life Eternal / Depends alone upon the Universal hand & not in us / Is aught but death In individual weakness' (*FZ* 104:8–10, E 361–2).

Good and bad forces are now clearly split: Christ, Los with Enitharmon, Jerusalem and Beulah against Orc's angry desire, Urizen's desperate defences, and Vala's deluding seductiveness. Satan's character is developed as the final form of the defensively judging, Urizenic mind. Blake Christianises his earlier retaliatory cycles, absorbing them into a redemptive pattern: Satan condemned to death 'as a murderer & robber'. Vala, the evil mother, appears in her final form as the whore of Babylon, now clearly identified with the forbidden 'Fruit of Urizens tree', the poisonous mother-breast.

The support provided by Christian ideas apparently enabled Blake to give full rein to his fantasies of mutilation. Vala's daughters, Rahab and Tirzah, enact a sadistic fantasy of torture. They bind and maim Man to keep him from escaping their influence.

If thou dost go away from me I shall consume upon the rocks
These fibres of thine eyes that used to wander in distant heavens

Away from me I have bound down with a hot iron
These nostrils . . .

. . . .
Go Noah fetch the girdle of strong brass heat it red hot
Press it around the loins of this expanding cruelty
Shriek not so my only love.

(FZ 105:33–46, E 364)

This description is only a more vicious version of Enion's manipulations of Tharmas's fibres. Enion, too, was afraid Tharmas would 'wander away' and attend to other females. But now sadistic acts appear as equivalent to the crucifixion of a Christ who represents all victims of female cruelty. Thus Los closely identifies with Christ; he puts Christ's body in the sepulchre he had 'hewn . . . for himself'.

Urizen, who might be expected to exult at his foe's crucifixion, is terrified by 'the female death'. He seems near realisation that Tirzah and Rahab's tortures represent what he most fears, castration and feminisation. He reacts by displaying male potency, embracing his mother, 'forgetful of his own Laws', and, since he is now expressing forbidden impulses, turning into an Orcian serpent. At the same time, Urizen's controlling defences take final shape: 'A form of Senseless Stone remain in terrors' (*FZ* 106:32, E 367). Urizen becomes paralysed when his ritualistic defences against impulse break down, much as the prepsychotic in similar difficulty becomes catatonic. In this state neither Urizen's humanity nor his laws seem dependent on 'his own power',[46] and the female correspondingly gains strength. Thus, for example, Los's blood-vessels dart from his body forming Enitharmon, and Vala becomes able to create the imprisoning forms of the natural world. The female's tyranny, however, is now tamed by Christ's redemptive scheme, which permits natural forms only so that they 'may be put off' when Man regains his power.

Blake now shows Man at his weakest, attended by Enion and Ahania. Ahania, with seeming sense, urges Urizen to give up his self-destructive masochism ('Will you seek pleasure from the festering wound or marry for a Wife / The ancient Leprosy' – *FZ* 108:13–14, E 369), yet she lingers lugubriously over Man's frightening position: 'His eyes sink hollow in his head his flesh coverd with slime / And shrunk up to the bones' (*FZ* 108:31–2, E 369). Her vision of Man evokes fears of devouring and mutilation: Orc's serpents explicitly attack Man's 'nether parts' while the famished poetic Eagle waits to finish him. Enion's answering speech suggests that male fears can be dissipated by banishing the independent female: 'Behold the time approaches fast that thou shalt be as a thing / Forgotten' (*FZ* 109:29–30, E 370). When Christ returns, the world will be rehumanised as male.

> So Man looks out in tree & herb & fish & bird & beast
> Collecting up the scatterd portions of his immortal body.
> (FZ 110:6–7, E 370)

This Night's first additions emphasise Rahab, the evil mother, while later additions suggest how Christ will undo her evil. Rahab, as Blake portrays her, is thoroughly evil and incapable of repentance. As earlier, it is incestuous desire that initiates retaliatory cycles. Rahab communes with Orc, her lover–son. In revenge, Urizen burns her, but she reanimates in new form.[47] In Blake's last addition, Los, now clearly identified with both Blake and Christ, benignly re-enacts Enion's earlier destructive maternal manipulations: he draws 'into wires the terrific Passions & Affections / Of Spectrous dead' (*FZ* 113:7–8, E 362). But, although Blake tries to control the fantasy of the destructive mother and give it redemptive meaning, woman's independent presence is still threatening. Enitharmon's daughters have a sinister quality. Their spiderlike weaving of the new bodies 'In soft silk drawn from their own bowels in lascivious delight' (*FZ* 113:10, E 362) resembles Rahab and Tirzah's preparation of 'webs of torture'. Only Christ, by offering himself to their knife and perpetually redeeming men, can oppose them.

NIGHT IX

This Night's rewritten version begins with apocalypse. Los, terrified by Christ's death, displays world-destroying potency: 'his right hand branching out in fibrous Strength / Seizd the Sun. His left hand like dark roots coverd the Moon / And tore them down' (*FZ* 117:7–9, E 372). Although Blake's inflated images insist on Los power, his apocalyptic violence suggests a defensive reaction, similar to Urizen's display of war-machines, rather than a confrontation with what is feared or a resolution of conflict. Blake's subsequent images of oppressors cruelly punished and females liberated echo the wish-fulfilling elements of the political prophecies. In line with Blake's rejection of the trouble-making female, however, incestuous ideas are purified. Thus the Sons of Eden descend into Beulah, and Enitharmon and Los (in the form of the Spectre and Urthona) share a spiritualised, shadowy embrace. Urizen's repressive books unroll and burn; Orc's desiring serpent body, mirroring their movements, unfolds and consumes itself; and Vala, the seductive mother, also burns.

Blake originally began the Night with an image of conflicted Man lying limply on his rock. In accordance with his other revisions, which transform images of vulnerability into images of power, Blake decided to put Los's godlike activity first. After the reassuring picture of Los's controlling strength, Blake can exhibit Man emasculated: 'O weakness & weariness O war within my members / My sons exiled from my breast' (FZ 119:32–3, E 374). Man's analysis of weakening conflict, like Blake's, emphasises father–son hostility. Man accordingly urges Urizen to improve relations with his children. Earlier, Urizen coldly manipulated Orc while pretending to care for him. Now Man wants Urizen to give up pretence and be a genuine 'Schoolmaster of souls', openly expressing both anger and love.

> That the Eternal worlds may see thy face in peace & joy
> . . . .
> While little children play around thy feet in gentle awe
> Fearing thy frown loving thy smile O Urizen Prince of light.
>   (FZ 120:22–5, E 374)

Furthermore, Man urges Urizen to relinquish his raging dragon-form (and similarly to let Orc self-destruct).[48] Before rehumanising, Urizen 'repents', not of the impulsiveness represented by his dragon-form but of his previous defensive preoccupation with the future. Here Blake suggests a rejection of modern civilised life: Urizen also repents of his city-building, shipping, and scientific exploration, wishing instead to return to a childhood garden devoid of the anxiety that apparently drove him to build civilisation.[49]

> Saying O that I had never drank the wine nor eat the bread
> Of dark mortality nor cast my view into futurity nor turnd
> My back darkning the present clouding with a cloud

And building arches high & cities turrets & towers & domes
Whose smoke destroyd the pleasant garden & whose
    running Kennels
Chokd the bright rivers burdning with my Ships the angry deep
Thro Chaos seeking for delight & in spaces remote
Seeking the Eternal which is always present to the wise
Seeking for pleasure which unsought falls round the infants
    path.

                                        (*FZ* 121:3–11, E 375)

Urizen's primary fear about the future was that Ahania would weaken and destroy him as Vala did man. To relieve this fear, Blake re-creates Ahania's nature (and, by implication, all female nature) according to a less threatening pattern. Her reunion with Urizen illustrates her change: before the now-youthful Urizen can embrace her, she falls dead at his feet. Her death has puzzled critics, but it can be understood psychologically as rendering her harmless: not only is she a corpse but also she bears no grudges and dies 'smiling'. Like all of Beulah's females, she happily accepts self-immolation. As Man explains to Urizen, the male principle, Christ, 'remains Eternal', while Beulah's females 'shall learn obedience [from Ahania's example] & prepare for a wintry grave' (*FZ* 112:13, E 376). The females' wintry death removes the source of Oedipal conflict and isolates them from the males when they are creatively working together.

Freed from the fear of the female and the son, Urizen's mind attains great flexibility, and he no longer needs to think in terms of binding and containing.

    What Chain encompasses in what Lock is the river of light
        confind
    . . . .
    Where shall we take our stand to view the infinite &
        unbounded.
                                        (*FZ* 122:22–4, E 376–7)

Imitating his thought, the universe explodes, hurling the dead up to judgement. Blake's earlier deprived children and rebel sons coalesce in one great figure, 'The Cold babe', who at once represents the pierced Christ and the rage-filled Orc. Crying furiously, the babe rends his oppressors 'limb from limb' while 'they beg . . . in vain' for mercy. The Christian context sanctions Blake's images of destructive violence. Christ himself appears triumphant in the sky with the 'four Wonders' and watches as a previous prisoner assaults his judge. Urizen participates in this destruction by ploughing up earthly 'cities' and the starry universe. The citizens, sown again as human 'seed', are relentlessly punished for past sins: kings, princes and warriors are hurled on 'unproducing sands & . . . hardend rocks' (*FZ* 125:11, E 379) where they cannot grow.

By making Urizen instrumental in punishing authority-figures, Blake brilliantly resolves the problem of guilt. Urizen, the deprived child and the rebel Orc act together. Orc literally dogs Urizen's footsteps: 'the flames of Orc follow the ventrous feet / of Urizen' (*FZ* 125:12–13, E 379). The image reverses earlier images of Orc attacking Urizen's vulnerable feet. And, as Urizen earlier starved Orc into submission, now Orc as companion-in-arms shares the wine and 'delicate repasts' brought by Urizen's daughters.

With Urizen and Orc now co-operating in virile activity, Ahania can safely rise from death. Blake suggests, however, that, as long as one has an impulse-ridden physical body, one is not really safe. Thus Man anxiously wishes to put off his newly risen body, and Urizen responds to the suggestion of still-present danger by confining Luvah and Vala permanently in the genitals, warning them never again to set 'their Dominion above / The Human form Divine' (*FZ* 126:9–10, E 380). What this means, I think, is that they must never again disturb the harmony between men (or in each individual's mind) by inciting the father's overthrow. Blake's illustration (*V* 126) indicates the ever-present danger of Oedipal impulse: Orc, as a huge-eyed ghost, beats with his phallic third leg against the thighs of a helpless man.

Besides repudiating incestuous desire, however, Blake also represents incest in a purified form, defensively isolated from the 'reality' of male relatedness, in a dream-sequence. The Beulah dream-episode also continues Blake's wish-fulfilling recasting of woman's nature by showing the once-terrifying Vala humbly seeking guidance from Luvah, her Christlike teacher and master. Using her fear of death (in the illustration, Time awaits her with his sickle), Luvah leads her to worship him and promises her survival after death. Specific narrative elements reverse or cancel threatening images in the earlier Nights. Vala's 'new song' of innocent harmony with nature, for example, structurally opposes the opening evocation of earthshaking horror; Vala's gratitude to Luvah for food and care –

My Luvah here hath placd me in a Sweet & pleasant Land
And given me fruits & pleasant waters & warm hills & cool
    valleys.

(FZ 128:21–2, E 382)

– replaces her earlier destructive insatiability as a female–dragon in
Night II. Though Blake's insistence on Vala's transformation is
supported by allusions to the soul, Christ, and prelapsarian innocence, the accompanying illustrations suggest her reluctance to be
reformed. The illustration (*V* 128) accompanying Vala's 'new song',
for example, shows her sleeping, not singing, exotically dressed,
more a seductive Indian dancer than a worshipful Eve.

Blake's uneasiness about Vala's reformation may stem from a
disjunction between his conscious and unconscious concerns:
although ostensibly rejecting both incest and Oedipal struggle and
presenting an idealised natural innocence, he also presents an
incestuous fantasy. The guilt and fear this fantasy arouses makes
Beulah not only beautiful and satisfying but also full of 'sweet
delusions', and 'Despair'. The incestuous fantasy itself occurs in the
Beulah dream, when Tharmas and Enion are reborn as Vala's
children and become lovers. Blake recasts earlier characterisations of
the rejecting mother (Enion averts her eyes from Tharmas) and of the
desiring son (Tharmas as child–lover resembles the Emblems' despairing son) in an ideal form. Vala, as the longed-for benevolent
mother, leads her younger counterpart Enion to Tharmas, comman-
ding her to look at and be good to him. Earlier, Enion had looked
away, like previous rejecting females, causing Tharmas's loins to
fade. Enion's withdrawal behind her veil suggests that the emotional
significance of Vala (pronounced 'Veila') is the mother (or sister)
hiding herself from the sight of her son (or brother), Vala's insistence
now that Tharmas and Enion may 'look' cancels Urizen's prohibitions about sexual looking and removes the veil – or taboo – between family-members. But, although incest is gratified here, Blake
suggests that gratification is possible only in a dream, separated from
the sleepers' 'Eternal reality'. When the Eternals awaken, they
disperse Luvah and Vala through the atmosphere, in effect cancelling
the dream union.

When Luvah is exhaled, he is separated from Vala and drawn back
into relationship with Urizen and the other Eternal men. Luvah's
reinstatement as the Eternals' dutiful wine-server suggests repentance

of his original rebellious attempt to trade the heavenly wine for Urizen's horses. Tharmas, too, appears now among the men. Blake's chief remaining problem, given his view of woman as inevitably producing conflict between men, is how to keep her as gratifier while ridding himself of her as a troublemaker. Although he tries to imagine woman with a changed nature, images of evil, either in her or caused by her, seem to arise almost obsessively despite his intentions. Enion's reunion with Tharmas is an example of how Blake begins on a hopeful note and ends with horror. Her reappearance is carefully orchestrated. Blake uses the same imagery (groans, sobs, rattlings) that he used to represent Tharmas's dissolution after his separation from her, but in reverse order, suggesting that event's redemptive 'undoing'. Enion's subsequent willingness to be a good mother is shown by her flowing milk, which generates a host of dependent creatures. Yet the idea of mother seems still inextricably tied to the idea of fraternal rivalry: many of the creatures are armed for war, and the illustration (V 132) shows two males fighting: a large-eyed Orcian ghost throws his spear against a paternal Albion with awe-inspiring genitals. Between his legs, a smaller man grovels before a seductively naked Vala.[50] Blake's continued difficulty in imagining a lasting solution to male–female relations is reflected in the Eternals' horrified response to Enion's reappearance: 'They shudderd at the horrible thing / Not born for the sport and amusement of Man but born to drink up all his powers' (FZ 133:6–7, E 386). Seeing Enion, the Eternals cannot help thinking of the now seemingly inevitable fall, when man, weakened by sex, slept, 'Forsaking Brotherhood & Universal love'. Woman has no place in the all-male family, where 'in his brothers face / Each shall behold the Eternal Father & love & joy abound' (FZ 133:25–6, E 387).

Blake's ambivalent treatment of woman continues in his description of the destruction of Vala, now identified as the great whore. Her destruction now is inconsistent with her earlier reformation, but it illustrates Blake's fluctuation between good (obedient virgin) and bad (malevolent whore) images of the mother. An important function of apocalyptic violence now becomes clear. By participating in universal destruction, the men actively inflict on others what the female 'whore' (and her 'beast') once did to them. As a reaper, for example, Urizen wields the scythe of the sibyl mother who threatened both father and son with death in Gates.

Tharmas, too, gets a turn at active mastery. He threshes out nations and stars from their husks, repeating in a new context his body's destruction by Enion. Vala's punishment as Mystery represents punishment for all females, including Enion, who repressed or tortured the infant male. Blake's illustration (*V* 134) of a female monster with a serpentine tail assimilates the previous female dragons with the biblical whore and beast. But now the rapacious female is ridden and seemingly mastered by a nude male. Blake emphasises man's release from the clutches of the female by a concluding allusion to the Declaration of Independence. Freed from the whore, Mystery, even the black slave will return to harmonious life with his brother man.

Luvah also gets his chance to avenge what Vala did to him. Throwing off his crown of thorns, he gathers the whore's 'Legions' into his wine-press. There, the suffering of the human grapes repeats, under Luvah's control and without threat to him, the 'distracted ravening desire' of the outcast mother, Enion. Blake's vision of Luvah's wine-press is the most concretely sadistic of the apocalypse series. Urizen's instruments of torture, 'The Plates the Screws and Racks & Saws', now become Luvah's and, following his orders, his daughters lacerate and whip their victims.

There is something basically unsatisfying, at least to me, about Blake's indulgence in sadistic fantasy with the self-righteous implication that sadism is necessary to ensure eventual peace. The watching creatures engage in an orgy of cruelty. They drink in Mystery's death-agony, as earlier they sprang up ready to struggle for Enion's milk. They 'Dance around the Dying & they Drink the howl & groan / They catch the Shrieks in cups of gold' (*FZ* 136:40, 137:1, E 390). Their jubilation underscores the Night's theme of apocalyptic justice; if one was once deprived of milk, he will now drink blood. Blake's image of frenzied small creatures also suggests ways in which infantile deprivation colours subsequent love with vengeful cruelty. Blake identifies the destruction of the grape bodies with sexual play.

> These are the sports of love & these the sweet delights of
>   amorous play
> Tears of the grapes the death sweat of the Cluster the last sigh
> Of the mild youth who listens to the luring songs of Luvah.
>   (*FZ* 137:2–4, E 390)

The creatures' excited dancing itself suggests sexual excitement: they dance naked, flaunting their bodies, denying both shame and compassion. The variety and ordinariness of the dancing creatures suggest that no one is immune to Luvah's frenzy.

Blake now repudiates both unbridled desire and its regressed expression in cruelty: Luvah is put out as dung on the ground and what is left of him is banished, along with Vala, to a Beulah dream-world 'till winter is over'. This isolation of Luvah's sadism parallels Blake's earlier isolation of the incestuous dream in Beulah. Without such isolation, brotherhood is impossible. But, although Blake suggests a change in man's nature – each of the four Zoas is shown in redeemed form – it rests on the premise that woman's nature can also be changed. As the Night draws to a close, Blake replaces the images of the destruction of Tharmas's body in Night I with the image of a submissive Enion working industriously at her loom. Only then is Blake able to see his vision of 'New born Man'.

7 Blake's *Milton*

Blake's *Milton* was written at the same time as the last Nights of the heavily revised *Vala*. Blake strongly disclaims responsibility for his poem. It was written, he says, 'from immediate Dictation, twelve or sometimes twenty or thirty lines at a time without Premeditation & even against my will'.[1] Although we need not take Blake's account of spirit dictation literally, the poem in fact displays a confusion and a density of meaning that are characteristic of unpremeditated or unconscious thought: to unpack one page thoroughly would require a small book. Because this density makes parsing of much of the text impracticable, we shall concentrate instead on Blake's psychological themes.

Not surprisingly, Blake continues to express the idea, central in *Vala*, that murderous females engender conflict between men, but *Milton*, unlike *Vala*, stresses the relationships between the men themselves. This emphasis probably derives from the poem's close relation to Blake's life-situation at the time. The poet William Hayley had become Blake's patron, and Blake seems to have suffered a critical loss of self-esteem in becoming dependent on Hayley. Blake incorporated his relationship with Hayley and its attendant fears into his poem, a stratagem that served to allay his fears and to restore his self-esteem.

Hayley's patronage began when he commissioned Blake to do a portrait of his dying son, Thomas. Hayley's attitude toward Blake, although kind, was clearly paternalistic and, indeed, patronising: '[Blake] pursue[s] his art . . . under my auspices, and as He has infinite Genius with a most engaging simplicity of character I hope he will execute many admirable things.'[2] After Blake had finished Thomas's portrait, Hayley continued to give Blake engraving work, as well as to find him jobs among his aristocratic friends. These friends, particularly Hayley's cousin, Lady Hesketh, openly disapproved of Blake, thus adding to his feeling of humiliation at being a dependent artist.

One of Blake's tasks was to illustrate Hayley's *Ballads*, which are clearly the works of an inferior poet. Still, Blake was grateful for the work; he seems at first to have considered Hayley as a sort of benevolent older brother, praising his 'brotherly affection'.[3] They met when Hayley was about to lose a son who was also an artist, and the idea that Blake would somehow replace Thomas was probably unconsciously present to both Hayley and Blake. Ultimately, however, Blake's love for Hayley changed to hatred. Blake began with a suspicion that Hayley's benevolence was motivated by envy and ended by suspecting Hayley of instigating a plot to have him hanged for sedition.

In *Milton*, Blake expands his quarrel with Hayley into a myth of cosmic rivalry and usurpation. Hayley as Satan covets the harrow of Palamabron–Blake. *Milton*'s 'Preface' immediately introduces the concepts of rivalry and usurpation by announcing the rivalry of the Bible with the classics and denouncing the classics as the product of theft. By modelling his attack on Milton's earlier attack on the Augustans, Blake prepares us to accept Milton as a good father or brother who will eventually endorse Blake's 'Bible' against the 'Stolen and Perverted Writings' (M 1, E 94) of the Grecophile Hayley. Blake follows his opening statement of theme with a call to arms: young artists must retain their integrity and refuse to work as 'Hirelings' oppressed by 'fashionable fools'. Blake concludes with an example of his own poetic art, which is also a statement that if true artists band together and fight, they can build Jerusalem in 'Englands green & pleasant land'. The 'Preface' as a whole sets up an analogy between Hayley's use of Blake's instrument (the harrow) and the Greek theft of the original inspiration of the Bible.

The poem's first major section after the 'Preface' is an opening song by the Bard. In the Bard's song, Blake creates a mythic context into which he will set Hayley–Satan's theft. The song notes that the poet Los created three classes of men at the time when Albion, Universal Man, was murdered by Envy. These classes – the Elect, the Reprobate and the Redeemed – reflect the conflict between fathers and sons: in terms of psychological dynamics, the Elect represents the father, while the Reprobate and the Redeemed suggest his angry or compliant sons. The action of the classes is given particular illustration in the body of the poem, where Blake identifies Hayley and Milton as the Elect, Rintrah as the Reprobate, and Palamabron as the Redeemed. Blake suggests that the conflict represented by the classes is reproduced in some way in the structure of art. Moreover, he indicates what the classes mean psychologically by inserting a series of examples of Oedipal conflict between his introduction of the classes and his explanation of them.

In the first example, Blake describes Los's binding–creation of the paternal figure. Urizen. Subsequently, Los has a rebellious son, Satan, who is plainly going to perpetuate the Oedipal cycle of guilt and retribution. Subsequent interpolated plates bring in the pernicious female, who initiates male conflict; the dangerously seductive 'Daughters of Albion' take the men they choose 'into their Heavens in intoxicating delight'. Blake's juxtaposition of the females' choice of men with a statement that 'the Elect cannot be Redeemed', but are 'Created continually / By Offering & Atonement in the cruelties of Moral Law' (*M* 5:9–12, E 98), suggests that election means female choice. This choice is followed by guilt on the part of the chosen as well as by persecution of others with moral law. The females, led by the 'cruel Virgin Babylon', perpetuate the classes by torturing the victims of moral law, just as earlier Enion and Enitharmon destructively manipulated the bodies of their sons.

The vignettes of Oedipal conflict not only exemplify the effects of the creation of the classes; they also allude to the current rivalry between Blake and Hayley. Thus, Los, standing up for Blake–Palamabron, tells Satan to forget about trying to drive Palamabron's harrow. And the Bard intervenes with an elliptical description of a triumph that can be explained by reference to Blake's work with Hayley.

Between South Moulton Street & Stratford Place: Calvarys foot
. . . .
Resounded with preparation of animals wild & tame
(Mark well my words! Corporeal Friends are Spiritual Enemies)
Mocking Druidical Mathematical Proportion of Length
     Bredth Highth
Displaying Naked Beauty! with Flute & Harp & Song
Palamabron with the fiery Harrow in morning returning
From breathing fields. Satan fainted beneath the artillery.
                                        (*M* 4:21–8, 5:1–2, E 97)

The 'preparation of animals' here stands both for sacrifice and for Blake's engravings of animals for Hayley's book of animal ballads. Hence the sacrifice is improper, but the fact that the engravings will 'mock' mathematical proportions is Blake's true feeling: his illustrations will triumph over Hayley's mechanical verse. A triumph over mathematical proportion may have contained, in addition, a reference to Lady Hesketh's criticism of the proportions of Blake's animals.[4] In the subsequent lines (on plate 5), Palamabron's harrow stands not just for prophecy but for engraving, including Blake's engravings for Hayley's book. Thus the confrontation with Blake's work causes Satan to faint. Later it is explained that Satan was in fact shot by the 'artillery' of Elnyttria, Blake's emanation, when she defended him against Hayley's homosexual desire ('his soft / Delusory love to Palamabron'). The two explanations of Hayley's (Satan's) fainting are the same. The assertion of Blake's creative potency (as male, as poet, as harrower) defends against fears of homosexual passivity apparently aroused by Hayley's patronage and, for the same reason, Hayley is portrayed as the one who is passive, impotent and homosexual.

In all of the opening scenes, creation is linked to destruction, a connection that reflects the fact that, because of Oedipal rivalry, creative activity is equated in the unconscious with destruction of the rival, the father's body.[5] The same aggressive intent is evident in the concept of classes, which continues the attack in the realm of abstract thought. Blake's statement that the paternal Elect is non-existent, a 'Negative', is a means of destroying the father. The other two classes, the Reprobate and the Redeemed, embody the ambivalence of sons toward their fathers. Rintrah, the Reprobate, though he takes his name from *Marriage*, where he plays a different role, stands for filial rage and rebellion. Palamabron is the Redeemed. He stands for filial guilt that contains the rage and turns it into pity. That the son is split into a raging and a self-mutilating part is the fault of the father. In *Marriage* the Just Man was evicted from Paradise by the hypocritical villain. In *Milton*, Hayley masquerades as a brother 'while he is murdering the just' (*M* 7:23, E 100). In *Marriage*, Blake stresses the paternal villain's treachery in order to lessen guilt for his own attack on his poetic fathers. Similarly, in *Milton*, Blake stresses Satan–Hayley's envy. Actually, Blake's dependent position might well have caused him envy of Hayley's independence and unmerited success. To relieve himself of this envy, Blake may have projected it onto

Hayley, just as Satan projects unacceptable impulses onto Blake in the narrative: 'mildly cursing Palamabron, him accus'd of crimes / Himself had wrought' (*M* 7:34–5, E 100). Palamabron, on the other hand, gives Satan his harrow out of self-mutilating 'pity', after the triumph of Naked Beauty. When this guilty pity is put aside, the underlying anger appears. Palamabron reddens 'like the Moon in an eclipse' and prophesies Hayley's despair and death. The moon-metaphor suggests his rage at being overshadowed. Then Rintrah and Hayley–Satan also become 'angry & red', and fight. Jealous rage has been exposed in all the males, whom Enitharmon appropriately treats like scrapping children, kissing her youngest, Satan, and separating him from the others. Heaven's Assembly fears this rage and tries to remove it by condemning Rintrah. Los's violent rage at the verdict serves as illustration of the fact that repressing anger again is not sufficient. As long as fathers and sons – the classes – and their separate bodies exist, conflict will recur.

Once the father–son classes have been set up in conflict, each member goes through the same thing. Thus Satan illustrates the ambivalence expressed in Rintrah/Palamabron by separating into a raging form and a defensive form that is associated with 'The Science of Pity'. Pity here is both hypocritical pity for those one has suppressed and pity in the sense of self-emasculation through suppression of both creativity and anger. The defensively dead part of Satan appears as the 'Covering Cherub' that keeps man from Eden, while the still raging part of Satan enters a female womb-space and becomes reborn under female domination. Satan, after submitting to maternal repression, comforts himself by creating new victims; he 'Compell'd others to serve him in moral gratitude & submission.'[6]

Thus Blake shows the cycles continuing and returns to Hayley–Satan's charge of 'ingratitude' against Blake–Palamabron. Now the female Leutha takes the blame for the men's quarrel. With Leutha, Blake portrays both normal and homosexual reactions to Oedipal rivalry. On the one hand, he suggests the triangle of faithless mother and two rivals, with the troublesome Leutha lusting after the more potent male. In analysing her 'fault', Leutha links it to the incestuous desire that led to the fall: 'We are the Spectre of Luvah the murderer / Of Albion' (*M* 13:8–9, E 106). On the other hand, Leutha represents the homosexual and passive impulses that a child feels toward his father and that a man can feel toward another man. In both cases Blake represents himself as the stronger, admired male, Palamabron.

At this point, Blake introduces the redemptive concept of the Seven Eyes, which will watch over the fallen Satan's activities. However, like the classes, the eyes themselves embody father–son conflict; they are split-off aspects either of a punishing God or of his opponent Lucifer (Orc). Conflict will continue until Jesus's death atones for the extravagances of desire and results in a redemptive merger of the classes. Reconciliation means sexual sharing, and Elnyttria accordingly brings Leutha, Satan's emanation, to Palamabron–Blake's bed. The incestuous fantasy of sleeping with Satan's bride probably served a defensive function against fantasies of homosexual submission. Passive and homosexual wishes are projected onto Satan–Hayley, who admires and envies Palamabron and wants his love. That the ideas of incest and aggression against his rival aroused Blake's guilt is suggested by the ominous issue of the union with Leutha: Rahab, Tirzah and Death, who as murderous parents will carry on the cycle of retaliation.

The main body of the poem shows Milton descending to extricate himself and, through him, Man from the cycles of guilt and retribution in which the Bard's song shows him to be trapped. Blake's choice of Milton makes psychological sense. In *Marriage*, Blake recognised Milton as a poetic father and tried to transform him from a censorious presence into an ally, one of 'the Devil's party'. Now, Blake's quarrel with Hayley and particularly Hayley's accusations of 'ingratitude' aroused Blake's guilt. He defended against the attack of conscience by having Milton, an even stronger 'father', take his side. Blake–Palamabron's innocence is vindicated when his story, told by the Bard, motivates Milton's descent not as an accuser but as a forgiving double. When the Eternals doubt the Blakean Bard's words, he hides in Milton's bosom, where he can participate in his power. Milton decides to do what Blake most wanted him to do – rid himself of his condemning selfhood, fearing that it will judge him too. Milton identifies this part of himself with Hayley–Satan, and admits to similar envy and aggression. 'I in my Selfhood am that Satan: I am that Evil One!'

Blake recognises that all men, as part of the human condition, share in conflict and guilt. The men in whose lives the restraining superego predominates are just as hostile as their impulsive counterparts, but they are more hypocritical. They rationalise hostility under the cloak of moral righteousness. Blake's analysis of Milton's aggression contains the brilliant insight that it is easier to rationalise hostility when one is unconscious of it. One purpose of Milton's descent is to make him conscious of both anger and desire. This, in turn, alleviates Blake's guilt by making father and son suffer equally. Their common problem is how to neutralise woman's baleful influence.

Blake's symbolic account of Milton's development from childhood through rebellious adolescence to the status of mature artist repeats similar sequences in earlier works. Immediately after his descent, Milton is surrounded by maternal power like a child. His hermaphroditic shadow represents both repressive female attitudes (the churches) and a feminisation of Milton's body. The polypus also represents weakening feminisation and Man's oppression by external nature. The male element, though temporarily relinquished, remains reassuringly present in Eden as an 'Image Divine'. Against the threatening maternal images Blake once again sets the image of the nurturing Beulians. Milton's real self is sleeping, surrounded by females who 'feed / His lips with food of Eden' (*M* 15:14–15, E 108). However, the female threat is temporarily stronger than its benevolent counterpart. Albion is in paralysing despair from absorbing feminine precepts, Milton also absorbs their precepts, and his hardened body forms the universe's mundane shell, whose distortion of the natural world to fit moral ideas is reflected in the 'Rock Sinai'. Enitharmon and Los, frightened when they see Milton in this judgemental form, try to stop him. They do not realise that Milton will break free of this rocky female matrix (as Los did earlier) and exercise his creative humanising powers.

Milton's struggle with Urizen (*M* 18, *IB* 234 – Illus. 67) integrates images of aggression against the father's body with images of creative reconstruction. On the one hand, Milton attempts to re-create Urizen's body with red clay (an attempt clearly related to Blake's own work of engraving).[7] On the other hand, as a powerful naked youth Milton aggressively wrestles with the grey-bearded Jehovah. As an adolescent rebel struggling against father and conscience, Milton is manipulated by Rahab and Tirzah, who seductively urge him to usurp paternal power by becoming consort and 'king', and initiating a cycle of retaliation by restricting a younger rival 'with the Chain of Jealousy' (*M* 19:38, E 112). They simultaneously create the entrapping natural body and the false heavens of seduction and betrayal, which will formalise and perpetuate conflict. Tirzah resembles Delila[h], and Blake makes her echo Delila[h]'s speech from his

Illus. 67   *Milton*, plate 18

Samson sketch (E 435) when she tempts Milton: 'Come to my ivory palaces O beloved of thy mother! . . . & be thou King' (*M* 20:4–6, E 113). Milton resists the invitation, but Blake suggests the connection of the seductive mother with his own trial in a final image. Scofield, the soldier who had accused Blake, had appeared at the gate of Blake's garden. Blake now makes him appear before the gate of the biblical Reuben, who had assumed his father's sexual rights with his concubines. Thus Blake links the accusation of sedition with an accusation of coveting the father's sexual prerogatives.

In earlier works, struggle against paternal figures or their representative, conscience, always resulted in guilty paralysis. When Blake made his poetic father Milton fight his own split-off ('frozen') censorious attitudes, this reduced the necessity of a guilty reaction. In addition, Blake pleads his own utter unworthiness before the heavenly Father. 'But thou O Lord / Do with me as thou wilt! For I am nothing, and vanity' (*M* 20:17–18, E 113). Blake's statement serves to appease conscience, and in the following passage Blake makes it clear in fact that the 'Lord' he is propitiating is not external but internal. 'O thou mortal man. / Seek not thy heavenly father then beyond the skies: / There Chaos dwells' (*M* 20:31–3, E 113).

While Blake propitiates his conscience, Milton tries to evade its demands and enter the barred inner gate to Heaven (Satan's Seat). This gate suggests the Freudian censor. If one evades the guard, one arrives at the city of Golgonooza (in Albion's loins) through which there is access to Beulah's sexual gratification. Urizen, naturally, hinders Milton's approach to it.

Although his presentation is obscure, Blake suggests that Milton did briefly evade the censor (and Urizen) and engage in forbidden sexual activity in Beulah. Milton's divine form is expelled from Eden after the Eternals look down into Beulah and become 'fill'd with rage' (*M* 20:45, E 114). Considering the fact that Blake's fall often followed intercourse, that Beulah is the place of sexuality, that the Eternals observe something outrageous there, and that Blake has just been speaking of a territory outside morality, it would seem that the Eternals are enacting the part of Milton's own Jehovah casting out desire.

Los responds to the fall with a depression and a concern that his creative powers (his sons) will desert him under the influence of 'female' concepts of sin. His recollection of a prophecy that Milton will loose Orc 'from his Chain of Jealousy', thus ending the female-initiated cycles of crime and punishment, gives him the courage to descend to the barred gate in Udan-Adan'. The Ulro landscape, with its black lake formed by victims' tears, is a further concretisation of Los's depression. What Los confronts here is a fall or regression to sado-masochism initiated by fear. Ulro's repressive sadism is linked to anality through images of blackness and opacity, such as the black lake and the black cloud that exudes from Blake's foot (*M* 32, *IB* 248 – Illus. 68). In addition, Blake suggests homosexual ideas which he later modified into images of redemptive fusion between men: Blake's foot is 'the nether / Regions of the Imagination' (*M* 21:4–5, E 114), and when Milton penetrates it he creates a 'vast breach'. Milton's track, which in the illustration (*M* 36, *IB* 252 – Illus. 69) ends in a phallic tip, penetrates between hemispheres (of desire and sensuality) to enter the world of Los, Blake's foot. Perhaps because of the homosexual connotations of Milton's penetration, Blake denies conscious knowledge of it: 'for man cannot know / What passes in his members' (*M* 21:8–9, E 114). After the penetration, Blake is given the gift of a vision: the vegetable world appears as a bright sandal of 'precious stones'. This sequence suggests that receiving a vision is the psychological equivalent of being impregnated by the poetic father.

Total opposition to the black Ulro world of despair lies not in Milton but in the figure of Ololon, whose river 'of milk & liquid pearl' (*M* 21:15, E 114) opposes Los's black waters. With this 'sweet River', both nourishing and beautiful like the good mother it represents, Blake imagines satisfaction of the thirsts of all of his deprived characters, from Tiriel to Milton.[8] Beside this river, the divine family of previously outraged Eternals laments having driven Milton from Paradise. As an autobiographical statement, the self-accusation of the heavenly brothers because of their part in getting rid of their 'dead brother' Milton suggests the guilt one feels when a sibling – even one loved as much as Blake loved Robert – dies. It cannot be coincidence that Robert is resurrected as Blake's twin in *Milton*. This attempt to turn a brother into an alter ego and to deny enmity by fusion is paralleled in the body of the poem itself. The heavenly family transcends fraternal rivalry by merging the erstwhile rival Zoas into the figure of Christ. As Christ, the family is then able to share the maternal river: 'As One Man even Jesus / Uniting in One with Ololon' (*M* 21:58–9, E 115). In the next plates, Blake develops his idea of merger as a way not only of denying enmity but of

Illus. 68 *Milton*, plate 32

absorbing strength and other good qualities.

Blake now portrays a union with Los ('I became One Man with him arising in my strength' – *M* 22:13, E 116), which suggests a homosexual act: in the illustration (*M* 47, *IB* 263 – Illus. 70), Blake kneels and turns backward toward Los so that his face rests suggestively against Los's groin.[9] Blake's own genitals were inked over, not necessarily by him, with black ink, and later versions provide him with underclothes. The sexual implications here, however, seem to overlay a deeper fantasy of merger with an idealised figure. The similarity of Blake's stance to Urizen's stance (frontispiece to *Europe*) suggests that the person he wishes to become like,

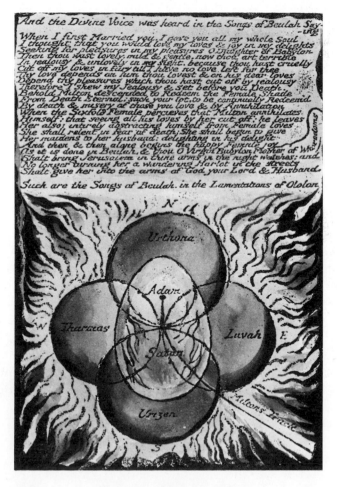

Illus. 69 *Milton*, plate 36

through merger, is the father. It is tempting here to turn to clinical examples, such as those of Heinz Kohut, of the way such fantasies may be expressed through sexual imagery.[10] One of Kohut's patients, a painter, derived strength from observing a powerful man's penis. This sexual 'looking' covered a need to merge with an ideal figure to shore up his self-esteem.[11] Visual (or, as in another case, sexual) merger resulted in a revival of lost infantile omnipotence, what Kohut calls the 'grandiose self'. A similar revival is clear in Los's statement that his union has cancelled out an original separation from the 'Eternal Bosom' and has returned omnipotence of thought: 'both Time & Space obey my will' (*M* 22:17, E 116).

Blake suggests that feelings of omnipotence are a necessary part of creativity. Following their merger, Blake–Los moves toward the city of art. He overcomes a need for vengeance against the paternal figure when Rintrah and Palamabron fruitlessly urge him to throw Milton into the furnaces. After vengeance is rejected, conflict must be dealt with through faith, which involves humility and sacrifice, and art, symbolised by Blake's merger with Milton and the poet Los. Although Blake tried to close the gap between faith and art, humility and imaginative omnipotence are difficult bedfellows.

Omnipotence constitutes a temptation to kill: Rintrah and Palamabron beg Los to destroy Milton. Los explains that he no longer needs to destroy Milton because he has embraced him: undoing of separation seems to be an alternative to destruction. But, although Los assures his sons of his benevolence toward this poetic predecessor, art, as Blake presents it in Golgonooza, is contaminated by hatred and envy. Here, though, Los the artist re-creates a body more consistent with desire; creativity retains its association with destruction. Los's workplace, Bowlahoola, suggests the bowels and the cruelty Blake associates with their functioning. Bowlahoola is 'namd Law' (*M* 24:48, E 119) because law institutionalises early impulses of cruelty and domination. Los's activities there recall his vengeful binding of Urizen. He performs his 'horrid labours', aided by thundering bellows and accompanied by cacophonic music which suggests a cruder form of body-noise. Bowlahoola is in effect both 'stomach', where eating and incorporating are represented by the digestive furnaces, and bowels, as its name suggests. By making Bowlahoola the site of creation, Blake links it not only with destruction but with the child's first bodily production: excrement.[12] Blake's radical thoroughness returns us to the body origins of

Illus. 70   *Milton*, plate 47

creativity and our feelings about what has been created. He imagines a situation, based on the earlier one, in which a male can outdo the female. The females can produce only an emasculated polypus 'without Thought or Vision', and Los must correct it through his art. Both Los's labours and his parallel work of apocalyptic destruction in the wine-press are attempts to deal with envy and rage by rationalising them as part of a redemptive plan. However, in spite of Blake's rationalisations and statements of principles of mercy and sacrifice, destructive impulses were a crucial part of his art. And in so far as he tried to exorcise these impulses by embodying them artistically he was only partially successful.

Los's creative–destructive work at his furnaces is matched by his task at the wine-press. Here, before destroying them, he analyses the three classes of conflicting fathers and sons and examines their effects on each other. In Blake's analysis, Rintrah and Palamabron suggest his own elated and depressed moods.[13] Palamabron's 'doubts and fears' and his oppression by the Elect refer both to Blake's quarrel with Hayley and to his alternation between self-doubt and megalomaniac confidence. Though Rintrah has unbounded confidence, he also expresses constant rage. Blake's own struggle seems to have been against both rage and doubt. In Los, who cautions his labourers against their destructive impulses, Blake imagines creative confidence freed from rage. Meditating on the imagination's power, Los returns to the child's animistic vision of the world, where every natural act is the result of man's will. But, in spite of Los's omnipotence, creation seems to include a destructive element. When Los embodies 'passions and desires', conflict and the hostile 'classes' are created simultaneously. And both the bodies and the classes must be destroyed.

The wine-press owes its form to the cycles of Oedipal guilt and retaliation: 'Luvah laid the foundation & Urizen finish'd it' (*M* 27:2, E 123). Los, as its director, retaliates in kind for what he once suffered passively. He imposes his words on others' minds just as earlier (in *Vala*) he and Blake had suffered from the Urizenic wheels crushing their brains: 'He lays his words in order above the mortal brain / As cogs are formd in a wheel' (*M* 27:9–10, E 123). The imagery suggests the aggression powering Blake-Los's need to impress his thoughts on other minds and recalls the parallel aggression in *Island* where Blake, having invented a new method of printing, swore that whoever rejects his works 'will not deserve to live' (E 456).

Island, moreover, foreshadows Blake's concern in *Milton* with the merger of good brothers and the defeat of bad ones. In *Island* he denied fraternal rivalry by the closeness between Quid–Blake and Suction–Robert – Blake's 'twin' in *Milton* – and, at the same time, expressed rage against others who, through envy, might not appreciate his works. These enviers, portrayed in *Island* as puppies and fleas, become the envious insects dancing around Los's press in *Milton*. Blake's later insistence that Robert had given him his method of printing in a dream not only denied brotherly competition but may also have covered Blake's derivation of his method from Cumberland. Hayley's change (in Blake's eyes) from a good, idealised brother into a hated thief suggests Blake's general tendency to alternate between love and hate. Increasingly he dealt with his ambivalence by exaggerating it artistically and splitting people into groups – either manifestly good or manifestly bad. All his hatred was then projected onto the bad: envy is all on the part of Hayley, who steals his harrow.

Pursuing the dynamics of envy, Blake's narrative moves from the wine-press to the land Allamanda or 'the sense of touch'. This land's harrowing – an act analogous to Blake's engraving – also expresses ambivalence. Blake portrays it as a 'cruel' rape of the Beulah heavens, an exertion of masculine force, which seems necessary in order to avoid 'Death Eternal'. Blake indicates that in all the arts creation is contaminated by aggression. Poetry is transformed into religion – that is, it takes part in the cycles of guilt and retaliation. Music, which Blake had connected with the noise of the bowels accompanying creation, is changed into law, the institutionalised urge to power, and painting into the sadistic surgery of Jack Tearguts.

Although he implies that the arts have an unfallen, undestructive form, Blake's analysis is appropriate to his own art. Perhaps he is able to characterise and confront sadistic impulses in creativity and sex so clearly because of his new conviction that they can be exorcised. His analysis precedes another attempt to describe Los's benevolent creation of bodies for the dead: 'Creating form & beauty around the dark regions of sorrow' (*M* 28:2, E 124). Blake emphasises the artist's ability to soothe the passions by creating artistic forms to house them: 'porches of iron & silver' (*M* 28:1, E 124). Finally, Los's sons create rich visions of eternity and barricade them against 'cunning or rage'.[14]

Los's reconstruction of time and space, however, suggests that art cannot solve problems of conflict and rage. A complete reconstruction of experience is needed that will make the satisfaction of basic needs central. Los's time, for example, is defined by satisfaction of the basic need for nurture. In between each of Los's moments stands a Daughter of Beulah 'To feed the Sleepers on their Couches with maternal care' (*M* 28:49, E 125). This conceptualisation literally insists that there is no time in which one experiences the maternal figure's absence. This in-between time becomes the moment in which the poet works – as well as the actual time-span of history. In making creation take place in the space-time where the mother nurtures, Blake suggests that creativity depends on the maternal environment. Los also reconstructs space. Man's experience of it becomes animistic like that of Piaget's child subjects, who insist that moon and clouds follow them when they walk:[15]

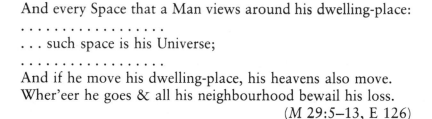

And every Space that a Man views around his dwelling-place:
. . . .
. . . such space is his Universe;
. . . .
And if he move his dwelling-place, his heavens also move.
Wher'eer he goes & all his neighbourhood bewail his loss.
(*M* 29:5–13, E 126)

Reconstructed time and space, then, re-establish the egocentric world of infant thought, where experience is interpreted through the body.[16] But Blake's ability to imagine a sympathetic, animistic world provided only a temporary respite from his awareness of man's separateness and vulnerability. Book One ends as 'Rahab and Tirzah pervert / Their [Enitharmon and her daughters'] mild influences . . . [and] Weave the black Woof of Death' (*M* 29:53–6, E 127).

In Book Two, Blake imagines the necessary maternal partner of the 'omnipotent' child, for it is the mother's loving response that enables the child to sustain feelings of omnipotence. 'Beulah to its Inhabitants appears within each district / As the beloved infant in his mothers bosom' (*M* 30:10–11, E 128). In his portrayal of the males 'resting' in Beulah, Blake maintains the fiction of omnipotence but transfers it from 'beloved infant' to admired poet. Blake gratifies the male's wish for nurture while simultaneously denying infantile dependence. Beulah's women are correspondingly weak and fearful of the inspired males. The female world of obedience is carefully separated from the male world of creation – man only drops in for a rest cure before continuing his virile forward progress 'thro' / The Bosom of the Father' (*M* 31:4–5, E 129). Although Blake denies his dependence on the Beulian female, his depiction of Mother Nature's admiration for the inspired lark suggests his dependence on maternal love and approval of his body and gifts. The bird's ecstatic song makes it an apt symbol for the poet; its shape and gravity-defying flight have also made it a traditional symbol for the phallus.

> Mounting upon the wings of light into the Great Expanse:
> . . . .
> His little throat labours with inspiration; every feather
> On throat & breast & wings vibrates with the effluence Divine.
> (*M* 31:32–5, E 129)

Even the paternal sun must admire the lark's song: 'the awful Sun / Stands still . . . looking on this little Bird / With eyes of soft humility, . . . and awe' (*M* 31:36–8, E 129–30). The inspired lark whose notes welcome the day recalls Blake's self-image in a Poetic Sketch as one whose 'notes Should Rise to meet the New born day' (E 438) if he could conquer his envy. Now, he conquers envy by ridding himself of rivals. Accordingly, the poet–lark is provided with admiring parents who concentrate on him alone. This wishful picture of parental love contrasts with Blake's portrayal of the cruel treatment given the 'Divine Voice' by his female.

> I thought that you would love my loves & joy in my delights
> . . . .
> Then thou wast lovely, mild & gentle. now thou art terrible
> In jealousy & unlovely in my sight, because thou hast cruelly
> Cut off my loves in fury . . . .
> (*M* 33:2–7, E 131)

The 'Divine Voice' is disappointed because his bride has not fulfilled the fantasy of the sexually generous wife–mother, which Blake first developed in *Visions*. In this context, Milton's 'self-annihilation' suggests a voluntary annihilation of the sexual passion that puts him in the female's power. Paradoxically, his withdrawal not only returns her to him but also forces her to be generous.

> When the Sixfold Female perceives that Milton annihilates

Himself: that seeing all his loves by her cut off: he leaves
Her also: intirely abstracting himself from Female loves
She shall relent in fear of death: She shall begin to give
Her maidens to her husband: delighting in his delight

. . . .

As it is done in Beulah, & thou O Virgin Babylon
    Mother of Whoredoms
Shalt bring Jerusalem . . .

. . . .

Shalt give her into the arms of God your Lord & Husband.
                                            (M 33:14–24, E 132)

When Milton rejects 'these Heavens builded on cruelty' (M 32:3, E 130), he is rejecting the Beulian heavens governed by female sexual choice as well as the Urizenic laws that punish rival suitors. But Milton's Spectre still suffers sexual frustration, tracking his emanation 'thro' the snow & the wintry hail & rain' (M 32:5, E 130). Blake's Notebook poem 'My Spectre' reveals the autobiographical source of Milton's words. The drafts describe a jealous unforgiving female who murders the speaker's 'sweet loves'. In spite of this, the speaker's spectre follows her footsteps just as Milton's Spectre does. Milton becomes Blake's alter ego sharing his sexual difficulties and expressing his anger against the Hayley who murders 'by undervaluing calumny' (M 32:7, E 130). In a later lyric sexual intrigue and a murderous rival are connected: Blake implies that Hayley tried to murder him, and perhaps to seduce his wife.

And when he could not act upon my wife
Hired a Villain to bereave my Life.
                                            (E 497)

Apparently, Blake's tormenting images of dangerously jealous female and murderous 'friend' could only be subjugated by the idea of voluntarily annihilating the conflicted impulsive part of the self. By accepting annihilation, as Jesus does, one becomes free to accept the reward of unlimited love. However, Blake also protected himself against the feared destruction, stating that, although individuals perish, 'their Forms Eternal Exist, For-ever. Amen' (M 32:38, E 131).

Milton's self-annihilating descent is paradoxically both a voluntary purification and an ejection from Eden. It is to cancel out

Milton's ejection that Ololon descends, thus making good the wish for forgiveness that Blake demonstrated in 'My Spectre'. Her descent leads her into the centre of Blake's most negative image of the female, the polypus: within it, a shadowy mother and sinister females spin bodies foredoomed to conflict. Blake describes the way the harmonious pursuits of men (mental 'War & Hunting') are changed by a process that seems the reverse of sublimation into the sadistic physical violence of the impulses. And here Blake refers again to his conflict with Hayley: 'Brotherhood is changd into a Curse & a Flattery' (M 35:4, E 134). Ololon's wish to get past the polypus to Golgonooza represents Blake's attempt to return to higher forms of 'warfare'.

Ololon appears in a compliant female form that cancels out the murderous images of Rahab and Tirzah. She enters Blake's garden at Felpham, where he had written his visions of 'Natures cruel holiness', as a twelve-year-old virgin. Milton's Shadow opposes Ololon's attempt to become compliant by 'condensing all his fibres'. The Shadow contains within it all the elements that compose the cycles of guilt and retaliation and that make defensiveness necessary: tyrannical fathers, seductive moon-goddesses, secret rites, and sacrificed children. Blake stresses the murderous mother's importance in these cycles by showing her as 'Mystery' in Satan's breast, inhabiting a landscape whose burning pits and poisonous fountains reflect the dangers of her body. Her murderous cruelty is defined as the source of Blake's own impulses of rage and envy: she offers only poison in her cup, just as earlier, in Blake's sketch, the poet longing for a 'Cooling Drop' was offered only filth.

Blake, having described the mother–whore who initiates conflict, depicts an end to the cycles of retaliation: Milton as father, 'black, severe & silent', confronts the 'gorgeous' Spectre of Satan as rebellious son. Satan, conditioned by female philosophy, tries to provoke Milton to annihilate him. Milton refuses to play the game of envy and repression. Blake's solution to conflict as he states it here is annihilation of self rather than one's rival. But what does this mean in Blake's poem? When self-annihilation was mentioned earlier in connection with the jealous female, it suggested getting rid of the sexual passion that puts a man in her power. Now Blake suggests a complementary meaning – giving nurture and, perhaps, sex to another man.

In plate 45 (*IB* 261 – Illus. 71), Milton, who, the text tells us, is

Illus. 71   *Milton*, plate 45

still fighting with Urizen (as father) while at the same time fighting the Spectre (as son), is no longer a rebel but an androgynous Christ supporting Urizen, who kneels with his face against Milton's groin. The position of the men suggests that Milton is comforting and perhaps letting himself be drained or cannibalised by Urizen. Urizen seems flaccid,[17] and Milton appears radiant, not depleted. Although speaking about it continually, Blake nowhere shows us the self-annihilation the poem seems to be moving toward.[18] Instead, Milton strips off everything opposed to the Blakean imagination and emerges from his rotten robes as an inspired man to whom Ololon 'vows obedience'. Milton, having subordinated Ololon, becomes Blake's ally against all who threaten his self-esteem and art: 'the tame high finisher of paltry Blots' will no longer dare 'to mock with the aspersion of Madness' the 'Inspired'. Doubters of the imagination, whether poetasters or rationalists, become in Blake's rhetoric killers who 'to gratify ravenous Envy ... murder time on time' (*M* 41:17–20, E 141).

Now, for the first time, Blake suggests his solution for the problem of woman. If conflict between men is to cease, she must stop existing. Sexual organisation, 'the Abomination of Desolation', must disappear 'Till Generation is swallowed up in Regeneration' (*M* 41:25–8, E 141). But, although Blake announces the end of sexual organisation, male sexuality continues to stand as a model of the human, while the female is either incorporated or isolated restrictively in Beulah. By suggesting incorporation as a possibility, Blake moves toward the idea more fully developed in *Jerusalem* of an androgynous being. In the idea of androgyny Blake recalls a stage in early development in which male and female were not clearly distinguished but appeared only as active and passive tendencies. Thus Ololon asserts that the pernicious sexual organisation only covers a fruitful interplay of opposites. When Ololon, as a dove, dives into Milton's Shadow in the climatic scene, her action suggests the rebirth of the passive principle in the male. Ololon's transformation from virgin to dove also suggests the destruction of the cruel 'virgin' mother. Blake's images reverse the implications of rape in *Vala*. Whereas Enion's transformation into serpent–bird signified absorbing Tharmas's masculinity, the virgin Ololon gives up her phallic female will and re-enters the male as a harmless dove. At the same time, the non-virginal part of Ololon, which represents her compliant Beulah self, descends in bloody clouds that signify that her marriage with Milton has been consummated. Jesus simultaneously descends in a 'Garment of War', six thousand years of history, the time in which male and female alternately are pierced and bleed. Blake's apocalyptic rhetoric insists that this time is over, but, as we shall see in *Jerusalem*, the cycles continue to repeat themselves obsessively in his imagination.

8   *Jerusalem*

Jerusalem is a poem *par excellence* about the conflict between love and hate, and between rage and forgiveness. Yet honest readers approaching it for the first time are oppressed and confused by the eddying, repetitive quality of the narrative and the mass of 'minute particulars' with which it is constructed. An understanding of the poem's inner dynamics, however, can provide a thread through Blake's maze. The chief psychological problem posed by the poem is how to reconcile the father, Albion, with the son, Los. The difficulty is their mutual suspicion and hatred, which are linked to their desire for exclusive possession of the mother, Jerusalem.

Blake's use of images from *Gates* to delineate the figures of Los and Jerusalem (in the Notebook sketches they were youthful traveller and beloved wife) suggests his return to an earlier statement of the problem with a new solution. There, the traveller–son, seeking union with his beloved, was balked by a man-eater and a bloodthirsty maternal sibyl. As Blake reordered the emblems, he tried to resolve conflict with the father by seeing him as a common victim of the mother. But this essentially pessimistic idea did not satisfy Blake. In *Jerusalem*, therefore, Blake more clearly directs rage toward the mother as a castrating phallic female, and then, through the persona of Los, rescues the father from her. The concept of Christian forgiveness, which is used to deal with any residues of rage, also covers a fantasy of sexual sharing. The reconciled men, merged into one figure, share the embraces of a chastened and obedient Jerusalem.

Jerusalem opens with Albion's refusal to share his emanation Jerusalem with Christ. This initial selfishness sets the pattern for Los's conflict with Albion. Los alternates between rage and a loving wish to forgive Albion. Los's 'murderous thoughts' clearly arise from the supposition that his 'stolen' bride is in Albion's 'pleasure garden'. Albion, then, not only refuses to share his emanation with Christ but, at least in Los's fantasy, steals the brides of other men. Although Los tries to resist the evil thoughts suggested by his Spectre, he is tormented and symbolically punished for them by 'Terrors in every Nerve, by spasms & extended pains' (*J* 7:7, E 148). The illustrative vignette describing Luvah's passion melted in the furnace suggests that the constant secret punishment going on in Los's body is directed against his sexuality – in other words, that it is a form of castration.

Los fights his murderous thoughts in two ways: by evoking Christ's aid ('O that I could abstain from wrath! O that the Lamb / Of God would look upon me and pity me in my fury' – *J* 7:59–60, E 149); and by reconstructing experience through his art. Much of chapter 1, addressed to Blake's 'public', concerns Los's work in Golgonooza, city of art. A major problem with art's reconstruction of experience, however, is that, fuelled by rage and guilt, it results not in transformation but in representation of disturbing conflicts. Los shows his Spectre the torments going on within his creative furnaces and sorrowfully admits, 'I now am what I am: a horror . . . Behold what cruelties / Are practised in Babel & Shinar' (*J* 8:18–20, E 150). The cruelties that Los observes in history originate in the same murderous rage he feels inside himself. Therefore, his Spectre 'saw now from the outside what he before saw & felt from within'. Los's insistence that he is 'inspired', that both his torments and his creative labours are only for 'Albions sake' (*J* 8:17, E 150) is an attempt to relieve his guilt over the murderous impulses expressed through his creative work. Los's – and Blake's – self-accusation persists and is projected onto the figure of the Accusers, who deny Los's inspiration and start a war to punish genius. All but three of the Accusers are named after men who participated in Blake's trial.

The Spectre functions like a harsh superego; he arouses fear and 'mighty Shame'. Shame is the inverse of the poet's triumphant display of his 'Giant forms' within his poem. Los's insistence that he has broken shame's 'fetters' has a biographical root in Blake's victory over the 'Spectrous fiend' who fettered his feet, interfered with his art, against conscious wishes to perfect it, and subverted 'conjugal love'.[1] I would suggest that Blake's 'fiend' was a result of his own inner war with guilt, and that it was his grasp of the principle of forgiveness that brought him victory over it. Since he felt competitive and hostile toward figures like Sir Joshua Reynolds, it is perhaps significant that his 'enlightenment' came the day after visiting the Truchsessian picture-gallery, when 'Suddenly . . . I was again enlightened with the light I enjoyed in my youth, and which has for exactly twenty years been closed from me as by a door and by window shutters.'[2]

Blake's insistence on his suffering for exactly twenty years is important, since it refers back to the year of his father's death. It would have been natural for Blake to feel guilt over his father's death because of death-wishes toward him. Retrospectively, Blake dates the fiend's interference with his work and sexual life from this time. Moreover, Blake's trial for sedition against the king was probably experienced as punishment for all his earlier struggles with paternal figures, Hayley included. Hayley's help in gaining Blake's acquittal may have provided the stimulus for his conversion-experience. The first fruit of 'enlightenment' was a new confidence and pride in his work.

In *Jerusalem*, however, Blake presents conflict as unresolved; Los must struggle desperately with his 'murderous thoughts' against Albion. Still, it is the wish to save Albion, to revive the dead father, that now justifies Los's exercise of his art. And it is Blake's Christian motive and wish to unite with his readers 'wholly One in Jesus' that he stresses in his opening preface, where he begs his audience to love and forgive him 'this energetic exertion of my talent' (*J* 3, E 144). His request to his readers not to take his enthusiasm for 'presumptuousness or arrogance' (*J* 3, E 144) echoes his earlier letter to Hayley: 'Dear Sir, excuse my enthusiasm or rather madness, for I am really drunk with intellectual vision whenever I take a pencil or graver into my hand.'[3]

But neither Hayley, Blake's public, nor Los's Spectre was ready to forgive artistic enthusiasm. Los's Spectre persists in shaming him by calling Enitharmon Los's 'Great Sin', for, as sister–bride, she is closely linked to Los's incestuous wishes. Los reacts to the Spectre's accusation by creating 'the Spaces of Erin', perhaps in an attempt to give the female a redemptive role, but his efforts are subverted by his inability to control the natural female as mother or bride: 'animated and vegetated, she is a devouring worm' (*J* 12:3, E 153).

Los also struggles against shame to complete Golgonooza as a home for Jerusalem, Albion's emanation. Here Jerusalem is the bride of the Lamb and of Los, too, in so far as he is identified with Christ. Lambeth (Lamb's House), the place where Blake wrote his revolutionary prophecies, is personified in a figure who prepares Jerusalem's furniture and whom she loves: 'Lambeth! the Bride the Lambs Wife loveth thee' (*J* 12:41, E 154). Although highly purified and allegorised, Los's creation of Golgonooza still bears the marks of incestuous fantasy, and it therefore is threatened by a landscape of 'Malice: Revenge: / And black Anxiety' (*J* 13:42–3, E 156). In his effort to create an artistic form to contain Jerusalem, Los is also continually threatened by negative images of the mother. Albion's seductive daughters, for example, 'wooe Los continually to subdue his strength' (*J* 17:10, E 160).

Now Blake begins to shift blame for the fall onto the pernicious female. Los and Albion are both her victims. To illustrate, Blake repeats the tale (from *Vala*) of Vala's seduction of Albion and Man's reduction to 'a little grovelling Root' (*J* 17:32, E 160). The results of seduction are guilt, shame, and sexual disease. Albion is overcome:

> I have no hope
> Every boil upon my body is a separate & deadly Sin.
> Doubt first assaild me, then Shame took possession of me
> Shame divides Families. . . .
>
> (*J* 21:3–6, E 164)

Albion here is a brother of Los and of every man whose fall is caused by seduction. Albion's fervent wish 'That the deep wound of Sin might be clos'd up with the Needle' (*J* 21:13, E 164) is a barely disguised wish for the closing up of the dangerous female genital. Albion is horrified at the discovery of infantile sexuality in his daughters.

> . . . Cordella! I behold
> Thee whom I thought pure as the heavens in innocence & fear:
> Thy Tabernacle taken down, thy secret Cherubim disclosed
> Art thou broken? Ah me Sabrina, running by my side:
> In childhood what wert thou? unutterable anguish! Conwenna
> Thy cradled infancy is most piteous. O hide, O hide!
> Their secret gardens were made paths to the traveller:
> I knew not of their secret loves with those I hated most.
>
> (*J* 21:19–26, E 164–5)

Moreover, their willing seduction is analogous to his own and similarly incestuous in its meaning. He blames Jerusalem and her daughters for inciting Luvah against him; the illustration (*J* 21, *IB* 300 – Illus. 72) shows them being punished for this action; naked, they are being whipped by a naked man with a cat-o'-nine-tails.

Albion's sadism covers guilt over his own incestuous desires. Vala cleverly draws his attention to his secret 'Sin'. And Albion admits the truth of Vala's accusations by his masochistic response. He urges her to use her castrating knife and 'drain my blood / To the last drop' (*J* 22:29–30, E 166). Simultaneously, he calls Jerusalem 'Daughter of my phantasy! unlawful pleasure' (*J* 23:2, E 166). She becomes an incestuous shape projected on his night-time curtain – an autoerotic dream. Jerusalem entreats Albion as 'my Father & my Brother' to share her with Christ.

Albion vacillates between repentance ('I have erred') and renewed intransigence. In the midst of Albion's struggles Blake interjects a scene whose intensity and content suggest a transformed memory:

> What have I Said? What have I done? O all-powerful Human
>   Words!
> You recoil back upon me in the blood of the Lamb slain
>   in his Children.
> Two bleeding Contraries equally true, are his Witnesses
>   against me
> We reared mighty Stones: we danced naked around them:
> Thinking to bring Love into Light of day, to Jerusalems shame:
> Displaying our Giant limbs to all the winds of heaven! Sudden
> Shame seizd us, we could not look on one-another for
>   abhorrence: the Blue
> Of our immortal Veins . . . fled from our Limbs.
>   (*J* 24:1–8, E 167)

Blake attributes this experience to Albion, but Los's struggle against shame and Blake's display of 'Giant forms' are clearly related to it. Earlier, Blake linked Los's shame with the murderous thoughts that interfered with his creative and redemptive wishes; here, loving impulses cause shame. It is because the men's exhibitionistic display of their naked bodies has an erotic purpose, 'to bring Love into Light', that it causes extreme shame and 'abhorrence'.

By juxtaposing this scene with shedding Christ's blood, Blake

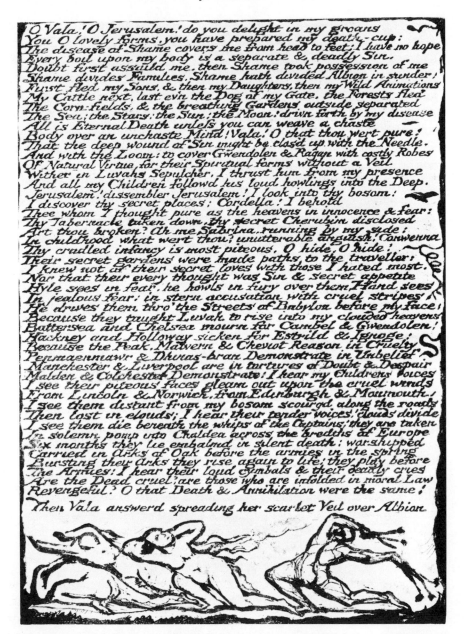

Illus. 72 *Jerusalem*, plate 21

suggests that crucifixion is a defensive substitute for an act of love between Albion and Christ. Albion's need to defend himself from awareness of his love's homosexual component explains his difficulty in passively submitting to Christ's embraces. The fear of behaving like a female to another man is also expressed by Albion's sons when they resist brotherhood as 'soft complacencies' of weakness. Instead they also want to crucify Jesus. Although these homosexual fears must have been shared to some extent by Blake, he resisted them, and continued to portray woman as the real enemy and crucifier of Man. Chapter 1's final full-plate illustration (*J* 25, *IB* 304 – Illus. 73), derived from Poussin's *Martyrdom of St Erasmus*, shows Rahab, Tirzah and Vala drawing out Man's intestines in a visual variation of Vala's earlier manipulations of his phallus.

The entire chapter can be seen as an apologia 'To the Public', including Hayley, and, in imagination, Blake's father, for Blake's enthusiastic display of 'Naked Beauty'. This display, like the exhibition of the naked body, provokes shame because of its connection with murderous and sexual impulses toward the parents. Blake depicts in sequence the possibilities of Oedipal responses. Los's murderous rage against Albion is the first and most 'natural', but, as we saw, the resultant shame and guilt contaminate Los's (and Blake's) art. Los's attempted seduction by the daughters and Albion's seduction by Vala represent incestuous desire as a type of bewitching that unites fathers and sons as victims. Finally, Albion's mixed recollection of crucifixion, exhibited nakedness and love represents the possibility of desire between father and son, along with the defence that gratifies desire in a distorted and sadistic way.

In chapter 2, addressed 'To the Jews', Blake explores Albion's rational and moralistic defences against both incest and homosexuality: 'unnatural consanguinities and friendships / Horrid to think of when enquired deeply into' (*J* 28:7–8, E 172). Since these impulses are expressed in art, Albion also condemns 'Every ornament of perfection, and every labour of love' (*J* 28:1, E 172). And, Blake clarifies further, 'Albions Sons / Must have become the first Victims, being the first transgressors' (*J* 28:23–4, E 173).

Albion's condemnation of an art associated with unlawful passions echoes Blake's own self-condemnation when he was fighting off inexplicable 'melancholy'. 'I myself remember when I thought my pursuits of Art a kind of criminal dissipation . . . which I hid my face for not being able to abandon as a Passion which is forbidden by Law

And there was heard a great lamenting in Beulah: all the Regions
Of Beulah were moved as the tender bowels are moved: & they said:

Why did you take Vengeance O ye Sons of the mighty Albion?
Planting these Oaken Groves: Erecting these Dragon Temples
Injury the Lord heals but Vengeance cannot be healed:
As the Sons of Albion have done to Luvah: so they have in him
Done to the Divine Lord & Saviour. who suffers with those that suffer:
For not one sparrow can suffer. & the whole Universe not suffer also,
In all its Regions, & its Father & Saviour not pity and weep
But Vengeance is the destroyer of Grace & Repentance in the bosom
Of the Injurer: in which the Divine Lamb is cruelly slain:
Descend O Lamb of God & take away the imputation of Sin
By the Creation of States & the deliverance of Individuals Evermore Amen

Thus wept they in Beulah over the Four Regions of Albion
But many doubted & despaird & imputed Sin & Righteousness
To Individuals & not to States, and these Slept in Ulro.

Illus. 73   *Jerusalem*, plate 25

& Religion.'[4] Blake later felt that 'the immense flood of Grecian light & glory' transformed art from a crime into 'Law & Gospel'.[5] Nevertheless, Greek 'light' without the concept of forgiveness failed to relieve Blake's guilt or rid him of the 'fiend' that tormented him. Peace could be experienced only by embracing his tormenter as a brother, a concept, as we saw, that implies a fraternal union against the 'Female Will'.

Following Albion's analysis of female will, Vala taunts him with her control ('The Imaginative Human Form is ... Born of the Woman to obey the Woman' – *J* 29:49–51, E 174), and, looking at her, Albion becomes feminised: 'how my members pour down milky fear ... all manhood is gone!' (*J* 30:3–4, E 174). Los undertakes to save Albion by investigating the nature of woman's power: 'what may Woman be? / To have power over Man from Cradle to corruptible Grave' (*J* 30:25–6, E 175). His tentative answer is that her power derives from sexuality: 'Consider this O mortal Man! . . . said Los / Consider Sexual Organization & hide thee in the dust' (*J* 30:57–8, E 175).

Woman's power is such that only Christ can prevent man's emasculation: the Divine Hand limits the fall in order to keep man male. Thus reassured, the reader observes Albion's sons fall under Tirzah's power. The Eternals, also observing, remark that now 'a Man dare hardly to embrace / His own Wife, for the terrors of Chastity' (*J* 32:45–6, E 177). This inhibition of sex also destroys art and science, which 'cannot exist but by Naked Beauty displayd' (*J* 32:49, E 177). Los amplifies the connection by blaming Albion, presumably under female control, for attacking 'our secret supreme delights' and forbidding 'with Laws / Our Emanations'. Albion, unable to respond either to Los or to Christ, freezes defensively into 'petrific hardness' and again wants to sacrifice Jesus.

Now, Albion becomes dangerous ('He hath leagued himself with robbers! . . . Envy hovers over him' – *J* 36:13–14, E 180), and Jerusalem is hidden from him in Blake's beloved Lambeth. Although fully Christianised, Blake's protection of Jerusalem is a variant of the fantasy of the mother saved from a tyrant by the poet–son. The primitive nature of the underlying fantasy is brought out by Blake's allusions to the nursery tale of Jack the Giant-killer. 'Hark! hear the Giants of Albion cry at night / We smell the blood of the English! . . . The living & the dead shall be ground in our rumbling Mills / For bread' (*J* 38:47–50, E 183). The Accusers' world, in which 'a mans worst enemies / Shall be those of his own house and family' (*J* 41:25–6, E 186–7), is the early world of Oedipal conflict and can be transcended only by enormous efforts. Blake counterposes the bloodthirsty giants to an ideal of intellectual warfare in which 'the Soldier who fights for Truth, calls his enemy his brother' (*J* 39:41, E 183).

When Los tries to break down Albion's defensive moralism by showing him that 'the accursed things were his own affections' (*J* 42:3, E 187), Albion responds, as Satan did in *Milton*, by crucifying all who have shown 'ingratitude' to him. 'Ingratitude' here seems to stand for the whole web of Oedipal 'sins' that merit 'vengeance deep'. Albion's condemnation of ingrates reminds us not only of Hayley's accusation of his dependent, Blake, but also of the risks a still-dependent child takes in expressing his feelings. Years earlier, in 'A Little Boy Lost', Blake had depicted such a child burned at the stake for confessing he loves himself more than his father and brothers. The little boy's defiant resistance to parental expectations echoes Blake's revelation that 'Corporeal Friends' are 'Spiritual Enemies'. And, as might be expected, Albion is now recognised as the spiritual enemy.

Blake again shifts blame for paternal cruelty onto the female in a flashback, in which Albion creates his 'Sexual Religion' of guilt and banishes Luvah after his seduction by Vala. Los comments that sexuality must be transcended: 'Humanity knows not of Sex: wherefore are Sexes in Beulah?' (*J* 44:33, E 191). Entering Albion's bosom to investigate and 'search the tempters out' (*J* 45:5, E 192), Los sees the seductive Vala contending with Jerusalem for possession of Albion. Under Vala's auspices, Albion's sons set up temples of punishment where men mingle in sadistic acts rather than brotherly love. Vala calls Jerusalem 'harlot', presumably because instead of exclusion and punishment she wishes to share her love with both father and sons. Albion is unable to resolve his inner conflict; he abandons hope and, swooning, is received into Christ's arms. Although auspicious, this union does not signal a solution; Albion accepts the embrace only because he is weak and dying – his law continues to operate. Jerusalem must again hide from him, roused by 'maternal love' for the sons threatened by Albion's law. The chapter ends with a request for Christ's active intervention to wipe out 'remembrance of Sin' so that the family may be reconciled.

Chapter 3, 'To the Deists', investigates the impact of irrational impulses of rivalry and hatred on creativity. It opens with Los, dominated by a desire for vengeance, building Golgonooza. Blake's preface insists that everyone has these negative emotions and they cannot be made to disappear by declaring (as the Deists do) that man is naturally good. If man suffers from a too-harsh conscience, he also suffers from a glossing-over of his destructive impulses. The rejection of irrationality in dream and religion without understanding its force in mental life was perhaps the primary mistake of eighteenth-century rationalists, and it prepared the way for reaction. Blake insists on man being born 'Satan' and 'altogether an Evil' (*J* 52, E 198), in the context of eighteenth-century optimism. His insistence that even the most pious 'are Men of like passions with others' (*J* 52, E 199) prepares us for Los's mixed motives in building Golgonooza. Thus, for example, Los's wish to save Albion runs parallel with an inadmissible wish to hide Jerusalem from Albion's sight. This unconscious wish is rationalized as a duty to protect the emanations from Albion's rage. But Albion reacts instead to the underlying wish, with thoughts of 'deadly revenge springing from the / All powerful parental affection . . . Seeing his Sons assimilate with Luvah' (*J* 54:9–11, E 201).

In another way, too, Blake opposes current ideas of the goodness of human nature. Los, as artist–visionary, wishes to usurp the female's generative function by recreating the body in accord with his desires. Not surprisingly, the females object and declare war, but he manages to 'retain his awful strength' (*J* 55:2, E 202) and continues to investigate the source of their power in a meditation on the female mysteries of birth and nursing. Los himself illustrates the driven curiosity of the child when faced, without explanation, with a new sibling: 'tell me where found / What you have enwoven with so much tears & care? . . . Remember! recollect!' (*J* 56:22–5, E 204). The Daughters of Albion's answer, 'it came / And wept at our wintry Door' (*J* 56:26–7, E 204), recalls tales of children found under cabbages or brought by the stork. As if to show how this 'discovery' occurred, Gwendolyn becomes a maternal 'Clod of Clay', and 'finds' the great Merlin as an infant worm. The underlying idea is of female witchery transforming once-omnipotent man into a being 'Subservient to the clods of the furrow!' (*J* 56:36, E 204). The value of the idea of finding or transforming is that it makes the female secondary. She hides, obscures, or mutilates what pre-existed in divine form. As the Daughters explain, they feared the Divine Vision and so covered it with a 'fleshly Tabernacle'. Later, afraid of the boy's sexual impulses, they become castraters and mutilators. Blake portrays the females, drunk with blood, cutting into men's bodies and brains (*J* 69, *IB* 348 – Illus. 74): even 'Horses: Oxen: feel the knife' (*J* 58:9, E 205). In this process, men harden toward one another and take out their frustrations in war.

Blake now imagines an interruption of the vicious natural circle. Los takes control of generation and recreates male and female to replace the 'Hermaphroditic' phallic female and feminised male. The true female, as Blake sees her, is neither seductive nor punitive, but gives herself to all men in order to create harmony. To illustrate what this generosity entails both from the female and from the truly unpossessive male, Christ presents a vision of Joseph forgiving Mary for adultery. The idea of adultery is linked in turn with feelings of guilt and pollution. Joseph hears the word 'pollution' disturbingly repeated in his sleep, suggesting an additional literal meaning of pollution due to erotic dreams or fantasies. The dream's moral, however, is mutual forgiveness of sin, for 'There is none that liveth & Sinneth not! And this is the Covenant / Of Jehovah: If you Forgive one-another, so shall Jehovah Forgive You' (*J* 61:24–5, E 210). Jerusalem, watching the vision, feels that she too is polluted but will be forgiven: 'If I were Pure I should never / Have known Thee; If I were Unpolluted I should never have / Glorified thy Holiness' (*J* 61:44–6, E 210).

Christ suggests that sexual liberty in the resurrected man will extend to a change of sexual role in which, presumably, he could enjoy the pleasures of being made love to by a male: 'Man in the Resurrection changes his Sexual Garments at will' (*J* 61:51, E 210). Vala, who reappears to fight the ideals of forgiveness and full sexual freedom, taunts Los with his lack of control over feminisation: 'Thou art / Thyself Female, a Male: a breeder of Seed: a Son & Husband ... O Woman-born / And Woman-nourished & Woman-educated & Woman scorn'd!' (*J* 64:12–17, E 213). Illustrating her power, Vala unites with Albion's glittering, angry Spectre, and the resultant feminised man ('A dark Hermaphrodite') goes on a rampage of destruction. The decision to crucify Luvah follows associatively, and Vala takes over as goddess of war.

This is Luvah's third crucifixion in *Jerusalem*, and this time Blake successfully shifts responsibility to the female. Albion's male children have only a minor part in a preliminary scene of torture which Blake

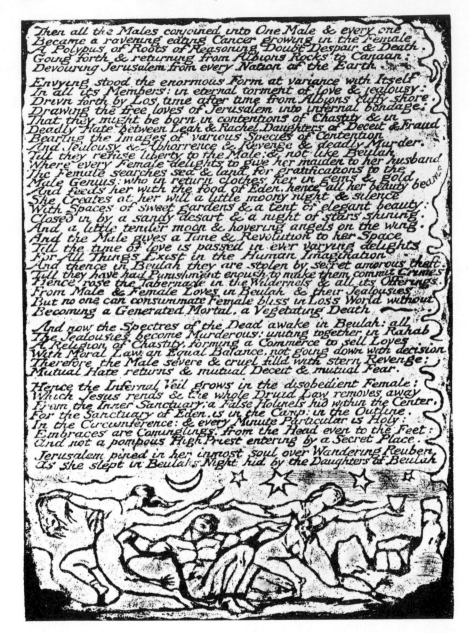

Then all the Males conjoined into One Male & every one
Became a ravening eating Cancer growing in the Female
A Polypus of Roots of Reasoning Doubt Despair & Death.
Going forth & returning from Albions Rocks to Canaan:
Devouring Jerusalem from every Nation of the Earth.

Envying stood the enormous Form at variance with Itself
In all its Members: in eternal torment of love & jealousy:
Drivn forth by Los, time after time from Albions cliffy shore
Drawing the free loves of Jerusalem into infernal bondage:
That they might be born in contentions of Chastity & in
Deadly Hate between Leah & Rachel, Daughters of Deceit & Fraud
Bearing the Images of various Species of Contention
And Jealousy & Abhorrence & Revenge & deadly Murder.
Till they refuse liberty to the Male: & not like Beulah
Where every Female delights to give her maiden to her husband
The Female searches sea & land for gratifications to the
Male Genius: who in return clothes her in gems & gold
And feeds her with the food of Eden, hence all her beauty beams
She Creates at her will a little moony night & silence
With Spaces of sweet gardens & a tent of elegant beauty:
Closed in by a sandy desart & a night of stars shining.
And a little tender moon & hovering angels on the wing.
And the Male gives a Tune & Revolution to her Space,
Till the time of love is passed in ever varying delights
For All Things Exist in the Human Imagination
And thence in Beulah they are stolen by secret amorous theft.
Till they have had Punishment enough to make them commit Crimes
Hence rose the Tabernacle in the Wilderness & all its Offerings,
From Male & Female Loves in Beulah & their Jealousies
But no one can consummate Female bliss in Loss World without
Becoming a Generated Mortal, a Vegetating Death

And now the Spectres of the Dead awake in Beulah: all
The Jealousies become Murderous: uniting together in Rahab
A Religion of Chastity, forming a Commerce to sell Loves
With Moral Law an Equal Balance, not going down with decision
Therefore the Male severe & cruel filld with stern Revenge:
Mutual Hate returns & mutual Deceit & mutual Fear.

Hence the Infernal Veil grows in the disobedient Female:
Which Jesus rends & the whole Druid Law removes away
From the Inner Sanctuary a False Holiness hid within the Center,
For the Sanctuary of Eden is in the Camp: in the Outline
In the Circumference: & every Minute Particular is Holy:
Embraces are Cominglings: from the Head even to the Feet:
And not a pompous High Priest entering by a Secret Place.

Jerusalem pined in her inmost soul over Wandering Reuben,
As she slept in Beulahs Night hid by the Daughters of Beulah

Illus. 74   *Jerusalem*, plate 69

uses to recapitulate his insight that guilt can force the aggressor to identify with his victim's impotence:

> While they rejoice over Luvah in mockery & bitter scorn:
> Suddenly they become like what they behold in howlings &
>   deadly pain.
>
> (*J* 65:74–5, E 215)

This time, however, Blake also suggests that murdering one's rival for the mother's love has the ironic result of internalising the mother as a Fury. The sons see 'their beloved Mother' Vala transfer herself from Luvah to them: 'their own Parent the Emanation of their murderd Enemy / Become their Emanation' (*J* 65:69–70, E 215).

Having, so to speak, taken over male bodies as instruments to create their female world of 'natural law', the Daughters give free rein to their sadism. Witchlike, they sit on the trial stones and cut their victims. Their phallic nature is indicated by the way they enter men's hearts 'in pomp' and erect temples there. The metaphor of pompous entrance recurs later in a description of sexual penetration. Blake not only repeats material from earlier chapters here but also brings in the Rahab and Tirzah material from *Vala*. Each idea or sequence of images seems to draw others with it in a potentially infinite series. At length, Blake returns to the image that began the sequence: 'Look: the beautiful Daughter of Albion sits naked upon the Stone / Her panting Victim beside her' (*J* 68:11–12, E 219). The implicit voluptuousness of the imagery is developed into the daughters' 'sporting', reminiscent of Salome, not with the head but 'in the skin of the Victim'. Albion's 'beautiful Daughter' examines 'Infants limbs', eats flesh, and drinks blood; she is both bewitching castrater and devouring mother. The warriors, fascinated – as Blake apparently was – by her behaviour and 'drunk with unsatiated love . . . must rush again to War' (*J* 68:63–4, E 220) against each other, not recognising their real enemy.

Blake now reintroduces the ideal of the female as gratifier and procurer of sexual pleasures for man. The evil daughters who 'refuse liberty to the Male' are compared to the Daughters of Beulah,

> Where every Female delights to give her maiden to her husband
> The Female searches sea & land for gratifications to the
> Male Genius: who in return clothes her in gems & gold.
>
> (*J* 69:15–17, E 221)

Blake's interest is clearly on the needs of the 'Male Genius': the male creates, the female gratifies. She has no independent existence and must accept his 'Fibres of dominion'.

This view of male–female relationships seems at first to be contradicted by Blake's enormous sensitivity to 'feminine' traits, such as tenderness and maternal care. Blake views these traits in two ways: on the one hand, they belong to the ideal female and allow her to care for the Male Genius; on the other hand, the poet can incorporate and use them in creation and in drawing close to other men. In this latter view, Blake anticipates the modern recognition of bisexuality and its special importance for creativity, which seems to arise as part of an inner dialogue between the male and female parts of the self. But Blake did not extend the right to express traits of the opposite sex to his females. When they do express them, they become threatening 'Female Wills' and must be destroyed. Even when they do not become phallic, their sexuality gives them a dangerous power. Finally, Blake considers their specifically female sexuality inferior to the total body sensuality of the child and holds them responsible for its loss.

Blake makes Christ sanction his vision by rending chastity's restrictive veil and reinstating this total body sensuality. In the restored Eden 'Embraces are Cominglings: from the Head even to the Feet; / And not a pompous High Priest entering by a Secret Place' (*J* 69:43–4, E 221). Blake's repetition of the image from the earlier passage describing Albion's daughters entering man's heart under-scores the connection between woman's power and genital primacy. When, at the poem's conclusion, Jesus re-establishes polymorphous sexuality, he effectively breaks the female's power over the male. Until then despite Los's work and some cheering visions of heavenly Canaan, Rahab triumphs. The chapter's end reveals her as mistress of the twenty-seven churches and heavens. The concluding illustration (*J* 75, *IB* 354 – Illus. 75) shows her, with Tirzah, as a crowned queen with genital scales and suggestions of a penis, embracing a seven-headed dragon. The facing plate shows Christ crucified, according to her will.

In chapter 4 Blake moves toward his apocalyptic solution. Con-tinuing the theme of the sexually generous female, Jerusalem recalls a time when she was enjoyed by the sons of the entire earth, including Christ:

And Rahab Babylon the Great hath destroyed Jerusalem
Bath stood upon the Severn with Merlin & Bladud & Arthur
The Cup of Rahab in his hand: her Poisons Twenty-seven-fold

And all her Twenty-seven Heavens now hid & now reveald
Appear in strong delusive light of Time & Space drawn out
In shadowy pomp by the Eternal Prophet created evermore
For Los in Six Thousand Years walks up & down continually
That not one Moment of Time be lost & every revolution
Of Space he makes permanent in Bowlahoola & Cathedron.

And these the names of the Twenty-seven Heavens & their Churches
Adam. Seth. Enos. Cainan. Mahalaleel. Jared. Enoch.
Methuselah. Lamech: these are the Giants mighty, Hermaphroditic
Noah. Shem. Arphaxad. Cainan the Second. Salah. Heber
Peleg. Reu. Serug. Nahor. Terah: these are the Female Males:
A Male within a Female hid as in an Ark & Curtains.
Abraham. Moses. Solomon. Paul. Constantine. Charlemaine.
Luther. these Seven are the Male Females: the Dragon Forms
The Female hid within a Male: thus Rahab is reveald
Mystery Babylon the Great: the Abomination of Desolation
Religion hid in War: a Dragon red, & hidden Harlot
But Jesus breaking thro' the Central Zones of Death & Hell
Opens Eternity in Time & Space; triumphant in Mercy
Thus are the Heavens formd by Los within the Mundane Shell
And where Luther ends Adam begins again in Eternal Circle
To awake the Prisoners of Death: to bring Albion again
With Luvah into light eternal, in his eternal day
But now the Starry Heavens are fled from the mighty limbs of Albion

Illus. 75   *Jerusalem*, plate 75

> . . . once the Four-fold World rejoicd among
> The pillars of Jerusalem, between my winged Cherubim:
> But now I am closd out from them in the narrow passages
> Of the valleys of destruction. . . .
>
> (*J* 79:58–61, E 233)

The female's sexual generosity becomes the base for an allegory of the decrease in political, social and religious liberty as the thorough-fare where men met in shared sexuality becomes, through the possessiveness of father, king and priest, a treacherous passage leading men to destruction. When Jerusalem shared herself with the sons, Blake implies, her 'secret joys' included the entire body:

> Wherefore in dreadful majesty & beauty outside appears
> Thy Masculine from thy Feminine hardening against the
>   heavens
> To devour the Human! . . .
> . . . O Vala! Humanity is far above
> Sexual organization. . . .
>
> (*J* 79:70–4, E 233)

Vala's explanation is couched in terms of the Oedipal conflict that accompanies genital primacy. Her 'beloved Luvah' (father and lover) set her to murder (read 'seduce and weaken') Albion. The 'murder'–seduction of man infantalises him, returning him to the female's power, and Blake accordingly describes the weakening of Albion's sons. The Daughters, in turn, change their lovers into vulnerable but greedy infants. Los himself becomes an 'infant horror' and will be drawn into Oedipal conflict by his newly formed (or melting) genitals: 'pangs of love draw me down to my loins which are / Become a fountain of veiny pipes: O Albion! my brother!' (*J* 82:83–4, E 238).

Nevertheless, Los combats the 'Patriarchal pomp' associated with the father's exclusive sexual rights with ideas of sexual sharing, as well as with ideas of incorporating 'feminine' qualities into renewed man. Thus Los reproaches Jerusalem for separating herself from Albion, and Los's emanation, Enitharmon, illustrates once again the difficulties of the female's separate existence. Enitharmon refuses Los's 'Fibres of dominion' and is jealous of his interest in Jerusalem.

> No! I will seize thy Fibres & weave
> Them: not as thou wilt but as I will, for I will Create
> A round Womb beneath my bosom lest I also be overwoven
> With Love; be thou assured I never will be thy slave
> . . . .
> In Eden our loves were the same here they are opposite
> I have Loves of my own I will weave them in Albions Spectre
> Cast thou in Jerusalems shadows thy Loves! silk of liquid
> . . . issuing from thy Furnaces. . . .
>
> (*J* 87:12–20, E 244)

Los patiently explains that Enitharmon must co-operate if he is to be united with the other men. However, Enitharmon is far from persuaded – 'This is Womans World' – and weaves the tabernacle of law 'That he who loves Jesus may loathe terrified Female love / Till God himself become a Male subservient to the Female' (*J* 88:20–1, E 244). Los's Spectre comments that the females' perverse love of 'mean abjectness' accords with the construction of their sexual organs, 'For I will make their places of joy & love, excrementitious' (*J* 88:39, E 245). Enitharmon, listening to the Spectre's description of her 'continually destroying in Family feuds' (*J* 88:40, E 245), enacts his words by scattering Los's 'love on the wind' and imprisoning Christ, Los's alter ego, in her 'Female Womb'.

Los and his creator turn this moment of defeat into a triumph of male planning. Sexual organisation is 'permitted' so that Christ can be born. Yet Christ is subject to the same troubles as Los. By virtue of his 'Maternal Birth' he becomes Satan in the sense of being dominated by the phallic female. His 'Maternal Humanity must be put off Eternally / Lest the Sexual Generation swallow up Regeneration' (*J* 90:36–7, E 247).

Blake's underlying logic leads him now to consider his personal satanic enemy, Hayley. Los sends his Spectre to all accusers of genius to tell them that in attacking him they are crucifying Christ.

> Go to these Fiends of Righteousness
> Tell them to obey their Humanities, & not pretend Holiness;
> When they are murderers: as far as my Hammer & Anvil
> permit
> Go, tell them that the Worship of God, is honouring his gifts
> In other men: & loving the greatest men best, each according

> to his Genius: which is the Holy Ghost in Man; there is no
> other God . . .
> He who envies or calumniates: which is murder & cruelty,
> Murders the Holy-one. . . .
>
> (*J* 91:4–12, E 248)

Furthermore, Blake extends his equation of envy with the murder of Christ to a parent's envy of his child: 'He who would see the Divinity must see him in his Children / One first, in friendship & love' (*J* 91:18–19, E 249).

Although this is marvellous poetry, we are given no psychologically convincing explanation of how Los's point of view triumphs suddenly over both the accusing Antichrist and the murderous and previously intransigent female. Blake's rhetoric creates an end to conflict simply by making Enitharmon announce,

> The Poets Song draws to its period & Enitharmon is no more.
> . . . .
> My Looms will be no more & I annihilate vanish for ever
> Then thou wilt Create another Female according to thy Will.
>
> (*J* 92:8–12, E 250)

And Los reaches a further insight that 'Sexes must vanish & cease / To be' (*J* 92:13–14, E 250).

Enitharmon makes a last effort to recall her sons to 'the Mothers love of obedience' (*J* 93:4, E 251), citing the example of Reuben, who 'found Mandrakes in the field & gave them to his Mother' (*J* 93:8, E 251). Albion, cold on his rock, oppressed by the Female Shadow, is Blake's countering example of the results a Reuben may expect from his phallic gift. The emblem of the famished eagle of frustrated genius that flies over Albion completes the example.

Since there seems no logical way out of the stalemate between Los and Enitharmon, Blake again resorts to inspired rhetoric. 'Time was finished! The Breath Divine Breathed over Albion . . . And England [the oppressive female] awoke' (*J* 94:18–20, E 252). When she wakes, she repents ('I have Slain him [Albion] in my Sleep with the Knife of the Druid' – *J* 94:25, E 252), and Blake's vision concludes. The Female and, by extension, the natural world return docilely to Albion's limbs: 'rejoicing in his indignation! adoring his wrathful rebuke. / She who adores not your frowns will only loathe your

Illus. 76   *Jerusalem*, plate 99

smiles' (*J* 95:23–4, E 252). With woman in her place, Albion is ready to meet Christ 'as Man with Man' (*J* 96:6, E 253).

In the final plates, Blake imagines a resolution of Oedipal conflict through Christian forgiveness and sacrifice. The energic source of this resolution is a fantasy of sharing the mother's love: Los as Jesus merges with Albion–Jehovah and embraces Jerusalem (*J* 99, *IB* 378 – Illus. 76). An alternate renunciatory resolution occurs in an early sketch which shows God the Father embracing Jesus as he accepts his Son's sacrifice. The sketch was based on a representation of the Prodigal Son, and it implies that only sacrifice or self-castration will make a son welcome to his father. Blake's final text brings out the sketch's sacrificial ideas by making Jesus offer his death as a supreme sign of love for Albion: 'Wouldest thou love one who never died / For thee' (*J* 96:23–4, E 253). Yet Blake alters the meaning of sacrifice by Los's being given 'sublime honour' and being joined by Albion in death. Their love death leads to the resurrection of the divine humanity.

Mutual forgiveness not only enables Jehovah and Jesus to unite and share Jerusalem, but precipitates a return to a completely 'human', death-free universe where thought is omnipotent and sensibility is fluid rather than confined to the genitals. Man rides a threefold sexual chariot, giving him the powers of an adult male, but his exquisitely sensitive nerves flow freely into paradisal 'Rivers of bliss'. His mind, extending or contracting at will, works 'Creating Space, Creating Time according to the wonders Divine / Of Human Imagination' (*J* 98:31–2, E 255). The fact that analogous modes of thought and body sensibility are present in every man's infancy does not detract from Blake's vision or its parallels in mystical thought. If anything, it helps explain the fascination of his ideas in a time in which people seem increasingly to feel alienated and helpless.

Conclusion

Jerusalem shows that Blake's obsession with sexuality was, if anything, stronger in his later prophecies than in the earlier ones. What has changed is the emphasis and the attitude. Sexual liberation has been replaced by forgiveness of sins as a means of salvation. Looking back at Blake's libidinal first phase, we can see that his shift from revolutionary to radical Christian is understandable not simply as a possible conclusion by him that revolution leads to tyranny or that power corrupts, but rather in terms of his inability to continue facing the guilt that the expression of aggressive and sexual ideas produced in him. In order to understand the force of Blake's guilt in the early period, we had to get beneath his defensive idealisations of energy and observe the strength and omnipresence of impulses of rage, envy and sadism. This was not always easy. Blake's defence against guilt at that time was a rhetoric of blame in which the tyrant father was always guilty, coupled with powerfully seductive images of sexual and aggressive energy: flaming, naked bodies, prisons broken open, females reddening like ripening grapes.

Blake's work had a coherence and integrity in the early prophecies perhaps partially because the inner conflict between drive and defence 'fit' so well with the outer theme of rebellion and paralysis. Dealing with inner conflict through externalising it by blaming the father and championing impulse permitted an unrestrained release of energy. For Blake, the glorification of impulse roused his imagination to produce concrete images of energy. Later, when he no longer wished to dwell on forbidden sexual and aggressive impulses and insisted instead on self-abnegation, he tended to produce less powerful, imageless abstraction.

By the time of *Vala*, Blake seems to have reached a stalemate. His

293

work became locked into a repeating pattern of impulsive struggle and melancholy defeat. He had expressed incestuous desire with perhaps more clarity than any other poet, but the suffering caused by his sexual and aggressive wishes seemed to get stronger as he became more aware of them, and his idealisations of energy became less able to protect him. *Vala* marks a crucial turning-point because in it he consciously repudiates the incestuous act at the heart of his concept of liberated sex and describes it as the original sin and cause of the fall. From this time on, his defensive misogyny grows and he rails against the female while drawing closer to the father.

Renouncing incest was equivalent for Blake to giving up poetry, because for him exhibiting his 'Giant forms' meant successfully competing with the father for the mother's sexual favour. The conflict between his conscious wish to embrace the father in forgiveness and his continued wish to embrace the mother *and* to write poetry celebrating that embrace is central to *Jerusalem*. It is not strange that the 'drama' of *Jerusalem* is one of poem-making. The act of writing poetry is the last hiding-place for the wish to kill the father and commit incest. Los's creative efforts in *Jerusalem* show that Blake was becoming increasingly aware of his poetry's deepest sources in impulses of rage and envy. The conflict between these impulses and the avowed salvational purpose of the poem may have led Blake to conclude that his work must be self-annihilating, no longer necessary once salvation has been achieved.

Los's struggle to build Golgonooza is the dramatically effective organising theme in *Jerusalem*, because the psychological tension between ambivalent feelings of love and hate, impulse and defence, that it involves is clear. Los's struggle is moving, too, because in his desperation we can sense Blake's own obsessive anxiety, his despair at the hatred and desire that kept contaminating his work in spite of the highest moral intentions. While desire and rage were clearly present in Blake's early works as well, his attitude toward them has changed radically. At the time of *Marriage* he said that hate was built into the structure of things and was as necessary as love for creation. Now he no longer seems able to accept hatred, although it is present in his hero's actions, and his chief aim appears to be avoidance of guilt. *Jerusalem* itself is a long defence against an accusation of guilt by an omnipresent Spectrous accuser. The defence takes the form of an exoneration of the act of writing poetry – a plea to the reader to excuse Blake for 'the energetic exertion of my talent'.

There is no question that Blake was aware of the impulsive content of his work. Albion, acting as accuser, condemns art – the decorations of Eden – as 'unnatural consanguinities and friendships / Horrid to think of when enquired deeply into' (*J* 28:7–8, E 172). Blake's chief defence against both this and the accusation of hostility is to plead a special mission: he is inspired and working to save Albion. This defensive reasoning is often mimicked by readers who assume that Albion misunderstands or is slandering Los, but the accusation is Blake's own. Los's incestuous and hostile motives become evident when his actions parallel actions in earlier work that have a clearly sexual meaning. In *Urizen*, for instance, Los hid Enitharmon to keep her away from his son and admitted Oedipal rival, Orc. Now, as part of his struggle against guilt, Blake rationalises a similar act. Los, building Golgonooza, thinks of hiding Jerusalem there in order to 'protect' her from Albion. Similarly, veiled sexual references take the place of earlier direct sexual activities and religious concepts are expressed in sexual imagery. The motivation for Los's anger against Albion, for instance, is never clearly expressed; there is only a passing reference to the possibility that Albion has stolen Los's bride Enitharmon and hidden her in his 'pleasure garden'. Again, the poem begins with a religious idea of Albion's being unwilling to accept the divine vision which is expressed in terms of sexual rivalry with Christ. Albion is unwilling to share his bride with the Son.

As the work of art nears completion, so does the incestuous project. Blake disguises this from his reader and himself by concentrating instead on hatred of women and an increasing closeness between the men who must fight off the seductive and sadistic female together. At the poem's conclusion, redemption is portrayed as a sexual consummation, an embrace between Jerusalem and Albion– Jehovah, which is incestuous because Los, Blake and Christ are imagined as participating, through merger with the father, in the embrace of the mother.

The ending of *Jerusalem* illustrates Blake's final unwillingness to accept substitutes for his original desire. While the ordinary man eventually accepts the fact that he cannot possess his mother but can instead imitate his father by taking a wife, Blake as poet insists on participating with the father in the primal scene. The 'solution' worked out in *Jerusalem* of drawing close to the father, not, as it appears, on the basis of a renunciation of incest but in order, secretly, to consummate it, was worked out against strong forces of inhibition. The strength of these forces was probably responsible for the fact that from this time on Blake stopped writing poetry almost entirely and became an illustrator of the works of others – works great enough to meet his needs for monumental significance but still works where the basic structure is stated by others. There, in his famous illustrations to the Book of Job and Dante, Blake's 'Giant forms' were not exposed in rivalry but were offered in what Frye calls an attitude 'of critical acceptance'.[1] Perhaps because he was no longer responsible for the outline of the 'drama', the obscurity that marred the poetry of *Jerusalem* disappeared and his forms became clearer, less eccentric, and more universal than before.[2] Moreover, what makes the illustrations to Job particularly successful is the solution of an artistic problem, the relation of text to illustration, in terms of Blake's wish to be truly reconciled with the father. In the illustrations to the Book of Job, unlike Blake's earlier illustrations to Gray and Young, text and illustrations are literally interwoven and perfectly fused.

Thus, while the sexual and emotional content of Blake's work remained fairly constant, his defences underwent change with a resultant change in his overt themes and the surface of his art. His early defensive strategies allowed him to express forbidden impulses overtly by projecting blame and idealising the forbidden impulses. (This early work was characterised too by an idealisation of ambivalence and a drive to bring opposites such as reason and desire together in some sort of mythic 'marriage'.) When, under the increased pressure of both bizarre fantasy and guilt, he turned to Christian ideas for a solution of conflict, he became less mythic, more analytic and allegorical.

He also became less successful artistically. This is not because allegory or Christian ideas cannot be the basis for great art. Rather, Blake's poetry seems to decline, for a variety of interconnected reasons. His awareness of his poem's latent significance kept threatening to break through his defences. This made him exaggerate the potential defects of the artistic method he was using. For instance, repetition and splitting off of subsidiary characters that mirror the primary ones are characteristic of allegory. Blake carries both of these to an extreme, which suggests his drivenness. The same excesses occur in his piling up of symbolic or illustrative details and correspondences far beyond what the reader is able to absorb. These devices, when used economically, serve to keep emotional content under control. The parts of Blake's poem in which he overuses these devices are instead arid as well as tedious.

An opposite problem occurs through Blake's breaking of narrative progression and throwing his narrative into a state of frustrating chaos. Ordinarily, as Angus Fletcher points out in his book *Allegory: The Theory of a Symbolic Mode*, sequential narrative has a calming effect on the reader by keeping anxiety away from the surface.[3] Blake's turbulent surface has an irritating and anxiety-producing effect on the reader that has been widely recognised. But it seems irrelevant and moralistic to deal with it by saying that Blake is justified in tormenting his reader with confusing rhetoric in order 'to separate the sheep from the goats, the saved from the damned, the forgiving, faithful readers from the accusing, rational ones'.[4] A more realistic response to Blake's obfuscations is to recognise that increasing pressures of inhibition were responsible for *Jerusalem*'s maddening obscurity. This obscurity not only veils Blake's meaning; it also forces the reader to endure a similar frustrated longing: he wants to get at Blake's redemptive message and he cannot unless, as one critic puts it, he recognises the narrative as 'a veil to be . . . ripped away from the drama' revealing the perfect form of the freed Jerusalem and bringing on 'the apocalypse of vision' – re-enacting in literary fashion the act with which Blake was obsessed.[5]

It is hard to avoid the conclusion that Blake, aware of the latent significance of his poem and in conflict over it, expressed his ambivalence by a form of sabotage. He felt compelled both to write the poem and to undercut it. The resulting rhetorical chaos is unsuccessful. It contradicts the unspoken requirements of the mode he is working in. It suggests by its obtrusive presence a defence that failed. The most successful parts of *Jerusalem* are those where Blake uses his earlier defensive techniques of denial and projection instead of obscurity, and conflict remains clear.

It is evident then that conflicting wishes and impulses – to write, not to write; to renounce, not to renounce one's desires – plague the creation of *Jerusalem*. Perhaps Blake's courageous persistence in completing the work is ironically his clearest redemptive message.

Notes

NOTES TO THE INTRODUCTION

1. Robert Southey, cited in S. Foster Damon, *William Blake, His Philosophy and Symbols* (Gloucester, Mass.: Peter Smith, 1958) p. 246.
2. David V. Erdman, *Blake: Prophet against Empire* (New York: Anchor Books, 1969) p. 3. See also Jacob Bronowski, *William Blake: A Man without a Mask* (London: Secker & Warburg, 1944), and Bernard Blackstone, *English Blake* (London: Cambridge University Press, 1949; Hamden, Conn.: Archon Books, 1966).
3. Northrop Frye, *Fearful Symmetry: A Study of William Blake* (Princeton University Press, 1969) p. 424. Frye is by far the most brilliant, though not the most recent, practitioner of this kind of criticism.
4. Thus, for example, the illustrations for *Vala* can be related to alchemical symbols but not to Blake's psyche. See Piloo Nannavutty, 'Materia Prima in a Page of Blake's *Vala*', in *William Blake: Essays for S. Foster Damon*, ed. Alvin H. Rosenfeld (Providence: Brown University Press, 1969). *William Blake's 'Vala'*, ed. H. M. Margoliouth (Oxford: Clarendon Press, 1956), sees the sexual drawing as illustrating 'Urizen's idea of what Ahania really is, i.e., sin' (p. 144). John E. Grant, who has clarified the visual details of the perverse or orgiastic 'erotic fantasy' Blake portrays, comes to the disappointingly tame conclusion that 'Blake . . . seems to have observed more clearly than most libertarians in the 18th Century how the pursuit of natural happiness tends to lead insensibly toward a quest for the unnatural' – 'Visions in *Vala*', in *Blake's Sublime Allegory*, ed. Stuart Curran and Joseph Anthony Wittreich, Jr (Madison: University of Wisconsin Press, 1973) p. 184.
5. These exceptions do suggest, however, that at least some readers are becoming aware of the necessity of attending to the emotional content of Blake's poems and his sexual obsessions. Mary Lynn Johnson and Brian Wilkie ('On Reading *The Four Zoas*: Inscape and Analogy', in *Blake's Sublime Allegory*, ed. Curran and Wittreich, p. 203) suggest that the artistic coherence of *The Four Zoas* depends on 'patterns in the psyche'. Jean H. Hagstrum takes another look at the perverse sexuality of Babylon in 'Babylon Revisited', ibid., p. 101. Finally, John Sutherland, in 'Blake: a Crisis of Love and Jealousy', *PMLA*, Jan–Mar 1972, p. 425, suggests that 'the extent of Blake's preoccupation with sexual love may need critical attention'.
6. Since the completion of my book there has been a new and welcome concern with psychological issues. Christine Gallant, *Blake and the Assimilation of*

Chaos (Princeton University Press, 1978), has joined W. P. Witcutt, *Blake: A Psychological Study* (London: Hollis & Carter, 1946), and June Singer, '*The Unholy Bible': A Psychological Interpretation of William Blake* (New York: G. P. Putnam's Sons, 1970), as a thoughtful example of Jungian criticism. Gallant is perhaps too optimistic about Blake's ultimate success in mastering his inner chaos, but she does illuminate some of his defences, particularly his relationship to Urizen's controlling rationality. Now, in addition to the two Freudian articles by Randel Helms – 'Orc: the Id in Blake and Tolkien', *Literature and Psychology*, 20 (1969) pp. 31–5, and 'Blake at Felpham: a Study in the Psychology of Vision', ibid., 22 (1971) pp. 57–66 – there are articles like Morris Dickstein's 'Blake's Reading of Freud' in *The Literary Freud: Mechanisms of Defence and the Poetic Will* (New Haven, Conn., and New York: Yale University Press, 1980). There is also Diana Hume George's *Blake and Freud* (Ithaca, NY: Cornell University Press, 1980), which sees Blake both as anticipating major Freudian concepts and as improving on Freud by adding a dimension of liberty. While Gallant's analysis of individual early lyrics is excellent, I think she underestimates the degree to which Blake's ideas of liberty were dictated by his sexual fantasies – and so the opposite of free. Similarly, her rationalisation of Blake's hostility towards women distorts her reading of the prophecies.

7. Anne K. Mellor, *Blake's Human Form Divine* (Berkeley, Calif.: University of California Press, 1974) p. 336.

8. James Rieger, 'The Hem of their Garments: the Bard's Song in *Milton*', in *Blake's Sublime Allegory*, ed. Curran and Wittreich, p. 260.

9. As Frye observes: 'Hence, while no one could be less of an ascetic than Blake, the premise from which the ascetic starts is also his. The body is "vile": it is the body of a peeled ape, a witch's cauldron of tangled tissues and sodden excrement cooking in blood' (*Fearful Symmetry*, p. 194).

10. Roger R. Easson, 'Blake and His Readers in *Jerusalem*', in *Blake's Sublime Allegory*, ed. Curran and Wittreich, p. 312.

11. Stuart Curran, 'The Structures of *Jerusalem*', ibid., p. 339.

12. When John Sutherland ('Blake and Urizen', in *Blake's Visionary Forms Dramatic*, ed. David V. Erdman and John E. Grant (Princeton University Press, 1970) pp. 244–62) suggested ways in which the late Blake took on Urizen's defences, his restrained attempt was greeted with typical misunderstanding and horror at 'the astonishing conclusion that in opting for "the great and golden rule of art" . . . Blake "could argue freely (in effect) for Satan and for Urizen"!' – Morton Paley, *Blake Studies*, 4 (Fall 1971) p. 98.

13. S. Foster Damon, *A Blake Dictionary: The Ideas and Symbols of William Blake* (New York: Dutton, 1971) p. 309.

14. Damon, *William Blake*, p. 98.

15. Ibid.

16. Ibid., p. 99.

17. Damon, *A Blake Dictionary*, p. 196. Damon's reference to Shelley also suggests that Blake was participating in a common 'Romantic' justification of incest. But, however common incestuous themes were among other poets, for Blake with his intensely private vision these themes would seem to come primarily from his inner life. Even if they were available in the culture, the force of their meaning and their effect for Blake would have to depend on his personal views and needs and not merely on the attractions of a literary convention.

18. Norman O. Brown, *Love's Body* (New York: Vintage Books, 1966) p. 151.

19. Norman O. Brown, *Life against Death* (New York: Vintage Books, 1959) p. 176.

20. I am indebted to Frederick Crews for this observation. See his *Out of My System: Psychoanalysis, Ideology and Critical Method* (New York: Oxford University Press, 1975) p. 33.
21. Ibid., p. 55.
22. Ibid., p. 33.
23. Harold Bloom, *The Anxiety of Influence: A Theory of Poetry* (New York: Oxford University Press, 1973) p. 29.
24. Ibid., p. 11.

NOTES TO CHAPTER 1: 'AN ISLAND IN THE MOON'

1. Mark Schorer, *William Blake: The Politics of Vision* (New York: Vintage Books, 1959) p. 140. Northrop Frye, like Schorer and Damon, is shocked to 'stumble upon three of the most delicate and fragile of the Songs of Innocence' in the midst of 'a Gargantuan nightmare' (*Fearful Symmetry*, p. 182).
2. Damon, *William Blake*, p. 3.
3. Erdman, *Blake*, pp. 126–7. This idea, as we shall see, is partially true; but Erdman does not give enough attention to the Songs' surface innocence or the reasons for their striking difference in tone and style from the earlier satire.
4. Hubert J. Norman, cited in Damon, *William Blake*, p. 34.
5. Erdman, *Blake*, p. 101.
6. St Augustine, *Confessions*, trans. William Watts (London: William Heinemann, 1812).
7. Text-references to *Island* give the chapter followed by page numbers in Erdman.
8. Erdman, *Blake*, p. 102n.
9. Crabb Robinson, quoted in M. H. Abrams, *Natural Supernaturalism: Tradition and Revolution in Romantic Literature* (New York: W. W. Norton, 1971) p. 25.
10. The yellow vest is a comic foreshadowing of the spectre Tharmas's golden serpent-scales in *Vala*, and corruption's rape of flesh is echoed in Tharmas's rape of the earth-mother Enion.
11. The figure of Suction–Robert here may be a conflation of two siblings, Robert and another brother, christened Richard. Bentley and others believe Richard died in infancy when Blake was five. Gilchrist, on the other hand, assumed him to be Robert, recorded erroneously. Whether Robert or Richard was closest to Blake in age is in a sense irrelevant to any *images* of rivalry he presented. The intensity of such feelings in relation to actual siblings might be questioned by readers who imagine that by the age of five a child's anger and envy of a nursing infant is bound to be diminishing. But this depends entirely on the individual case. We do know Blake's extreme sensitivity about other childhood issues, such as discipline. Therefore, even if Blake was ten years older, Robert's birth, following that of the other sibling, could certainly have revived feelings of exclusion and jealousy. Psychodynamically, such feelings can be evoked throughout life by situations like the original one.
12. *Blake's Visionary Forms*, ed. Erdman and Grant, p. 27n.
13. Erdman, *Blake*, p. 90.
14. Ibid., p. 99.
15. For documentation of the relation between Blake and Flaxman, see G. E. Bentley, Jr, 'Blake's Engravings and his Friendship with Flaxman', *Studies in Bibliography*, 12 (1959).
16. *The Letters of William Blake*, ed. Geoffrey Keynes (Cambridge, Mass.: Harvard University Press, 1968) p. 39.

17. As is often the case with Blake's humour in *Island*, the sequence concerning Steelyard and the maiden forecasts a similar situation in a later poem. In *Vala*, Man falls when he walks 'Among the flowers of Beulah . . . and [sees] Vala the lily. . . . There he reveld in sweet delight among the Flowers' (*Blake's 'Vala'*, ed. Margoliouth, p. 43).
18. Erdman, *Blake*, p. 104.
19. Ibid., pp. 120–2.
20. Martha W. England, 'Apprenticeship at the Haymarket', in *Blake's Visionary Forms*, ed. Erdman and Grant, p. 23.
21. John Beer, *Blake's Humanism* (New York: Barnes & Noble, 1968) p. 22.
22. There are connections in Blake's text between scientific investigation and other forbidden activity. During the downgrading of Jehovah in chapter 2, the islanders discuss the propriety of using sacred names, particularly Jehovah's, in a secular context. Tilly Lally asserts that there is no harm in it, and Inflammable agrees with the remark: 'no [harm] I have a camera obscura at home' (*IM* 3, E 433). Although this remark seems like a *non sequitur*, it is related to the forbidden quality of looking. The point of Inflammable's comment is that the exploration of forbidden subjects, whether nature's image or the deity's attributes, is legitimate.
23. *Blake's 'Vala'*, ed. Margoliouth, p. 56.

NOTES TO CHAPTER 2: 'TIRIEL' AND 'THEL'

1. Critics have been unable to date these works precisely. Most seem to agree now that *Thel* slightly preceded *Tiriel*, both being written about 1789, with *Thel*'s mottos and plate 6 being added around 1791. For the purposes of our argument it does not really matter; Blake was obviously considering both sides of his fantasy at very nearly the same time.
2. Frye, for example, sees *Tiriel* as a 'tragedy of reason'; Damon sees *Tiriel* as 'the ancient religion of law empowered by the curse'; and Gleckner sees it as Blake's systematisation of previous notions of 'non-innocence' in the figure of father–priest–king (see Frye, *Fearful Symmetry*, p. 242; Damon, *William Blake*, p. 306; and Robert F. Gleckner, *The Piper and the Bard: A Study of William Blake* (Detroit: Wayne State University Press, 1959) p. 145).
3. The line citations and plate numbers of *Tiriel* are from G. E. Bentley, Jr, *William Blake, 'Tiriel': Facsimile and Transcript of the Manuscript, Reproduction of the Drawings, and a Commentary on the Poem* (Oxford: Clarendon Press, 1967). I have not reproduced the brackets that Bentley uses around his end-line punctuation of Blake's lines.
4. See, for example, Sigmund Freud, *Three Contributions to the Theory of Sex*, trans. A. A. Brill (New York: Nervous and Mental Disease Publishing Co., 1930) p. 55.
5. Nancy Bogen, 'A New Look at Blake's *Tiriel*', *Bulletin of the New York Public Library (BNYPL)*, 74 (1970) p. 161.
6. Bentley, *William Blake*, '*Tiriel*', p. 24.
7. See Bogen, in *BNYPL*, 74 (1970) pp. 153–65. Recently Bogen pointed out that Har's shifting age permits a twofold relation to the mother-figure – as child and as consort. She derives this relation from a myth of a Cuthite moon-goddess and her consort–child. The myth illustrates the incestuous pattern more openly than Blake did in *Tiriel*, but it does not explain the ambiguous relationships; it may even distract from the psychological implications of Blake's text. The strivings

that created the myth were fully alive in Blake's psyche though the myth undoubtedly gave him support and added confidence in presenting them.

8. See Mary S. Hall, '*Tiriel*: Blake's Visionary Form Pedantic', *BNYPL*, 73 (1969).

9. Sigmund Freud, 'Medusa's Head', *Collected Papers*, ed. and trans. by James Strachey, vol. v (New York: Basic Books, 1959) p. 105. At the same time the multiplied phallic snakes deny castration. This phallic aspect of the Medusa is what links her to the weaponed Amazon. It shows up in myth. Myrina, queen of the Amazons, rules over a country of Gorgons.

10. Erdman, *Blake*, p. 137.

11. Bentley, *William Blake, 'Tiriel'*, p. 16.

12. Erdman (*Blake*, p. 206) implies, rather misleadingly I think, that the three male figures were drawn separately from the old man and daughters; he refers to these as 'other sketches evidently made at the same time'. But what is important is that the figures were originally the family-group of *Tiriel*.

13. As we noted in Chapter 1, under the apprehension of the 'dark horrors' of revolution Blake himself felt the need of the support of his friend Flaxman.

14. A similar message is contained in the paintings of Queen Emma (1778) and Jane Shore (1779), where women accused of adultery are vindicated and their accusers discomfited.

15. Air, which is taken in like milk, functions well as a metaphor for the mother's pervasive presence, which is why Hopkins calls it this 'nursing element' – *Poems and Prose of Gerard Manley Hopkins*, selection, intro. and notes by W. H. Gardiner (Harmondsworth, Middx: Penguin, 1953) p. 54.

16. Erdman, *Blake*, p. 143.

17. John Milton, *Paradise Lost*, ed. Merritt Y. Hughes (New York: Odyssey Press, 1935) Book x: 556–70.

18. The earliest readers, among them Yeats, saw the poem as an allegory of an 'unborn' soul fearful of the sorrows of the flesh. In this tradition, Frye saw Thel as signifying anything unborn, from a baby to a vision. Others, such as George Mills Harper in *The Neoplatonism of William Blake* (Chapel Hill: University of North Carolina Press, 1961) and Kathleen Raine in *William Blake* (New York: Praeger, 1971) p. 52, took the allegory to be specifically Neoplatonic and connected the final part with the descent of Persephone to Hades. More recently, Michael J. Tolley has pointed out, I think correctly, that, while frame elements may be Neoplatonic, the idea of self-sacrifice at the core of the poem is clearly Christian – '*The Book of Thel* and *Night Thoughts*', *BNYPL*, 69 (1965) pp. 375–85. Other recent critics, with varying success, have examined Thel's personal qualities in relation to the values of Blake's states of innocence or experience.

19. Fantasies of a virgin mother derive ultimately from an infantile desire to deny the parents' intercourse. See, for example, Sigmund Freud, *Sexuality and the Psychology of Love* (New York: Collier Books, 1963) p. 85.

20. One difficulty with Blake's thought here, which is evident if we put clichés about beauty of sacrifice to one side, is that it is based on a false equation: nurture equals death. It is one thing to recognise that nurturing and dying are parts of one ecosystem and quite another to equate them one to one. This equation forms the core of childhood fantasies of injuring or even killing the mother through too greedy sucking or biting.

21. See, for example, Mary Lynn Johnson, 'Beulah, "Mne Seraphim", and Blake's *Thel*', *Journal of English and Germanic Philology*, 1970; or Robert F. Gleckner, 'Blake's *Thel* and the Bible', *BNYPL*, 64 (1960) pp. 573–80.

22. Andrew Marvell, *Selected Poetry and Prose*, ed. Dennis Davison (London: Harrap, 1952) p. 83.

23. Though it is tempting to picture Thel as encountering her unconscious or buried self in the pit – this idea was suggested to me in a written communication by Mary Lynn Johnson – I doubt that Blake was interested in Thel as a woman in quest of her identity. Rather, like many of his other characters, he was interested in her as an expression of his own (conscious and unconscious) anxieties. When he did not identify with her in this way, he saw her as either potential nurturer or potential Female Will.

24. For example, Mellor in *Blake's Human Form Divine* says the plate represents Blake's 'not very successful attempt' to 'interpolate into *Thel* his growing conviction that Innocence must . . . pit itself against the evils of tyrannical lawgivers' (p. 32).

25. *Letters of Blake*, ed. Keynes, p. 41.

26. Gleckner, *The Piper and the Bard*, p. 162.

NOTES TO CHAPTER 3: THE CASE FOR IMPULSE

1. For example, Damon (*William Blake*, p. 89) sees Blake's imagination in terms of Christian faith that traditionally must dominate reason. Frye (*Fearful Symmetry*, p. 195), with more sophistication, assimilates Blake's emphasis on the body to Christian doctrines of resurrection. Erdman (*Blake*, p. 175), looking at Blake from a historical viewpoint, sees in *Marriage* the struggle of a political radical. Nurmi finds the philosophical poet at work expounding the two tenets necessary for salvation: the idea of the expanded senses and the doctrine of contraries – Martin K. Nurmi, 'Blake's *Marriage of Heaven and Hell*: a Critical Study', *Kent State University Bulletin*, 1975, p. 15.

2. Gleckner, *The Piper and the Bard*, p. 186.

3. Ordinarily, a child moves away from his ambivalent feelings toward a more consistently loving attitude to his father when he renounces his desire to possess the mother. At this point, paternal prohibitions are internalised as the child's conscience. Blake seems unwilling to accept either disappointment of his original wishes or the validity of paternal prohibitions. Thus his view of the father continues to be highly ambivalent.

4. Max Plowman's analysis of *Marriage*, although mainly descriptive, does suggest the way in which Blake casts his work as a lesson or sermon with statement and example – facsimile edition of *The Marriage of Heaven and Hell* (London: J. M. Dent, 1927).

5. Blake's illustration, however (*MHH* 2, *IB* 99), introduces the idea of forbidden or stolen fruit, which his account of the expulsion denies. He presents it in a highly ambiguous way so that we do not know if we are to take it in a positive or negative sense: is it redeeming or stolen (a filched bird's nest?) and possibly harmful? Blake's ambiguity suggests both. The idea of theft prefigures one of *Marriage*'s central preoccupations and specifically the question of whether the Devil stole from God or whether Messiah built heaven with 'what he stole from the Abyss'.

6. *Letters of Blake*, ed. Keynes, pp. 74–5.

7. See Erdman's note in *Blake* (pp. 188–90) for the identification of Rintrah as a counter-revolutionary.

8. See, for example, Nurmi (in *Kent State University Bulletin*, 1975, p. 31), who sees Blake's pairing of directly opposing emotions as irrelevant to his main argument.

9. My ideas about Blake's struggle with Swedenborg and other predecessors were

confirmed by reading Bloom's *Anxiety of Influence* and his *A Map of Misreading* (New York: Oxford University Press, 1975).

10. Bloom's note in David V. Erdman (ed.), *The Poetry and Prose of William Blake* (New York: Anchor Books, 1970) p. 811.

11. Freud, *Three Contributions*, p. 20.

12. Witcutt, in his Jungian study of Blake, interprets this passage as evidence of a personality-disintegrating trauma in which reason was swamped by 'narcissistic delight in the beauty of his [Blake's] own body' (*A Psychological Study*, p. 57).

13. Nurmi, in *Kent State University Bulletin*, 1975, p. 38.

14. Blake's later use of the caterpillar – 'The Catterpillar on the Leaf / Reminds thee of thy Mothers Grief' (*GP*, E 265) – shows the extent to which Blake associated it with mother-destroying greed, an association first brought to my attention by the British analyst Marion Milner ('Joanna Field') in her book *On Not Being Able to Paint* (London: William Heinemann, 1950) p. 80.

15. See Herbert Marcuse, *Eros and Civilization: A Philosophical Inquiry into Freud* (New York: Vintage Books, 1955) ch. 2.

16. Harold Bloom, *Blake's Apocalypse: A Study in Poetic Argument* (Garden City, NY: Doubleday, 1963) p. 83. Though it is possible here and throughout *Marriage* to translate images of father–son conflict into intrapsychic terms of Super-ego versus id, I find my terms more useful for this text with its predominance of external rivalries (with Milton and Swedenborg).

17. Ibid., p. 830.

18. In Piaget's description, the child in his early years colours and forms the world through his emotions, literally animating all things with gods. As the child matures, he becomes more aware of the material qualities of the objects and his projections onto nature return inside. However, religious and moral forces (God and law) may still seem external – Jean Piaget, *The Child's Conception of the World*, trans. Joan and Andrew Tomlinson (Paterson, NJ: Littlefield, Adams, 1960).

19. First nature is animated as gods or parents who protect and punish; then, when more is learned about the natural world, influence moves to the moral sphere, where, as Blake saw, 'precepts were credited with divine origin' and priests took over to punish and reward (see Sigmund Freud, *The Future of an Illusion* (New York: Anchor Books, 1964) p. 25).

20. Critics have in general interpreted the viper negatively. See, for example, Damon, *William Blake*, p. 324; Bloom, in Erdman, p. 812.

21. See Dr Phyllis Greenacre, 'A Study on the Nature of Inspiration', *Journal of the American Psychoanalytic Association*, 12 (1964), for a discussion of the prototype of inspiration as it occurs in childhood in the phallic phase. Particularly illuminating is the connection she notes between the child's interest in the unseen force of air (the eagle's feathers of air) at this time and his genital sensitivity and magical thoughts about the penis as an independent and awe-inspiring representative of the self. (Such awe occurs in Blake's admonition, 'When thou seest an Eagle. thou seest a portion of Genius. lift up thy head!' – *MHH* 9:54, E 37.)

22. I think Erdman's reading of the illuminations as progressive stages of the etching-process is too literal and more orderly than Blake's own correlations of etching and the creative process.

23. Blake's anger at chastisement and, presumably, his reworking of it in fantasy, does not imply that his father's conduct to Blake was excessively harsh or unsympathetic – most scholars have concluded the opposite. Blake, nevertheless, was extremely sensitive to authority, even if exercised by a benign father, and he may have tried to master anger by reworking his earlier (psychically

painful) subordination in fantasy. His inability to bear even ordinary restraints is borne out by the alleged story of his father keeping him home from school. Like most fathers, Blake's probably had his failures in trying to discipline his son before they came to a pattern of freedom for him. The story holds that, 'He despised restraints so much that his father dared not send him to school. Like the Arabian horse, he is said to have so hated a blow that his father thought it most prudent to withhold from him the liability of receiving punishment.'

24. But see Morris Eaves, 'A Reading of Blake's *Marriage of Heaven and Hell*, plates 17–20', in *Blake Studies*, 4 (1971), for a different view of Blake's progress. According to Eaves, Blake and the Angel are looking down at the city of art from angelic perspective.

25. Nurmi, in *Kent State University Bulletin*, 1975, p. 56, suggests that, in the same spirit, Blake is turning Swedenborg's doctrine of marriage against him, since Swedenborg had said that marriage based on dominion appears as open strife after death.

26. David V. Erdman, 'Reading the Illuminations of Blake's *Marriage of Heaven and Hell*', in *William Blake: Essays in Honour of Sir Geoffrey Keynes*, ed. Morton D. Paley and Michael Phillips (Oxford: Clarendon Press, 1973) p. 201. I am much indebted to Erdman's careful description of significant details.

27. Nurmi, in *Kent State University Bulletin*, 1975, p. 63.

28. Robert Essick, 'The Art of William Blake's Early Illuminated Books' (PhD dissertation, University of California, San Diego, 1969) p. 135.

29. Ibid., p. 140.

NOTES TO CHAPTER 4: FATHERS AND SONS

1. See, for example, Erdman, *Blake*, pp. 228ff.; or Frye, *Fearful Symmetry*, p. 240.

2. Erdman, *Blake*, p. 240.

3. This figure has been interpreted as a female (flower–nymph), but it is derived from the clearly male Cupid, and the curves of its flower stem (akin to the phallic stem in *Thel*) suggest masculinity.

4. Melanie Klein, 'The Psychogenesis of Tics', in *Love, Guilt and Reparation and Other Works, 1921–1945* (New York: Delacorte Press, 1975; Boston, Mass.: Seymour Lawrence, 1975) pp. 114 and 126.

5. Yeats later took the white-bird image to represent his poet hero and used the idea of maintaining whiteness for his oft-washed virgin unicorn. Both bird and unicorn were used in defence of the purity of the incestuous fantasy at the heart of *The Player Queen* – Brenda Webster, *Yeats: A Psychoanalytic Study* (Stanford, Calif.: Stanford University Press, 1972) p. 40.

6. Erdman, *Blake*, p. 247.

7. Her efforts, her 'silken nets and traps of adamant', foreshadow the efforts of the female in Beulah whose main activity is to search land and sea for gratification for the 'Male Genius'.

8. Schorer, *Politics of Vision*, p. 249.

9. Erdman, *Blake*, p. 228. Also see Henry Wasser, 'Notes on *The Visions of the Daughters of Albion*, by William Blake', *Modern Language Quarterly*, Sep 1947.

10. Mary Wollstonecraft, *Vindication of the Rights of Women*, Penguin edn (Harmondsworth, Middx: Penguin, 1975) p. 109.

11. Ibid., p. 110.

12. Wollstonecraft may not have had an influence on Blake, but Stedman had. The reality of blacks suffering under tyrannical masters, and particularly his friend's

story of a black mistress taken from him by a cruel slaver, meshed with Blake's masochistic fantasies of Oedipal defeat and called forth strong sympathy. But, again, to see *Visions* as a translation into verse of Stedman's story, as Erdman does, seems to be a mistake of emphasis. Blake's fantasies were already there, ready to be excited by the brutal details of Stedman's narrative.

13. Erdman (*Blake*, p. 286), however, attributes these lines to disappointment in the Revolution.

14. *Letters of Blake*, ed. Keynes, p. 74 (emphasis added).

15. I think Blake here meant us to take Orc's part totally, and was not intending to convey the ambiguity of Orc's potential for good or evil. See, however, Morton D. Paley's argument to the contrary in *Energy and the Imagination* (Oxford: Clarendon Press, 1970) p. 74.

16. Erdman is correct when he points out that 'no form of the words revenge or vengeance appears in the Lambeth prophecies', but, in spite of Blake's conscious intent, vengeance is at the base of the fantasy structuring the work. See Erdman's valuable detailed essay, '*America*: New Expanses', in *Blake's Visionary Forms*, ed. Erdman and Grant, p. 113.

17. Orc's burning through heaven's gates is also a transformation into triumphant activity of his distressed impotence as he sits manacled in the wall's breach in *America*'s frontispiece.

18. Erdman ('*America*: New Expanses', in *Blake's Visionary Forms*, ed. Erdman and Grant) shows how Blake substitutes images of activity and sound for those of impotence and silence as the poem moves forward; at the same time, he accurately notes at every point the images that threaten to reverse this progression, thus creating what I call an eddying movement. Erdman more optimistically feels that, in spite of this 'to and fro' quality, freedom has made significant progress in the course of the poem.

19. Erdman has dealt in convincing detail with the historical allegory. I have followed his identifications of historical characters.

20. Michael J. Tolley, '*Europe*: "To those ychaind in sleep"', in *Blake's Visionary Forms*, ed. Erdman and Grant, examines the ways in which Blake bases his terrifying prophecy on Milton's ode celebrating the nativity, showing yet again how Blake tended radically to reverse (and revise) the meaning of his great predecessor.

21. John Sutherland, 'Blake and Urizen', in *Blake's Visionary Forms*, ed. Erdman and Grant, comments that in spite of negative elements 'one is immediately surprised by the degree to which the figure seems to be dignified – even glorified' (p. 248).

22. There are other connections between Los and Blake's Samson. For example, when he reveals his secret, he thinks of Delila[h]'s breast as a trustworthy haven, 'the ivory palace of my inmost heart' (E 435). In *Europe*, a breastlike rock appears beside the line 'Urthona [Los] takes his rest'; one figure leans against it while another, less fortunate, crawls toward it (E 3, *IB* 161). Enitharmon's fair but cold crystal house echoes Delila[h]'s deceptive palace breast. Moreover, Enitharmon's sky-palace belongs only to those sons and daughters who are obedient.

23. Tolley (see n. 20 above) draws attention to this and to Blake's deliberate contradiction of Milton's stanza in 'On the Morning of Christ's Nativity' (though he explains it differently).

24. Critics differ widely in assigning and interpreting these lines. Erdman thinks they are spoken directly by Urizen's sons (E 725), while Bloom (E 817) suggests an ironic reading: Los is speaking and imagining the reaction of Urizen's sons.

Tolley gives the entire section, 3:9–4:14, to Enitharmon. Both Erdman's and Bloom's interpretations make better sense syntactically than Tolley's for 3:9–4:9; Bloom's makes Los more active in savouring the envy he arouses, even to the point of enjoying Orc's supposed quiescence and his inability to act as a rival. But I think the evidence for Enitharmon's speaking the final lines is very great.

25. Tolley, in *Blake's Visionary Forms*, ed. Erdman and Grant, p. 115.

26. Irene H. Chayes, in her essay 'The Presence of Cupid and Psyche', in *Blake's Visionary Forms*, ed. Erdman and Grant, notes the alternating pattern of assault and retaliation in Blake's sexual myth (p. 230). She also traces Enitharmon's veil-lifting gesture on plate 4 to that of Psyche discovering Cupid and shows how what was originally a gesture of sexual curiosity develops into the evisceration of Albion by Venus in Blake's *Jerusalem*.

27. Critics have been bothered by her referring to the brothers as older than Orc when a few lines before he had been her eldest, but it is essential to the pattern of three brothers that Blake is about to use that they be repressive elders.

28. Gilray, in a political cartoon drawn on by Blake, brings in the implied relation to the mother by picturing Pitt as Death, protected by Queen Charlotte as his snaky-haired mother, Sin.

29. Perhaps we should see him as a spectral messenger of death: he rings his bell almost against the head of the dying girl, who rolls her eyes toward it as if hearing the voice of death.

30. *The Notebook of William Blake: A Photographic and Typographic Facsimile*, ed. David Erdman (Oxford: Clarendon Press, 1973) N 25.

31. See, for example, René A. Spitz, 'Metapsychology and Direct Infant Observation', in *Psychoanalysis, A General Psychology*, ed. Rudolph M. Lowenstein, Lottie M. Newman, Max Schur and Albert J. Solnit (New York: International Universities Press, 1966). Jean Piaget, from a slightly different viewpoint, tries to reconstruct the stages of the child's differentiation of himself and his actions from what surrounds him and his gradual awareness of discrete objects existing independently – *The Construction of Reality in the Child* (New York: Basic Books, 1954).

32. Blake equates this idea of punishment by enforced negative identity with the pain of individuation by describing both in the same words. Thus, Thurlow's pain is described as 'dismal torment sick', and, in a later poem (*The [First] Book of Urizen*), the nostrils, created as separate organs, are described as hanging 'in ghastly torment sick' (*U* 11:26, E 75).

33. Though the mood is definitely pessimistic, Erdman may be right when he points out that the web is less strong than the iron bonds of the text and can be broken by the tiny insects flying through it; but perhaps these are Enitharmon's obedient children who are portrayed throughout as insects.

34. Damon, *A Blake Dictionary*, p. 378.

35. The child is given a face in only one version. In a much later version used for an illustration to the Book of Job, Blake gives faces to both wife and children, producing a very different impression.

36. Copy G's unnaturally elongated penis is reproduced and discussed in G. E. Bentley, Jr, *The Blake Collection of Mrs Landon H. Thorne* (New York: Pierpont Morgan Library, 1971).

37. The Notebook poems and drafts are from *The Notebook of William Blake*, ed. David V. Erdman. They are designated in the text by N and the page number. Though I have included variants of words relevant to my argument, I have not tried to reproduce all the complicated word substitutions and cancellations of

the MSS. For these see Erdman's transcription. I am capitalising names (Rose, Lilly, etc.) for consistency, since Blake capitalises them in *Songs* though not generally in the Notebook.

38. Damon (*William Blake*, p. 100) cites this legend from Symons, who in turn gives no source.
39. This gesture links her with the threatening phallic sibyl in the illustration on plate 14 of *America* (*IB* 152); she gestures similarly toward the praying youth.
40. See John E. Grant, 'Two Flowers in the Garden of Experience', in *William Blake: Essays for Foster Damon*, ed. Rosenfeld, for some acute comments on the lover's masochism.
41. The unconscious link between phallus and mental powers may help to explain Freud's insistence that intellectual women suffer from penis-envy.
42. I am indebted to David Erdman for this view of the Bard's role. See the Introduction to his edition of the Notebook.
43. Rosenwald copy facsimile in the Pierpont Morgan Library.
44. Crabb Robinson, reported in Mona Wilson, *The Life of William Blake*, ed. Geoffrey Keynes (Oxford University Press, 1971) p. 72. At the time that Blake advocated community of women, he also asserted that he had 'committed many murders'. His lyrics suggest that these were variations of patricide.

NOTES TO CHAPTER 5: THE ORIGINS OF LOSS

1. I am indebted to W. J. T. Mitchell for this observation, although we understand the patterning from different viewpoints – 'Poetic and Pictorial Imagination in Blake's *Book of Urizen*', in *The Visionary Hand*, ed. Robert Essick (Los Angeles: Hennessey & Ingalls, 1973).
2. Thorne copy of *The [First] Book of Urizen* in the Pierpont Morgan Library.
3. Robert E. Simmons suggests that the whole of *America* is quite consciously an emotional, Orcian version of the events depicted in *Urizen* – 'Urizen: the Symmetry of Fear', in *Blake's Visionary Forms*, ed. Erdman and Grant.
4. What Simmons sees as symmetry abstractly constructed to show the negative, mechanical nature of Urizen's world, I take to reflect the deeply-felt emotional problem of identity and identification of Los as son with Urizen as father.
5. The British analyst Rycroft discusses a similar sense of alienation in the poet Leopardi. Rycroft speculates that disillusion first occurs in the context of the infant's relation to the mother. More particularly, if the infant fails to merge his wishful hallucination of the breast with the real experience of being nursed, he will not, as an adult, be able to value things as they are, and will instead construct illusions or substitute realities. If, on the other hand, the infant can merge the imagined and the real breast, later, as an adult, he will be able to use his imagination to enrich rather than substitute for reality – Charles Rycroft, 'On Idealization, Illusion and Catastrophic Disillusion', *Imagination and Reality* (New York: International Universities Press, 1968) pp. 36–7.
6. Perhaps in ironic contrast to the Miltonic 'spirit' that brooded over and impregnated the Abyss.
7. This repression is aided by readers who take the passage purely allegorically as Urizen's denial of joy in his intellectual activity. See, for example, Schorer, *Politics of Vision*, p. 240.
8. Bloom notes this as well as the ambiguity of Urizen's rejection of her (E 821).
9. Freud's case-history of the Wolf Man shows this regression in particularly clear form as well as being a storehouse of information about the negative Oedipal reaction and obsessional defence-mechanisms. See Sigmund Freud, 'From the

History of an Infantile Neurosis', in *Collected Papers*, trans. Alix and James Strachey, vol. III (New York: Basic Books, 1959) pp. 473–605.

10. The links in this passage between 'mud' torrents, birth and the hatching serpent are illuminated by the unconscious connection noted by Freud between faeces and baby that enables the sexually-curious child to construct a theory of anal birth. See Sigmund Freud, 'On Transformation of Instincts with Special Reference to Anal Eroticism', in *Collected Papers*, trans. Joan Riviere, vol. II (New York: Basic Books, 1960) pp. 164–72.

11. See Otto Fenichel's relevant description of fear of infection as a defence against feminine wishes of infection standing for impregnation in *The Psychoanalytic Theory of Neurosis* (New York: W. W. Norton, 1972) p. 209.

12. Erdman (*Blake*, p. 223) identifies Blake's branching tree with the Upas.

13. There, the nerves had been simply compressed by Urizen's bones, while his fantasies of 'prolific delight' had been hidden in a sulphurous fluid that settled into a white lake within the brain, a transformation of phallic sexuality into anal–sadistic rage.

14. See Paley, *Energy and the Imagination*, pp. 82–3.

15. Fred Weinstein and Gerald M. Platt, in their study of the French Revolution, *The Wish to Be Free* (Berkeley, Calif.: University of California Press, 1969), suggest that Robespierre's 'retreat to Authority' was in fact an effort to control his anxiety over feared punishment (pp. 109–36).

16. This and the following examples are taken from Weinstein and Platt, ibid., pp. 58–60.

17. Bloom, *Anxiety of Influence*, uses Los's swerve to illustrate the Romantic poet's necessary swerve away from his great predecessor, here Blake from Milton (p. 42).

18. Note, for example, Fenichel, *Psychoanalytic Theory*, pp. 250 and 322: 'The role played by respiratory symptoms in anxiety in general explains the fact that every anxiety, to a certain extent, is felt as a kind of suffocation.' In particular cases – in asthma, for instance – the suffocated breathing is a reaction to separation from the mother, 'a cry of appeal'.

19. See Donald Ault, *Visionary Physics: Blake's Response to Newton* (University of Chicago Press, 1974) p. 150. Ault notes that in *The Book of Los* 'physical concepts and images explicitly place severe restrictions on the activities of the protagonist' and that by this means Blake is attacking 'the imaginative lure of both Newton's and Descartes' systems'. But the reason this 'lure' was felt to be so threatening was its emotional associations.

20. There may also be the idea of forcing Urizen to experience sexual pleasure. As a weapon the orb resembles the globe, also fiery hot, with which Fuzon penetrates his father's loins.

21. All my references here are to Margaret Mahler, 'Notes on the Development of Basic Moods: the Depressive Affect', in *Psychoanalysis*, ed. Lowenstein *et al.*, pp. 152–67.

22. Mitchell (in *Visionary Hand*) describes the book's basic pattern as one of 'contraction and expansion'. The rather startling physical or athletic nature of the illustrations seems to be related to the early testing of the muscles and movement that accompanies the child's efforts to make the world his own. Blake reproduces this experience in Urizen's world-creation. And, as in *Tiriel*, the illustrations reflect a more positive aspect of the experience than the text.

23. I am indebted in the following discussion to David Erdman's masterly reconstruction of Blake's ordering, as well as to many of his observations. See *The Notebook of William Blake*, ed. Erdman.

24. Blake himself suggests that the leaf is the injured maternal body in his couplet 'The Catterpillar on the Leaf / Reminds thee of thy Mothers Grief'. As we have noted earlier, the caterpillar is closely related to *Thel's* infant worm and to *Tiriel's* serpent sons.
25. For a table of all Blake's orderings, see Erdman, *Notebook*, p. 64.
26. Erdman points out (*Blake*, pp. 204–5) that the head-clutching gestures of Earth and Air are the same as those of the threatened kings in *America*.
27. Ibid., pp. 202–3.
28. Mellor, *Blake's Human Form Divine*, p. 81.

NOTES TO CHAPTER 6: 'VALA' AND 'THE FOUR ZOAS'

1. For instance, in discussing Night VIIb Paley first notes 'traces of a new hope . . . Christian elements which are not part of added or later passages' (*Energy and the Imagination*, p. 121).
2. Johnson and Wilkie's essay 'On Reading *The Four Zoas*', in *Blake's Sublime Allegory*, ed. Curran and Wittreich, makes a pioneering effort in this direction. Their article has been superseded by a full-length study, *Blake's 'Four Zoas': The Design of a Dream* (Cambridge, Mass.: Harvard University Press, 1978), which appeared after my own manuscript was completed.
3. The extant lines that now describe Tharmas' dissolution, rebirth, and subsequent mating are written over seventy-two erased lines, which Bentley thinks form a unit: a previous short *Vala* poem or the core of what was to be a 'Preludium'. These lines are accompanied by carefully drawn illustrations that also serve to set them off from the rest of the Night.
4. Just as in *Gates*, the mandrake–infant loses his upstanding hair, symbol of his masculine energy, when he is plucked and put into the maternal apron.
5. Since I discuss the core of the early *Vala* and the MSS. illustrations, I shall refer to the poem as *Vala* throughout my chapter even when I am discussing late additions. The page numbers are from the Vala MSS. which the reader can find reproduced in G. E. Bentley's *Vala; or, The Four Zoas: A Facsimile of the MS, a Transcript of the Poem, and a Study of its Growth and Significance* (Oxford: Clarendon Press, 1963). For the reader's convenience, I have used Erdman's edition of *The Four Zoas* in *The Poetry and Prose of William Blake* (which includes *Vala*) for textual reference. The references are to page and line, followed by the page number in Erdman.
6. *Blake's Vala*, ed. Margoliouth, p. 160.
7. This is, incidentally, a brilliant analysis of the person whose hostile impulses and guilt are so strong that he or she cannot accept a gift with thanks.
8. Tharmas's change from pale white corpse to erect form 'in masculine strength augmenting' is incidentally analogous to Los's similar changes as he develops from sinking lungs weighted down by the white polypus to a fibrous form of 'impregnable strength'. The only difference is that Los weaves himself.
9. Her lack of pity at this point recalls the attitude of the rejecting queen toward the cupid son in *Songs of Experience*.
10. The sexual nature of the situation is disguised by allegorical necessity. As Bloom notes, it is understandable that Tharmas would shelter the emanations, 'for he is the guardian of the unsundered Innocence they seek to repossess' (E 855–6).
11. Grant, who describes these illustrations in detail, relates this monster to the female males of *Jerusalem* – John E. Grant, 'Visions in *Vala*: a Consideration of Some Pictures in the Manuscript', *Blake's Sublime Allegory*, ed. Curran and Wittreich, p. 157n.

12. Enitharmon's unresponsive body recalls the apathetic, rejecting mother of the Notebook sketches, just as her jealousy recalls the jealous Rose of *Songs of Experience*. There Blake had suggested the identity of the two figures by using his sketch of the turned-away woman to illustrate the Rose. Here, however, Enitharmon combines both figures in herself.

13. Enion's concluding lament also quotes Oothoon; perhaps in writing it Blake was recalling *Visions*.

14. At the same time as he darkens his picture of Urizen, he increases his reference to Luvah's irresponsible behaviour. Neither of them can succeed without Christ.

15. Note, for example, Johnson and Wilkie's description of the 'suicide of reason', in *Blake's Sublime Allegory*, ed. Curran and Wittreich, p. 215; or Bloom, E 871.

16. Grant, in *Blake's Sublime Allegory*, ed. Curran and Wittreich, p. 186. I am following his description of the scene because many of the details are not visible to me even in infra-red photographs.

17. Previously they were said to have been stolen.

18. Grant, in *Blake's Sublime Allegory*, ed. Curran and Wittreich, p. 189.

19. Ibid. Grant suggests that the object could be a 'female with an elongated neck'.

20. Grant (ibid., p. 191) notes the similarity of her manipulations to Rahab's torture of Albion; I would add to this a comparison with Enion's manipulation of Tharmas's fibres. David Erdman made the cautionary suggestion in a phone conversation that the 'unattached phallus' is an illusion created inadvertently.

21. Grant, ibid.

22. Blake himself associates the three fluids when he composes woman of 'blood, milk, and tears' (*U* 18:4, E 77). Enitharmon also suffers from separation; there is an illustration of her swimming, her right side exuding drops of blood.

23. Frye, in *Fearful Symmetry*, p. 293, though noting the Spectre's need to work with the real world, defines it as the will, 'the instrumentality of the mind'.

24. The flutes and lyres that Tharmas provides to cheer Los while he binds Urizen have an interesting parallel in a letter to George Cumberland (1796), in which Blake compares Cumberland's works to the sound of harp and flute that cheer on the work demanded by 'the Eternal parents' – *Letters of Blake*, ed. Keynes, pp. 26–7. In Night IV, the work encouraged by the flute is the son's binding of the father.

25. Even though it would have made little sense, because, as we have noted, she is already born.

26. See, for example, Fenichel, *Psychoanalytic Theory*, p. 221.

27. Ibid., p. 222.

28. Grant points out that their postures resemble those of the toasting male friends in Blake's *Night Thoughts* illustration.

29. However, see Johnson and Wilkie's *Design ₁ Dream* for their discussion of the text.

30. Fenichel, *Psychoanalytic Theory*, p. 476.

31. Blake here forms what Dr Silvano Arieti calls a primary class. Such classes (characteristic of schizophrenic thought) are not formed according to the rules of Aristotelian logic, but follow a primary process or palaeological pattern in which any things with a common predicate, in this case contraction, may be identified – *Creativity: The Magic Synthesis* (New York: Basic Books, 1976) pp. 66–76.

32. See Grant, in *Blake's Sublime Allegory*, ed. Curran and Wittreich, p. 169.

33. Damon defines Luban as 'the vagina, the Gate of Golgonooza which opens into this world' (*A Blake Dictionary*, p. 253). Johnson and Wilkie, in *Blake's Sublime Allegory*, ed. Curran and Wittreich, p. 224, wonder why Blake gives

Los jealousy as a motive. Understanding the Oedipal conflict that underlies Los's acts explains why.

34. See Ault, *Visionary Physics*, for an analysis of Blake's use of specific scientific concepts: 'vortexes', 'void'.

35. Grant, 'Visions in *Vala*', in *Blake's Sublime Allegory*, ed. Curran and Wittreich, p. 171.

36. Urizen's curse here echoes that of Tiriel, who explicitly suffered a brutal weaning.

37. It is important to realise that there were no emanations in *Vala*; the women were sisters, consorts or mothers. The emanation-concept acts, as Beulah does, to reduce the threat of the female, who exists only as an 'emanation' or part of man.

38. Blake's effective use of similarity to form a primary class here contrasts with the subsequent concreteness in his description of Orc's feeding, where the daughters knead bread on sagging clouds while icy rain pours down instead of milk. Both are examples of palaeological thought.

39. Yeats drew on this for his own expression of maternal deprivation, the bloodthirsty Seabars of 'The Shadowy Waters'. He took the Edenic fruit 'of many colors' for the same play.

40. Each new genealogy also produces new meanings for allegory-hungry critics. Margoliouth explains, for example, that Urizen and Luvah now appear at the same time because 'If you have Intellect as something distinct from the whole man, you cannot help having Passion distinct also' (*Blake's 'Vala'*, p. 137).

41. Paley (*Energy and the Imagination*, p. 160) finds Blake's attempt at solution here 'arbitrary' and 'unsatisfactory'. But in fact it makes as much sense psychologically as anything else. More to the point is its failure to accord with developments in the next Night, where Los is again bloodthirsty.

42. Originally scholars thought that Night VIIb came first, but Margoliouth, Bentley and, more recently, John Kilgore – 'The Order of Nights VIIa and VIIb in Blake's *The Four Zoas*', *Blake: An Illustrated Quarterly*, 12 (Fall 1978) pp. 107–15 – have convincingly argued against this. As Bentley notes, 'It is almost inconceivable that there should have been recognizable fragments of Christianity in the early drafts of *Vala* (*Vala or The Four Zoas*, p. 162).

43. As Bloom notes (E 885).

44. At some point Blake transposed parts I and II of Night VIIb so that it started with Urizen's megalomania, thus destroying its defensive connection to Vala's melancholy.

45. In the *Night Thoughts* illustration (*V* 101), Urizenic Death shoots a dart at an infant boy who is blissfully kissing his mother. Vala at this point sees Jesus as Luvah's murderer and pleads for a reunion in brotherhood and love, but reunion is impossible while she exists as the focus of conflict. And in a sense Jesus did murder Luvah, replacing him with a type of man who repudiates Vala's love ('Women, I know thee not').

46. See Silvano Arieti, *Interpretation of Schizophrenia* (New York: Basic Books, 1974) pp. 146–75, for some interesting clinical parallels to Urizen's disorder: John, for example, whose fear of committing terrible crimes inhibited every movement and who 'saw himself solidifying, assuming statuesque positions', like Urizen's stone form (p. 157).

47. Here, in his historical role, Urizen is Robespierre, who tries and fails to release man from religious (maternal) bondage in order to create a world of *fraternité*. The illustrations show instead the male crucified (*V* 111) or desperately dragging along a nude female with flaming breasts and vulva (*V* 112).

48. In spite of his rather complicated analysis of the split in Urizen between dragon-impulse and stony defence, Blake at times seems to return to early ideas of defence or restraint as unnecessary, as when he blames Urizen and his religion for the war: 'For war is energy Enslaved but thy religion / The first author of this war' (*FZ* 120:42–3, E 375).
49. Arieti points out that the ability to prospect the future is important in engendering 'the anxiety that is due to lack of security', but it is also tied to the 'reality principle' (*Interpretation of Schizophrenia*, p. 247). When schizophrenics lose the ability to anticipate the future, they also become incapable of dealing with their everyday environment.
50. Grant, 'Visions in *Vala*', in *Blake's Sublime Allegory*, ed. Curran and Wittreich, p. 197, suggests that these two are enacting the Judgement of Paris; certainly, the troubles caused by Venus are germane to Blake's vision.

NOTES TO CHAPTER 7: BLAKE'S 'MILTON'

1. *Letters of Blake*, ed. Keynes, p. 67.
2. G. E. Bentley, Jr, *Blake Records* (Fairlawn, NJ: Oxford University Press, 1969) p. 71.
3. *Letters of Blake*, ed. Keynes, p. 41.
4. Bentley, *Blake Records*, p. 102.
5. W. J. T. Mitchell is one of the few readers who have noticed the paradoxical equivalence of creation and destruction in the opening scenes of *Milton*. See his 'Blake's Radical Comedy: Dramatic Structure as Meaning in *Milton*', in *Blake's Sublime Allegory*, ed. Curran and Wittreich, p. 290.
6. Ironically, the Edenic Assembly has perpetuated this suffering of the innocent by their condemnation of Rintrah.
7. See, for example, *IB*, 234.
8. Ololoon's milky purity may echo the 'clear milky juice' which allayed the thirst of Milton's Samson in *Samson Agonistes – Paradise Regained, the Minor Poems and Samson Agonistes*, ed. Merritt Y. Hughe ʾew York: Odyssey Press, 1937) p. 576.
9. For a discussion of homoerotic love among figures in *Milton*, specifically on oral–genital conjunctions in plates depicting Los's appearance to Blake and Milton's rescue of Urizen, see W. J. T. Mitchell, 'Style and Iconography in the Illustrations to Blake's *Milton*', *Blake Studies*, 6 (1973) pp. 47–71.
10. Heinz Kohut, *The Analysis of the Self* (New York: International Universities Press, 1971) pp. 70–1, for example.
11. Ibid., pp. 158–9.
12. Freud has elucidated the unconscious equivalence of baby and faeces in 'Transformation of Instincts', *Collected Papers*, vol. II, pp. 164–72.
13. As described in his letter to Butts (*Letters of Blake*, ed Keynes, pp. 74–5).
14. Los's re-creation of the body as an artifact seems to clash with Blake's animistic view of Nature, but, as Piaget has shown, artificialism and animism occur together both in children's thought and in prescientific creation-theories. Both theories involve feelings of omnipotent control, such as Blake depicts in Los's reconstruction of time and space (see Piaget, *Child's Conception*, p. 358).
15. Ibid., p. 147.
16. Donald Ault, who notices Blake's return of perception to 'a primary bodily level', gives many suggestive examples of the way Blake sought to replace Newton's causality and logic with his own vision, using as a chief strategy the

idea that Newton's ideas were a parody of his own, i.e. that Newton, like Hayley, was a thief (*Visionary Physics*, p. 139).

17. Erdman (*IB* 261) notes his resemblance to the collapsed corpse of Abel.

18. I am indebted to Mitchell for this last observation (in *Blake's Sublime Allegory*, ed. Curran and Wittreich, p. 305).

NOTES TO CHAPTER 8: 'JERUSALEM'

1. Blake's naming the fiend Jupiter 'an iron hearted tyrant' is a clear reference to his own struggle with tyrannical father-figures and with guilt. His stress on Jupiter's being Greek is for another reason. At this moment, in his own art Blake was struggling against the aggressiveness associated with the creation and display of his 'Giant forms' by emphasising his positive intentions. Greek art, based on the display of the male body and lacking any redemptive emphasis, came to represent Blake's own rejected hostility put in historical terms: 'a Warlike State never can produce Art' (E 267).

2. *Letters of Blake*, ed. Keynes, p. 107.

3. Ibid.

4. Ibid., p. 37.

5. Ibid.

NOTES TO THE CONCLUSION

1. Frye, *Fearful Symmetry*, p. 425.

2. Anthony Blunt, *The Art of William Blake* (New York: Harper & Row, 1974) p. 87.

3. Angus Fletcher, *Allegory: The Theory of a Symbolic Mode* (Ithaca, NY: Cornell University Press, 1964) p. 288.

4. Roger R. Easson, 'William Blake and his Reader in Jerusalem', in *Blake's Sublime Allegory*, ed. Curran and Wittreich, p. 326.

5. Ibid., p. 324.

Index

315